MY LOOTING EYE

WERNER BÜTTNER
COLLAGES

black dog publishing
london uk

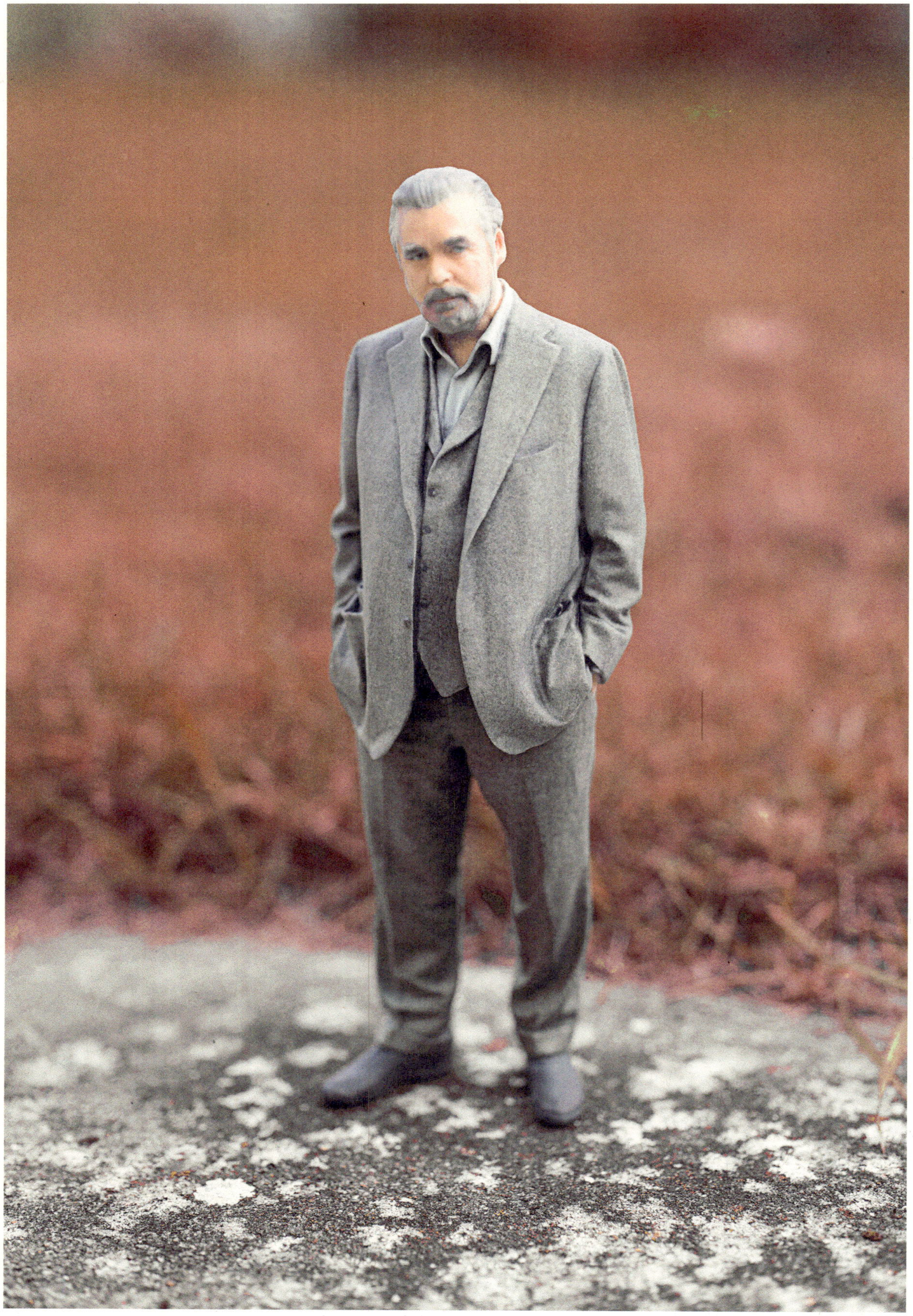

Part I

Gilda Williams

Werner Büttner's collages
From A to T (and back again)

A: A large adult panda—possibly overweight, possibly deranged—stares straight at us. Immense, black-ringed eyes appear unnaturally dulled and worried. The panda sits half-collapsed, pasted beneath an immense picture of glorious, golden fields of ploughed farmland. At the the very top is an oncoming 'cloud' of sliced prosciutto crudo*: blood red, and finely streaked with white animal fat.*

B: A beautiful—if minuscule—woman in a slinky red dress, emerges onto a tiny, ornate balcony. This small space is perched above three enormous soft-boiled eggs (each considerably larger than the woman herself) neatly presented on a clean blue-white napkin. This all floats beneath an immense ballo in maschera*-type wooden mask, itself sprouting thick green shoots, like hair. The whole is gently illuminated by a shaft of divine light, descending from heaven.*

C: A classically-trained male dancer in theatrical costume (ie, velvet bolero jacket; eighteenth century-style lace-front blouse; fake black curly beard; obscenely tight tights) leaps perilously... into the gaping mouth of a stony cave, its rough walls untouched by human hands, photographed in vintage black and white.

Blame the Surrealists, but we automatically presume that bizarre concoctions like these found in Werner Büttner's collages are akin to the "chance encounter on a dissecting table of a sewing machine and an umbrella": items tossed together 'randomly'. Panda bears and cooked meats; architecture and breakfast; ballet and geography: these may seem random pairings, but perhaps they are not. What method lies behind this madness?

In an attempt to get to grips with the logic behind Büttner's collages, at the end of this text readers will find an A–Z (or, more precisely, an A–T) lexicon which indexes the imagery chosen in Büttner's art: animals, foods, landscapes and more. The more we look at Büttner's collages, the more a mysterious logic seems to cohere in his world. I am curious to identify patterns in his choices, and spot where Büttner's images and interests cluster.

From the start, we observe that his collaged pairings often draw together and overlap the 'natural' with the 'cultural': in the three examples above, zoo animals (nature) with farm cultivation (culture); eggs (nature) with buildings (culture); stone (nature) with theatre (culture). Or, for example:

*D: Diplomat Thomas Cromwell, pictured in an Old Master-type painting (*culture*), is set alongside an enormous ancient tree trunk (*nature*) which seems to encircle his head like an asymmetrical halo in* Thomas Cromwell—half seinen König Frauen zu beseitigen *(*Thomas Cromwell—helped his king to get rid of wives*), 2013.*

F: In Liebevolle Erinnerung an den Krieg... *(*Fond memory of war...*), 2014, we find fascist-style monumentally carved war statuary (*culture*) standing to attention beneath a blackened, starry sky and a constellation of three gargantuan violets (*nature*).*

An oil painting coexists with the rings of a tree; mid-century figurative sculpture is blessed by giant purple blossoms floating in the heavens: plainly, in Büttner's work unrelated representations of 'nature' or 'culture' are forced to commingle in close proximity. But is this pairing the defining key behind this artist's collage tactic? How do Büttner's collages differ from his fellow collagists:

F: Fragmented body parts and infantile, regressive human behaviours—screaming, crawling, hiding, curling—pull together the sacred and the profane in Dash Snow's collages laced with youthful curiosity and frenetic sexuality.

G: Grotesquely oversized female erogenous zones (mouths, eyes) in Linder's collages interrupt idealised images of womens' bodies and faces, which are sometimes replaced by suggestive, organic things: blooming roses for heads; cherry-pink scoops of ice-cream for breasts.

H: Hannah Hoch forces together large heads with small bodies, positioning them into dangerous, unfamiliar or precarious positions.

J: John Stezaker joins together two (usually) unrelated found images—faces; postcards—and miraculously produces an uncanny surplus of meaning.

What about Büttner? If he is indeed like "a miserable dog marking a miserable territory"—as the artist puts it, self-deprecatingly—what are this territory's limits? What is the artist searching for in his selected images, such as found photos; magazines; catalogues; advertisements? And according to what unearthly logic are they combined?

Any simple formula regarding the mix of 'natural' and 'cultural' things breaks downs when we notice how, often, such a pair are joined by a third, more ambiguous element—a kind of punctum in the finished collage—which serves to complicate clear dividing lines:

K: In Die Diktatur des Bekannten *(*Dictatorship of the Known*), 2013, a Tuscan landscape of cypresses, golden fields and blue skies (*nature*) is interrupted by a little rose-pink satin brassiere, push-up style (*culture*), 'worn' by a wooden crest: an inanimate thing made to behave like a living woman's shoulders.*

*L: A long-haired mountain goat (*nature*) finds itself beneath a grand piano (*culture*) in* E und U, die Beiden Freunde *(*Classical and popular, two buddies*), 2005. However, the bottom half of the image is devoted to an incongruous ironing board and clean laundry: ironing being an activity that is yes, reserved for humans, but hardly qualifying as a 'cultural' pursuit.*

And so there are there in-between objects—like the brassiere's shield-shaped 'shoulders', or the domestic scene visited by a gravityless animal: these are stand-ins pointing towards human life but not entirely alive themselves. In fact, Büttner's attention regularly turns towards things that straddle life and death:

L: Leather: a living membrane—like skin—yet dead, like upholstery.

M: Meat: once alive, it now reeks of death, whether served grilled, steamed, roasted on a spit or—as Büttner seems to prefer—bloodied, butchered and raw.

Similarly, bodies break into pieces (disembodied hands are a favourite): the only whole 'living' human bodies belong to statuary or porcelain figurines—more akin to stone than flesh and blood. The few complete figures we often see only from the back, or from above, or hazily in silhouette. There are plenty of shelves or boxes for storage—but these are half-empty. The numerable dolls, cherubs and stuffed toys balance between the animate and the inanimate. Grinning skulls, kicking bones and soaring crucifixes can be the most 'alive' thing in the picture. There are plenty of accessories—gloves, hats, shows, wigs; these items waver between living, bodily protrusions and inert clothing.

Often images straddle the natural and unnatural worlds:

L: A Lego giraffe grins against a backdrop of sweeping sands in Da tobt was herzwärts... *(*Something's rampaging heartwards...*), 2004: the toy is expressive and friendly yet blocky and plastic in his manufacture; while the natural desert landscape seems artfully 'sculpted' by the wind.*

O: In Am siebten Tag aber war Ruhe... *(*On the seventh day, a bit of peace and quiet...), *2012, a swirling glass table lamp, shaped into a kind of curving wave, morphs at its base into a Dachshund sporting a hot-pink wig: the animal is denatured by the synthetic hairpiece, while the over-designed lighting recalls the open sea.*

P: A pink flamingo—gracefully bent, alive but looking artificial both for its garish colour and the 'boneless' curve of its neck—is framed by an enormous, ornate gate that is so ancient and weathered, it appears to have stood there for centuries, like a mountain. Ich verstehe sehr gut, warum die Alten Stunden in Gläsern zählten *(*I understand only too well why the ancients counted the hours in glasses*), 2004.*

P: In Die Blässe der Vollendung *(*The pallor of perfection*), 2013, a giant, demented baboon sits astride a balcony rail, looking very humanly tyrannical while lording over a sprawling built city beneath him which in contrast appears orderly and benign, like a natural landscape.*

*R: A rock formation (bizarrely recalling army-camouflage) includes a flat strip of wood panelling—hideous for its fake regularity—and an archaic equestrian figure, itself ancient like found stone yet stylised by human hand. (*Landpartie in grauer Vorzeit (Country outing in the dim and distant)*, 2004)*

*S: A super-skinny, almost withered (if not semi-mummified) Buddhist monk—half-dead save for his jaunty sunglasses—stands before a picturesque forest and above a pickle floating in a glass jar, inanimate yet looking suspiciously like a sort of eel-specimen preserved in formaldehyde. (*Ein brechreizfreies Leben ist nicht vorstellbar (A life without nausea is not conceivable)*, 2013)*

T: In Dieses Kind wird sich totsaufen... *(*This child will drink itself to death...*), 2013, a little-girl Mouseketeer wears a red-white checked dress and plastic Mickey Mouse ears, and is stationed before a slightly overgrown garden of formally shaped hedges. Is anything here* *'natural'? The living child is costumed as an animal who 'lives' only by virtue of cartoon animation; while the plant-life—once forced into geometric forms, but now unkempt—is neither satisfyingly cultured, not wholly abandoned to nature either.*

In all of these juxtapositions, questions regarding what is 'natural' and what 'cultured'—what is human/animal; animated/inanimate; living/dead—are quietly asked again and again. In light of these deliberate ambiguities, the alphabetical categories in the lexicon below are plainly troubled: does sushi fall under 'comestibles' or 'marine themes'? Does an equestrian sculpture belong to 'art' or 'equine themes'? Do mythological creatures count as 'fauna' or 'symbols'?

Moreover my method—sorting out Büttner's iconography, image by image—is unable to take into account, for example, Büttner's extraordinary usage of colour: his unerring shades of mint, tangerine and ox-blood, that serve to frame, even to dignify, the whole. Framing is central to these collages, and we note how many framing devices—arches, windows, actual picture frames—make their appearances. Landscape is a crowded category, and often the collage seems to create a kind of idealised place—a glade; a moonlit lake; majestic mountains—occupied by the wrong sort of life form. Scale is paramount: Big Bugs and tiny Modernist facades both look equally lost in vast ski resorts, while a vast church interior can prove claustrophobic for two copulating ladybirds.

Finally, things move, and move a lot. Ants march, rats drive cars, geese migrate—but most often objects, animals, and people hover or float, like the leaping ballet dancer that opened this essay, flying off-stage into a primordial cave. Rarely, however, do they fall. And, if they did, there are relatively few spiky or dangerous things in Büttner's world—the occasional sword notwithstanding. Things hover precariously, but Büttner always provides a soft landing: a plump sofa; a woman's curvaceous backside; a slice of cheese; or a freshly mowed, picture-postcard field.

Part II
An index of Werner Büttner's collaged universe

ACCESSORIES

eyewear — **sunglasses**, black, floating; **tortoise-shell frame;**
footwear — **high heels**, open-toed; **leather lacing**, close-up;
head gear — **bowler hat; cap**, on a skull; **cowboy; crown**, on a statue; **crown**, hovering above an allée of cacti; **'Chinese hat'**, formed by a heap of sand, in a bell jar, worn over medieval woman's head; **fedora**, perched on the edge of a black coffin, in a field of daffodils; **helmet**, London bobby type; **green leaf**, glued on head; **Napoleonic tri-corn**, pointed, worn by child; **red felt**, with decorative flower and ribbon band, atop despairing statue; **top hat**, worn by a rat driving a car; **woolly hat**, atop a snowman; **zebra print**;

ART

Classicism — **Brandenburg Gate; decorated ceramic**, Greek-type; **female busts**, statuary, a trio; **heads, emperor-type; gladiator**, statue; **interior; temple**, column facade;
music — **lyre player**, with boyfriend; **piano**, upright, with an oversized candle; **keyboard**, all-white; **piper**, stylised; **statue**, with musical notes; **violins**, hanging off a cactus;
statuary —
animals — **camels**, paired; **caryatid; cats**: mama and kitten; **Chinese Sumo lizard; dog**, on a tomb; **eagle**, stone;
cherub — **standing; winged**, in relief, above a green window;
classical — on **Brandenburg Gate; female bust; heads; Lincoln Memorial; Statue of Liberty**;
figurine — **cross-legged; despairing man**, wearing a red felt hat; porcelain, small; **figurine**, porcelain, Baroque clown rat with Pompadour wig; **gargoyle; gladiator-type; Holy Family**, wooden;
medieval-type — female bust, with musical notes; **medieval-type**, grotesquerie;
misc — **Easter Island-type; Egyptian obelisk-type, with a monkey face**, at its 'head'; **equestrian**, non-descript; **monolith-type**, stone; **nymph-type, Romantic; 'the thinker'**, Rodin, posed men in suits; **Venus of Willendorf**, full frontal; **winged**;

COMESTIBLES

carbohydrates — **baguette**, French; **fries**, French, doubled into an hourglass shape; **noodles; potatoes**, with meat and gravy; **sandwich**, cheese filling, impaled; **sliced white bread**, with jam-painted smiley face;
dairy — **cheese**, blue; Swiss, sliced; Swiss, with the artist's head poking from one hole; unidentified yellow; aging, on shelves; **eggs**, breakfast, soft boiled, with 'soldiers'; cracked, with chick; three; in a carton;
meat — and **potatoes; beef**, raw; **butcher's**, raw; **escalope**, on a plate, with lemon/parsley garnish; **hot dog; pig's head**, roasted; **pork**, raw;
root veg — **carrots**, in bundles; **potatoes**, boiled; **potatoes**, with meat and gravy; **sprouting**;

CONSTRUCTION

arch — ***Arc de Triomphe***, or just some plaster moulding; **door; pointed; window; with long-shadowed man;**
architectural details — **balcony**, ornate; **roof**, floating; **staircase**, iron, ornate, with green pillar; **urban medieval;**
brickwork — **arch** (upside down); **as a frame; as flooring; cell**; in a **window; L-shaped; small**, as frame; **white**, behind lap dog; as **wall;**
buildings — **aqueduct**, covered in vines; **beach huts**, in primary colours; **lighthouse; maquette**, late Modernist; **multi-storey parking facility**, concrete; **ruin**, in silhouette, at night; **urban medieval;**
church — **Modernist; country**, with giant bottle as *campanile*; **early Gothic**, in a forest; **spire;**
facade — **early Gothic**, church; **in perspective; Modernist**, multi-window;
house(s) — **beach-type cabin**, three, purple, very pitched asymmetrical roofs; **double-gabled**, white; **garden-tent-type; housing estate**, curved; **modest**, with drying laundry; **modest**, with lamp post; **made of hay;**

nestled, in a prawn's curled tail; **shed**; **suburban-type**, showing dormers and roof; **Tudor-type**, housing development;
space — **interior**, Baroque, empty; **interior**, church; **interior**, Modernist, with pool; **interior**, with corner; **outer**; **prison**, possibly ice-storage;
wall (see also *brickwork*) — **pegboard**; **stone**; **wallpaper**, flowery and pink, Victorian-**type**; **wallpaper**, lilac, classical trifleur pattern; **wallpaper**, William Morris-**type**; **wallpaper**, with Ken doll; **wallpaper**, striped, beige and brown; **woodpanelling**, with nipples detail.
window(s) — **arched**; **framed**, in white; on **facade**; **picture**, showing beach scene; **rectangular**, Modernist; **square**, modern; with **bars**; with **Christmas trees**; with **billowing curtain**; with **green shutters**;

CONTAINERS
boxes — **cardboard**, empty; full; with woman's outstanding cleavage; atop Statue of Liberty; worn by a man on a pogo stick; floating, over cherubs and sky; **stacked**, of appliances;
fences — **barbed wire**; **gate**, ornate; **ironwork**, and decorative pillars;
frame(s) — **Baroque**; **blue**, like a stylised door; **gold**, with horned man; **multiple**, frames inside frames inside frames **ornate**; **stone**, with red decoration; **tabletop-type**, showing a man holding a rifle; **with bloodied nose**; **with hammers**; **with jar**;
packaging — **Absolut Vodka**; **bottle cap**, folded; **Coke bottle**, in pieces; green wine bottle, as a campanile;
receptacles — **basket**; **briefcase**; **Red Cross bag**, worn by a snowman; **satchel**;

DECORATION
antlers — **horns**, on a newspaper 'head'; **moose**; **deer**, in the forest; **deer**, in silhouette; **distant antelope**;
bow(s) — on **bottles**; on a **wreath**; **red ribbon**; **ribbon**, as a tie;
Christmas — **extreme Christmas lights**, home exterior; **light-up deer**; **tinsel**, around head statuary; **trees**, in windows; **wreath**, atop a termite hill;
ladies haberdashery — **bikini**, blue; **bikini**, red; **coat**, suede, beat up; **gloves**, leather, worn by Alice Cooper; **gown**, polka dot; **scarf**, red; **seamstresses dummy** and measuring tape, coiled; **tights**, ripped;
mask — **golden**; **grotesquerie**; on a scribe; **'ethnic'-type**; **early Christian-type**; **like bricks**;

ELEMENTS, THE
air (see also *balloons*) — **smoke**; **soap bubbles**;
fire — **barbecue-type**, with roast pig; **candle**; **fireplace-type**, small, tame; metal
light — **extreme Christmas lights**, display, home exterior; **garden light**, with spike; **lamp**, stand-up; **light bulb**;
metal —
hardware — **hammers**; **silver bolts**, a large number, floating like a cloud; **trowel**;
heavy metal — **Alice Cooper**; **Iron Maiden**;
weaponry — **pistol**; **rifle**; **sword**, handheld; candlestick-type, impaling a cheese sandwich;
water — **as a spray**, released from a coiled snake; **flood**; **in drops**; **empty pool**, sloped; **faucet stream**; **filled pool**; **mirror-reflection lake**, with haunted house; **ocean**, nocturnal; **splashed**, on tyres; **water bottle**;

FAUNA
Big Bugs — **ants**, on the march; **butterflies**, in pairs; **dragonfly**; **ladybirds**, copulating; **ladybirds**, giant, in church; **mosquito**, fossilised; **mosquito**, on the roof; **termite**, hill; **unidentified**;
bird(s) — **black**, generic; **Canadian geese**; **dove**; **eagle**; **flamingo**; **owl**; **pigeon**, lone; **pigeons**, in cages; **ravens**, on a roof;
canines — **Bassett hound**, with flaying ears; **greyhound**, beneath a mug, floating; **hound**, literally in the doghouse; **Jack Russell-type**, staring a giant bone behind velvet ropes, meant to be comical; **terrier**; **wolves**, snarling; **wolves**, very large pack;
caprine — **goat**, cartoon-type; **goat**, cartoon-type with man; **herd**, aerial view;
deer — **Christmas-type**, illuminated; **stylised**, in a pack;
elephant — close up; on a white sofa;
equine — **a horse** knocked down, but getting up, heroically; with eyepatch, red; a **horseshoe**, tacked on a chair back; **equestrian statuary**, in bas-relief; archaic; **running horses**; **with Napoleonic rider**; **with zebra man**, and zebra;
feline — **black cat**, watched by Abraham Lincoln; **cartoon-type**, under equestrian statue; **lion**, large and dark, close up; **mama cat** and kitten, statuary; **tiger**, highly stylised and elongated;
frog — with Venus flytrap; fat and large;
hatching — **chick**, and cracked egg; **fish**; **insemination**;
marine — **fish, lone**; **fish**, paper cut-out; **fish**, platter, with lemon; **fish**, skin, close-up; **shells**, clam-type; **shrimp**, or prawn, large; **shark**, ripped in two; **sushi**;
ovine themes — **black-faced**, sheep, in bottom corner; **sheep**, grazing in a field;
panda — looking bored and a little psychotic, possibly drugged;
porcine themes — **dancing pig**; **oval-framed pig**; **overweight pig**, racing across snowy field; **raw pork**; **roasted pig**, on a spit; **supine pigs**; **wild boar**; ***prosciutto crudo***, sliced;
primate — **big chimp**, smiling; **chimp**, stuffed; **gorilla head**, atop an Egyptian obelisk;
reptiles — or **possibly a crustacean**, in dark landscape; **snake**, coiled, spraying water like a hose; **snake**, coiled with... a child?; **snake**, emerging from spiral pattern; **snake**, two-headed; **winged iguana**;
rodent — **rat**, in mosaic car;

FLORA
cactus — on **a field**; **potted**; **sprouting**, desert flowers; with **dripping violins**; **flanking a straight road**;
edible — **apple core**, floating over tiny house and large leaves; **apple core**, worn as a hat by a chimpanzee; **garlic**; **green pea**; **red berries**, small clump; **walnut**;
flowering — **blossoms**, pink; **daffodils**, field in bloom, with fedora hat and coffin; **daisies**, in a vase; **field of blooms**, white and purple; **orange rose**, large; **potted flowers**; **red rose**; **tulips**, in garden pots, interspersed with statuary; **tulip**, on a postage stamp;
forest(s) — at **dusk**; **birch**; **foggy**, with snarling wolves; **forest floor**; **generic**; **in silhouette**; **pine**; as background; in close-up; **with romantic sunlight**, streaming through x 2;
leaf(-ves) — in **a clump**, large, as background; **lone**, small, glued on someone's head; with **flowers**;
misc — **autumn foliage**; **botanical drawing**, foliage selection; **grass**, left to dry like hay; **house plant**; **pods**, beans, white; **shamrock**; **shoots**, green; **Venus flytrap**;
trees — **pine**, with church and pogo-stick man; **single**, staked, in front of a housing estate; **single**, surrounded by paving, in a garden;

GAMES AND TOY DEPARTMENT
balloons — **Jeff Koons-type**, blue dog; **child's party-type**, twisted into a dog shape; **red**, pinned to a window;
sports themes — **beach jogger**; **beautiful game**, the; **bodybuilder**; **gymnast**; **tennis balls**, spilled from a basket; **wrestlers**;
toys — **dice**; **Lego giraffe**, close-up; **Ken doll**, in the shower; **male doll**, puppet-type, with double chin and disembodied hands; **stuffed monkey**, on a toybox; **stuffed pig**, home made, bright pink, on a table;

HOMEWARE AND FURNITURE DEPARTMENT
bed — futon, empty; **bed**, wooden, modern, no mattress;
chair — **bench**, park type; **broken**, wood; **director's style**, with crucifix; **distressed leather**, brown; **floral pattern**; **garden-type**, with table; **leather**, designer type; leather, yellow; **white plastic**;
desk — with **empty drawers**; **kitchen sink unit**, Modernist;
knick-nacks — **clock**, small, mantelpiece-type; **clothes hangers**; **fork**; **life preserver**, red; **rolling pin**; **razor blade**;
lamp — table;
shelving — **archive-type**, messy; **low**, wooden, with books; **library, with gold-embossed bookspines**; with **cheeses**; with **skulls**;
sofa — **Chinoiserie-type**; **leather**, with a smiley face on a slice of white bread; **leather**, with a giant mosquito; **leather**, generic; **red**, beneath a field; **white**, with sleeping elephant; **white**, in a park;
soft furnishings — **armchairs**, floral pattern; **Empire-type sofa**, with yellow upholstery and canopy, seriously luxurious; **pillow**, beige, with comfy slippers; **'Orientalist'-type**, with cushions and throw rugs, seriously comfy;
stationery — **paper clip**, enormous; **pencil** very large; shavings;
table — **bedside-type**, white with gold trim, 'Princess' style; **round**, white plastic; with **garden gnome**;

HUMAN BEING
bones (see also *skull*) — **boneless body**; **dino skeleton**; **large**, admired by a dog and behind velvet ropes; **skeleton**, in hooded white cloak;
clown face — **on a chair**; **red**, oversized, on a woman's body;
couples — **Adam and Eve**;
disembodied — **bloodied nose**, with mouth; **decapitated matador**; **ear**; **knee and hand**, in meditation; **head**; **hand(s)**, holding a smiley face of slice white bread, holding baby birds; holding *'geschlossen'* sign; pinching another hand; **legs**, women's; **limbs**, child-like, wrapped in a... snake?; **trousers**;
fingerprint — really big; **skull**, with cap; Neanderthal; **skulls**, whole lotta;
hair — **Beatles-type mop**; **balding man**, with slipped toupee; **spiked**;
supine — **figure**, lying like a hot dog; **pigs**; **woman**, on the floor, with large clown face; **women**, on the floor, in spiral pattern;
Werner Büttner — with pencil and green towel;
woman — **cleavage**; **dancing**, in silhouette; **gymnast**; **lying on the floor**, with large clown face; in spiral pattern; **medieval-type**, bending over towards a basket; **torso**, black-and-white; **'tribal'**; **wearing red**, on a balcony; **wearing red 'coralline' dress**;

LANDSCAPE
aerial view(s) — of **a desert**; of **a football match**; of **a goat herd**; of **a jungle**;
desert — **aerial** view; **barren**; **Grand Canyon-type**, with a **long straight** road, floating above a red sofa; **sands**, with a country church and bottle campanile;
disaster (natural) — **floating house**, tidal wave; **roof blown**, seaside house;

field of flowers — **daffodils**; **field of flowers**, white and purple; **grassy**, fjord or prairie; **grazing land**, with sheep; **haystacks**, in a field, country church in the distance; **inflatable globe**, deflated, with shadow; **meadow**, with trees in the distance; with mountains in the distance;
fields — **agrarian**; **ancient**, with earth drawings; **cultivated**;
misc — **beach**, seen through a window; **city skyline**, with sunset and bridge, plus a highly stylized TIR truck; **cliffs**; **parkland**;
mountains — **at night**, beneath a calm midnight sky; **at sunset**; **at sunset**, with an antelope, *National Geographic*-type; **in silhouette**, beneath a purple/pink/yellow sky, slightly psychedelic; **snowy**; **very small**, long the bottom; **nocturnal**, figure against tree, lit by headlights, eerie as hell; empty forest road; **ocean**, nocturnal;
ocean — **floor**, fossilised; **parkland**; **path**, along water, straight; **ploughed fields**; **ocean waves**; **wave**, Hokusai-type; **of garden furniture**; **psychedelic sunset**; **red curving road**; **road**, straight, with telegraph poles; very curvy; into movie star's mouth; along farmlands; **road**;
snowy — **alpine**, postcard type; **field**, with a pig racing across it, beneath a big sky (see also *porcine themes*); **hill**, with grass peeking through; **stone**, strewn with jewellery;
trees — **bamboo**; palm, stretching to the sky; jungle-type, seen from above; staked and young, in a field;

MOVEMENT
flight — **bat**; **eagles**; **flock**, large, past a lighthouse; **Canadian geese**, in formation; **over chocolate**; **over ploughed fields**; **over pink blossoms** and intertwined giraffes; **solitary**;
weird wheels — **boring car**, on a cliff face; **car wreck**; **fishbowl** on wheels; **green antique**; **hot dog stand**, empty; **like a vase**, made of a tyre; **like a wheelchair**, ornate chair with tyres; **Model-T-type**, ambulance; **mosaic car**, driven by a rat;

PATTERN AND SHAPE
clump(s) — **of clay**; **of leaves**; **of berries**; **of coloured spices**;
geometry — **checks**; **spiral**, of women; **triangular**, bas-relief statuary; **triangular**, isosceles;
stripes — **as sky**; **collaged**, birch bark; **in a starburst pattern**, blue; yellow; beige; **like railway lines**, close-up; **painted**, purple and black, as a background; **stars and**; **thin**, as a background; **wash**, as background;
symmetry — **doubled brickwork**, L-shaped; **doubled jungle aerial view**, with floating roof; **doubled plate**, of French fries; **gate**; **shirt display**, and sliced shark; **frog**;
things in formation — **blue dragons**, in formation; **cheeses**, on shelves; **extreme Christmas lights**, home exterior; **folded shirts**, department store display; **flying geese**; **garden furniture**; **head statuary**; **logs or sticks**; **pigeons**, in cages; **rubber ducks**; **soldiers**, in silhouette, marching; **stacked boxes**; **skulls**, on shelves;
twinning — **armchairs**, floral pattern; **bas-relief statuary**, triangular; **bean pods**, white; **butterflies**; **camels**, statuary; **carpets**; **carrots**, in bundles; **cherubs**; **eagles**; **earrings**, with semi-precious stone; **Easter Island-type statuary**; **emergency exit men**, green; **foliage scraps**; **garden lights**; **golden masks**; **giraffes**, in love; **handkerchiefs**; **mannequins**; **pillars**, wooden, emerging from pillows; **pin-like creatures**, could be very long wooden spoons, with eyes; **planks of wood**; **potted flowers**; **sliced Swiss cheese**; **tents**; **tyres**, with splashes of water, 16; **slippers**; **surfers**, with Hokusai wave; **sushi**, salmon nigiri; **'the thinker'**, posed men in suits; **violins**, hanging off a cactus; **wolves**, snarling;

PLANET EARTH
geology — **cave**, with moss; **comet**, cartoon-type; **globe**, spinning; **icicles**; **soil**, close-up; **soil**, irregularly shaped; **rock formation**, in the desert; **standing stone**, precariously balanced;
rain — **drops**, on glass; **rainbow**, colour pattern; **raingear**; **umbrella**, red, in a rowboat;
sky — **big**, behind 'Big Fish' lettering; **blue**, **cloudy**, over grazing sheep; **darkening**, over a green field; **metaphysical-type**; **Northern Lights**; **postcard-type**, as background; alpine; **postcard-type**, behind cactus; **starry**, with Christmas deer;
stars — **Yasser Arafat**; **Marilyn Monroe**, glamour shot; **Marilyn Monroe**, look-alike; **Abraham Lincoln**;

SYMBOLS
cross/crucifix — **black cross**, with a light in the middle; **church-type**, small, in a corner, **Modernist**, in light; **red cross**, on a bag; **white cross**, big; **white cross**, small; **church-type**, small, in a corner; **wooden**, asymmetrical;
Deutschland über alles — **Joseph Beuys**, suit; **Brandenburg Gate**; **German flag**, colours; **medal**, war-type; **youth flag**, with Gothic typeface;
mythological creatures — **stange bearded man**; **Chinese dragons**, blue; **devil and angel**;
"the weight of the world" — **donkey**, with baskets; **old man**, with crates;

SEEN
from above — by **Abraham Lincoln**; by **a caged owl**; by **a flying owl**; by **a single eye**;
from the back — **a coat**, suede, beat up; **a horned man**; **a balding man**, with slipped toupee; one of two cherubs;
in silhouette — **bottle-shape**; **cowboy**; **crucifix**, small; **dancing woman**; **father and son**, hand in hand; **gargoyle**; **figures**, target-practice-type; **forest**; **goat**, cartoon-type; cartoon-type with man; **haunted house**; **long-shadowed man**; **man**, kicking giant potatoes; **men with briefcases**, stylised; **mountain range**; **soldiers**, single cut-outs; **surfers**, with Hokusai wave;

TYPOGRAPHY
graffiti — on **blackboard**, scholastic; on **chalkboard**; **scratched**; **painted**;
lettering — ***Bonne fete maman***; **embroidered**; **advertising-type**; **Arabic**; **'ART'**;
punctuation — **question marks**, in a pile;
signage — **'Al-Qaida'**; **'Big Fish'**, movie poster; **brass-plate type**; **CAFE**, **emergency exit**; ***geschlossen***; **GRILLBAR**, and roadsign; **neon**; **NO ARMS ALLOWED**; **ribbon-scroll-type**; 'sexy', white calligraphy type, with Holy Family; **traffic light** (green);

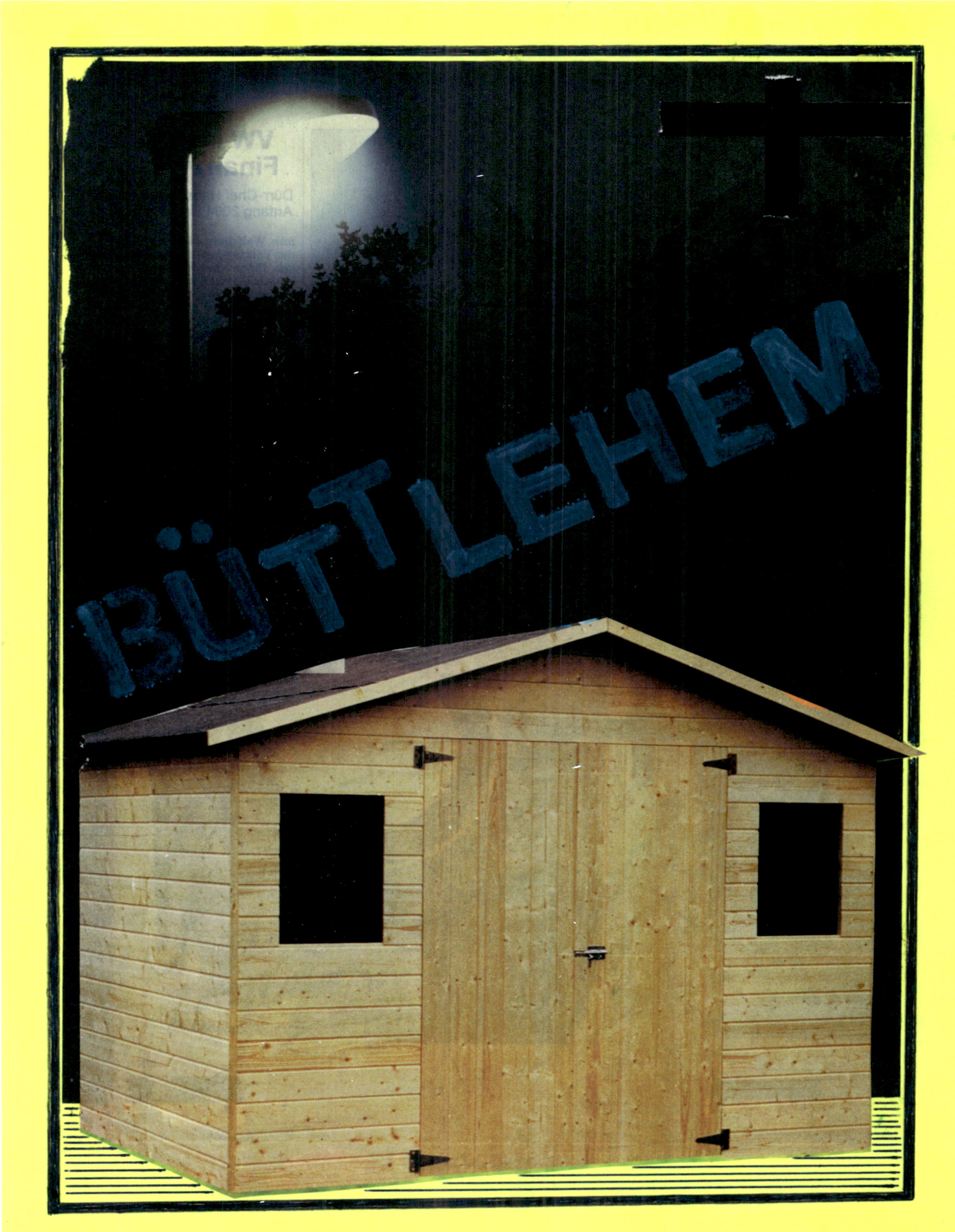

Büttlehem, 2001

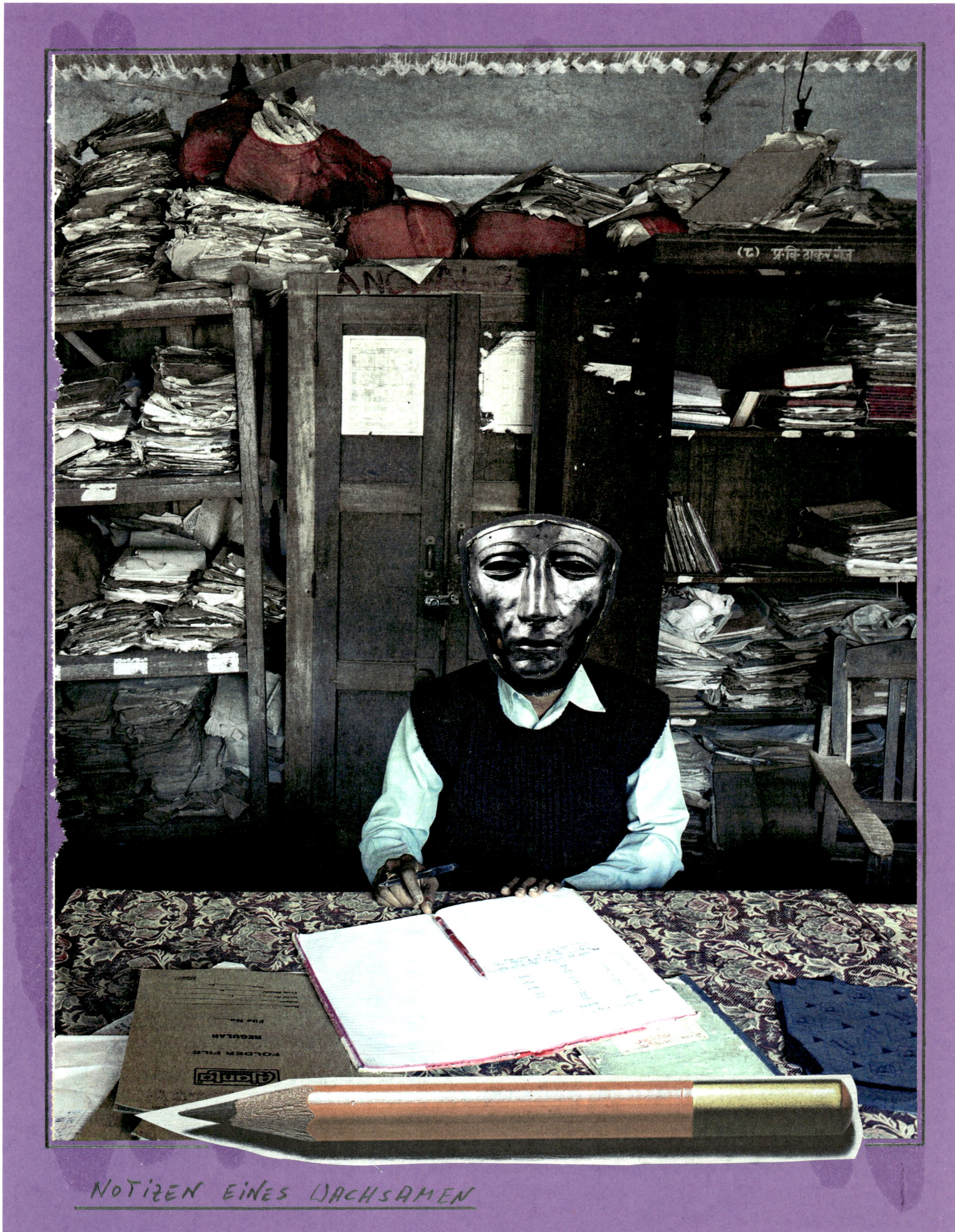

 Notes of a watchful man, 2004

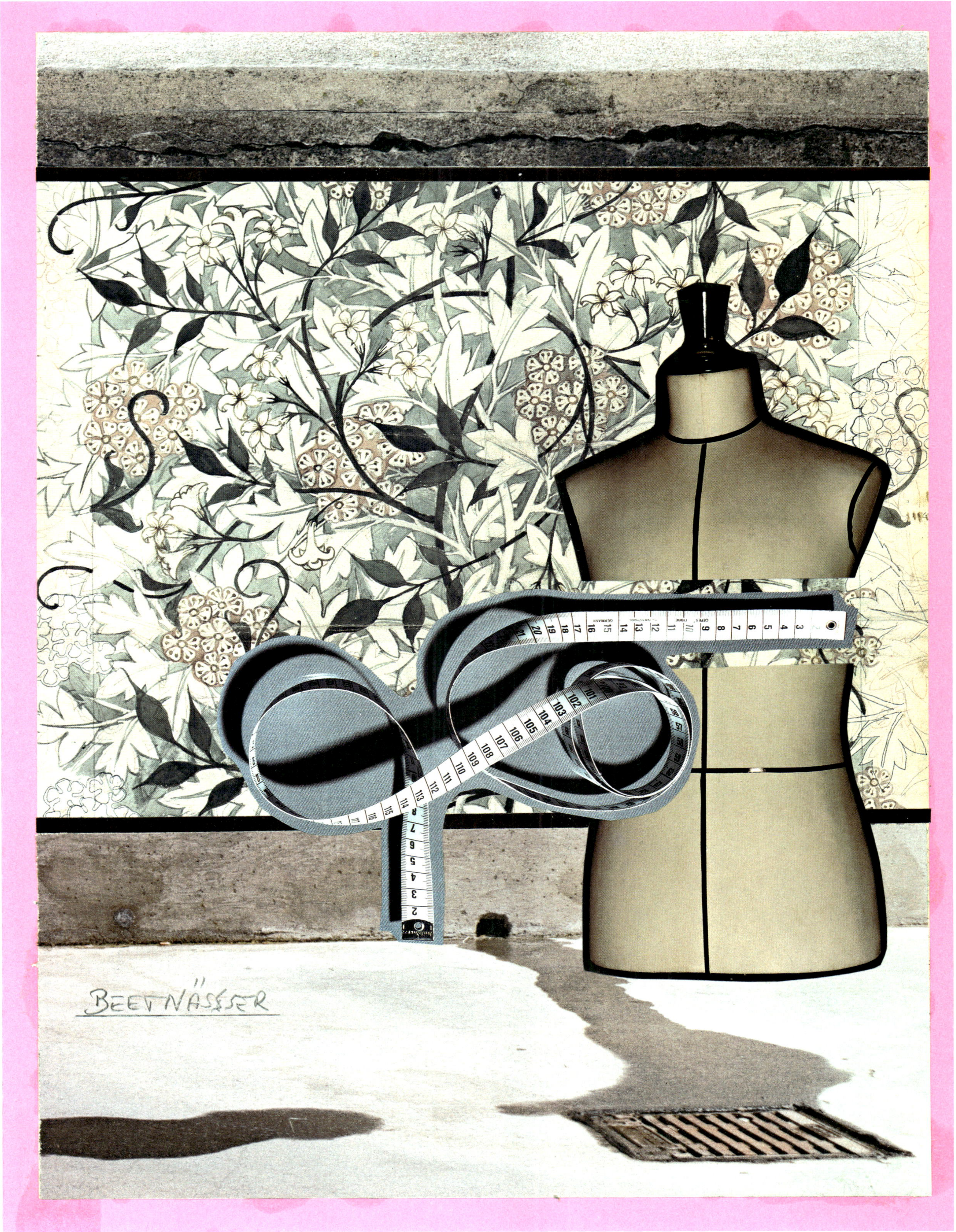

Flowerbedwetter, 2001

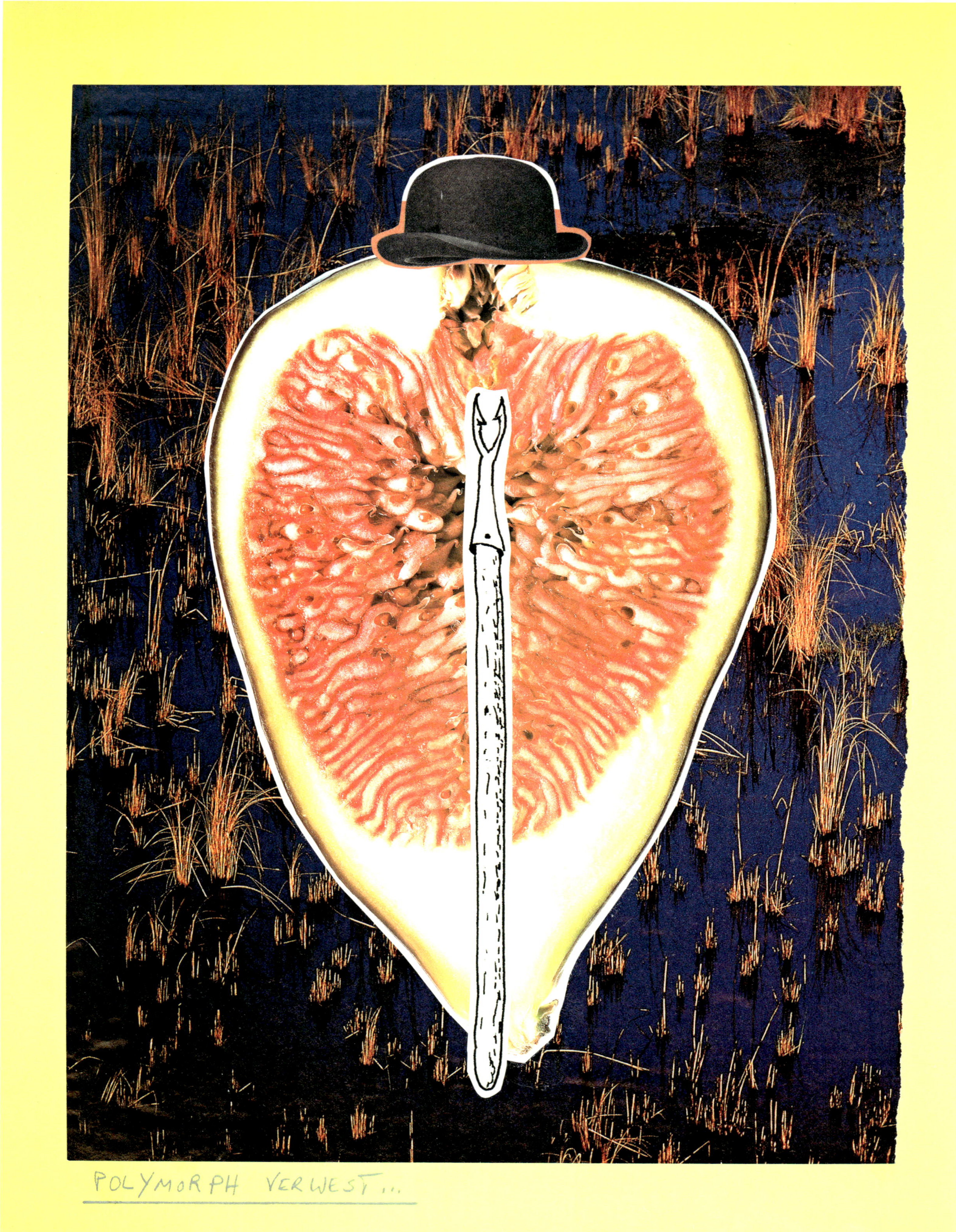

 Polymorphously putrid..., 2001

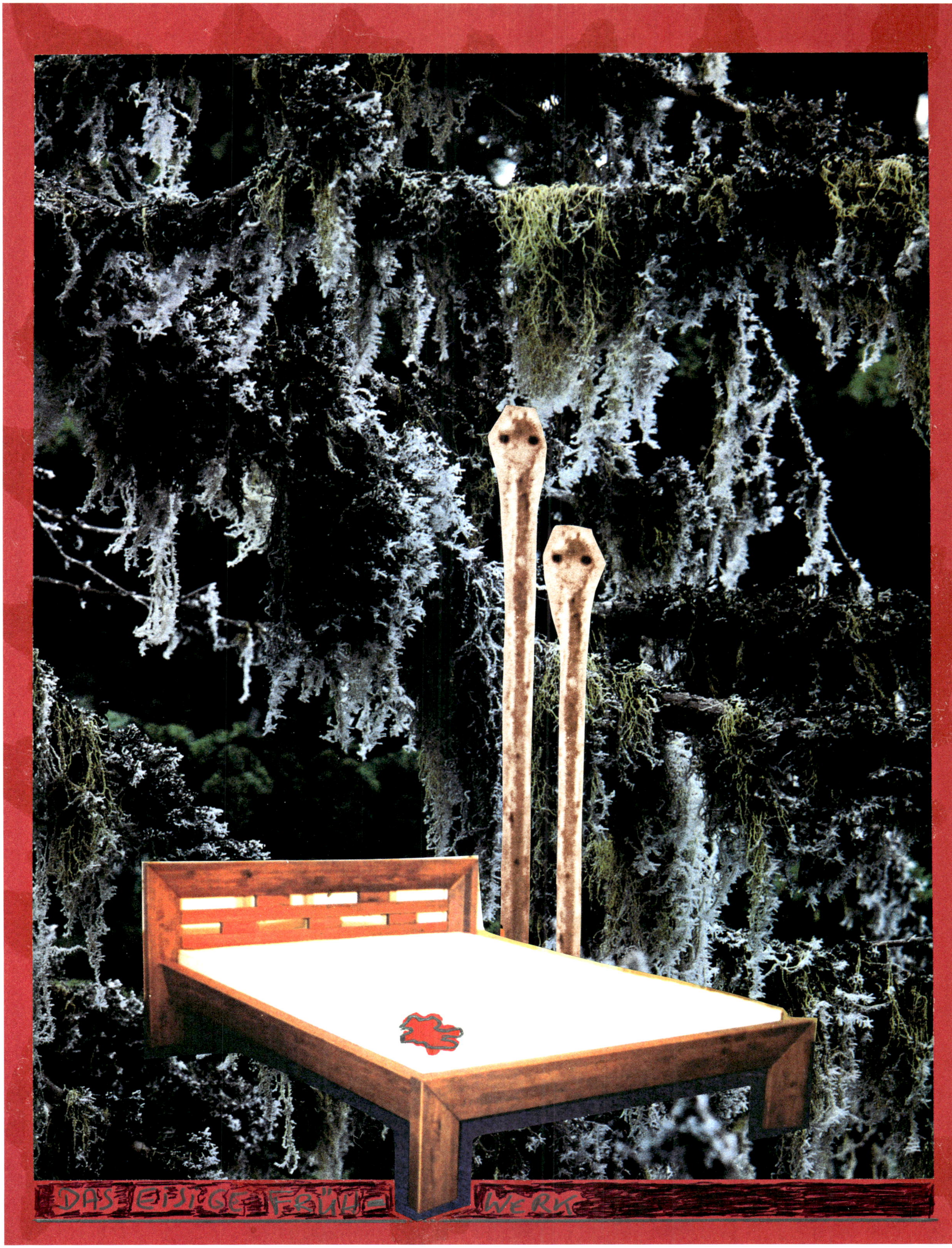

The icy early works, 2001

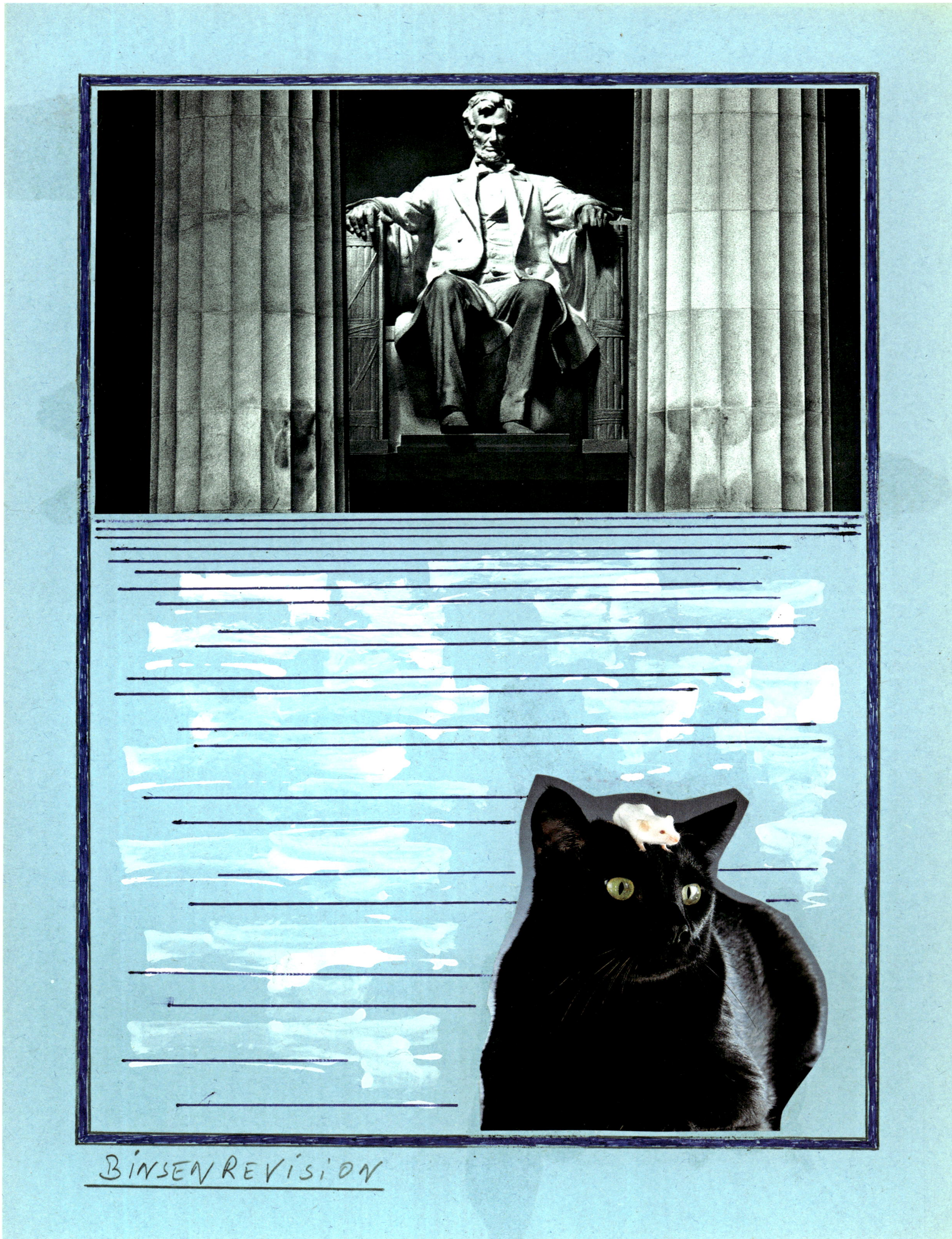

18 **Infernal audit, 2004**

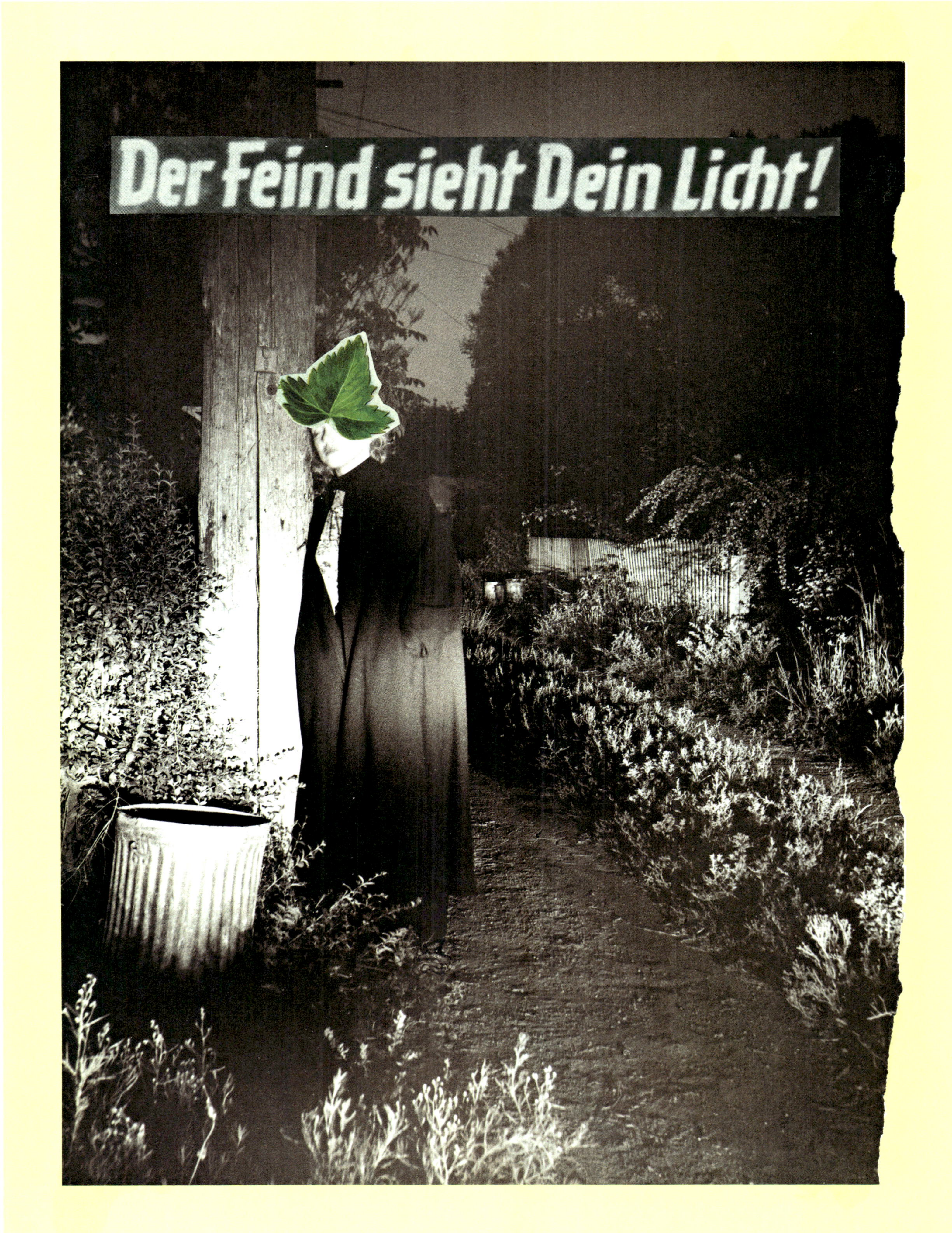

The enemy sees your light!, 2003

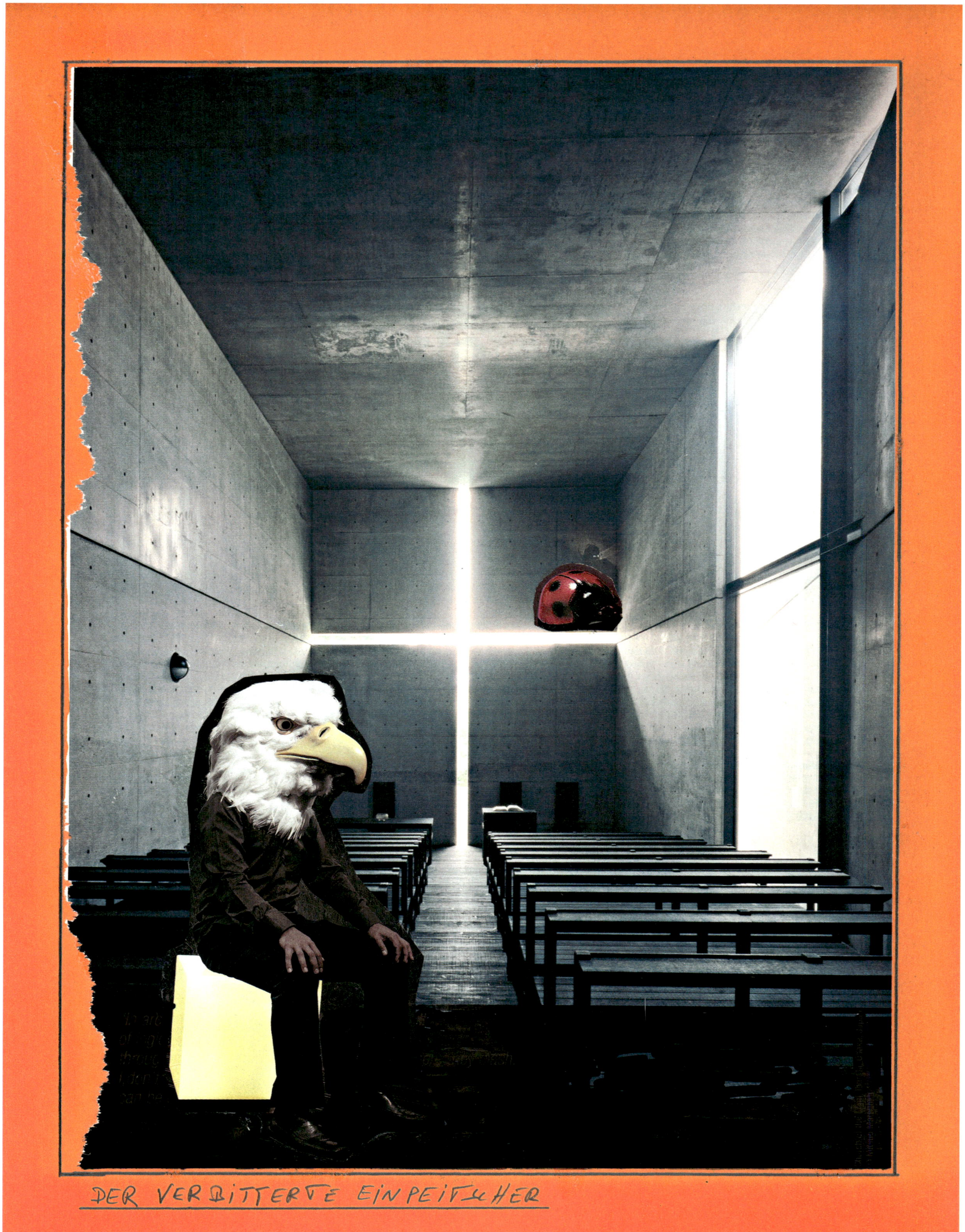

 The embittered firebrand, 2004

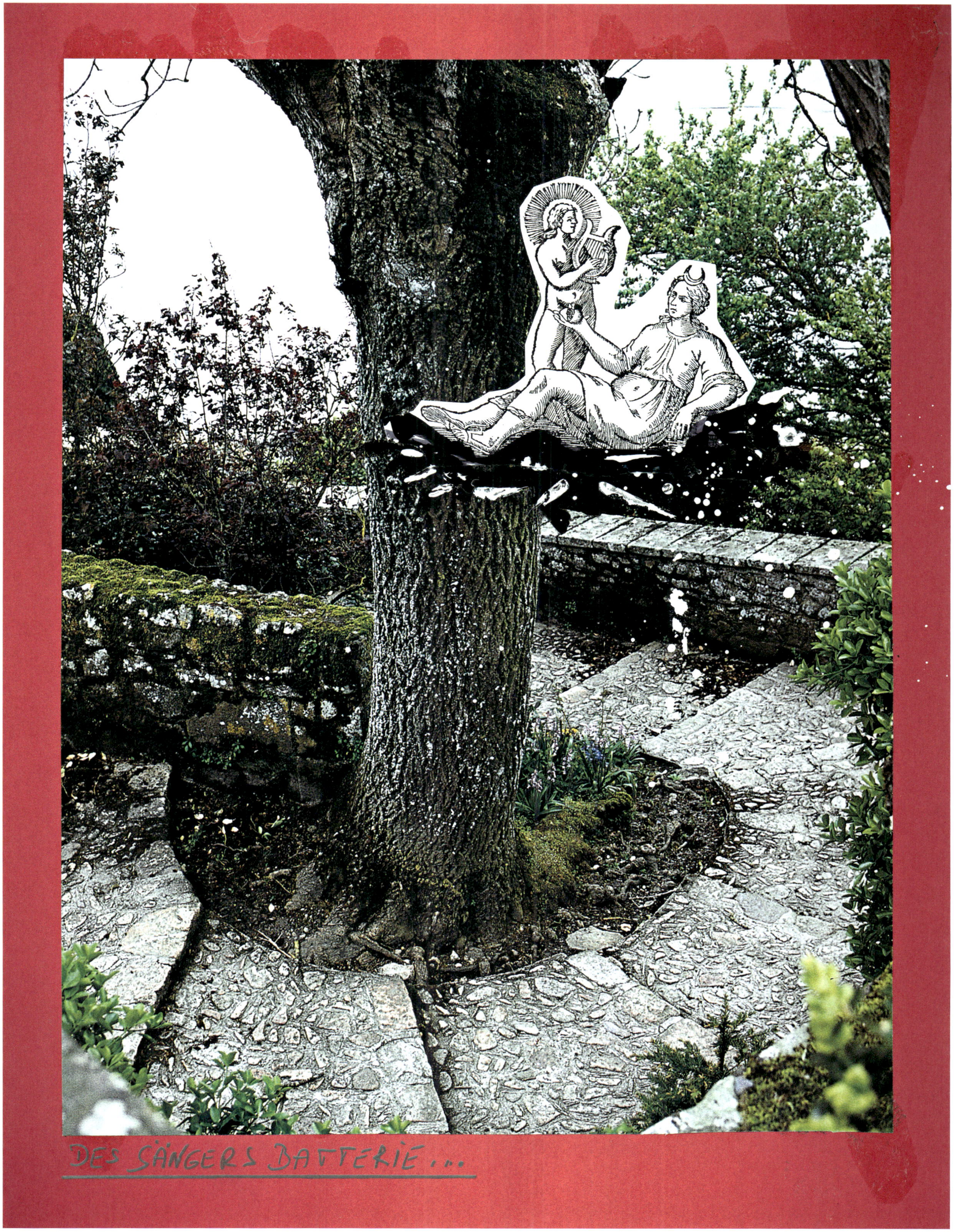

The singer's battery..., 2003

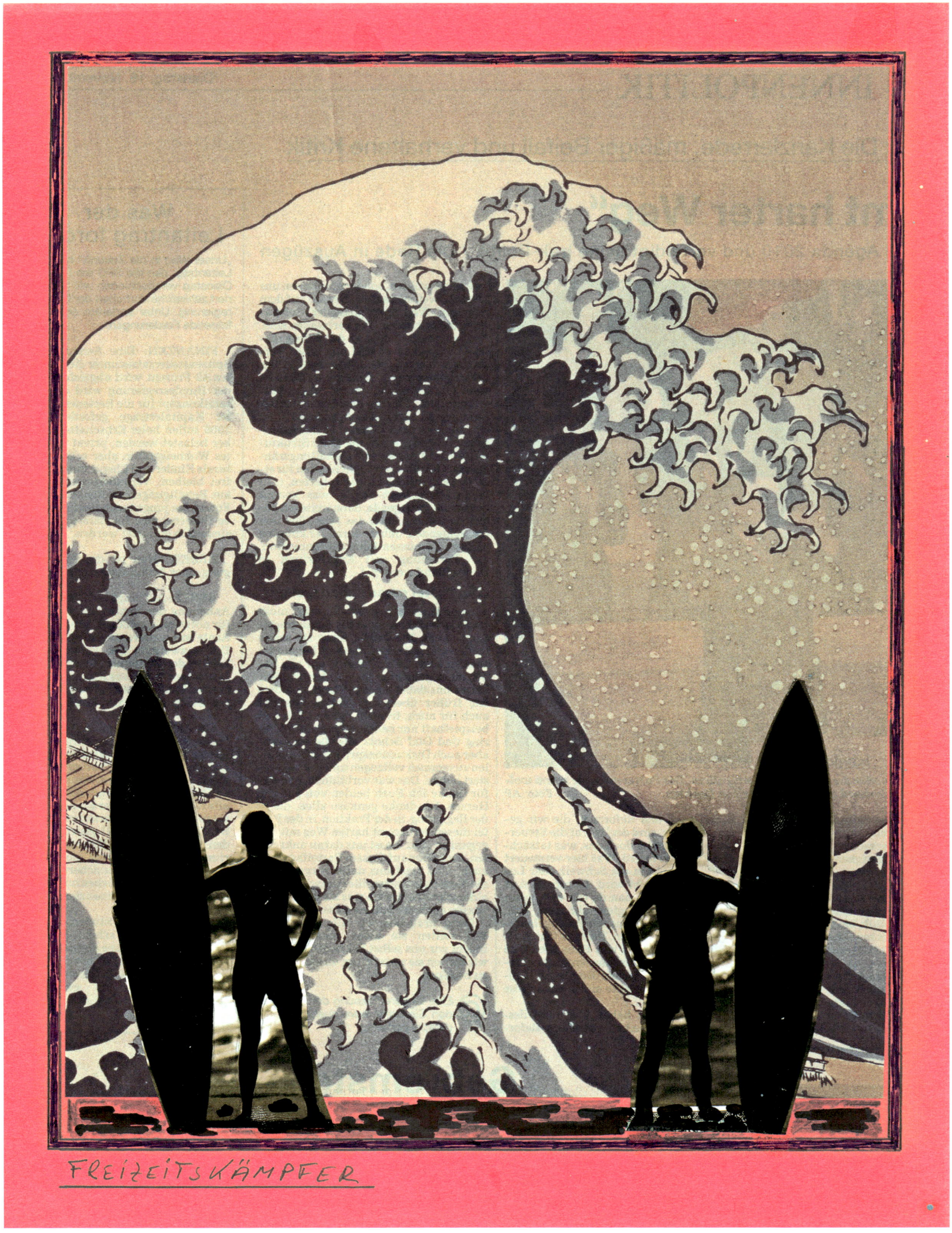

 Free-time fighters, 2003

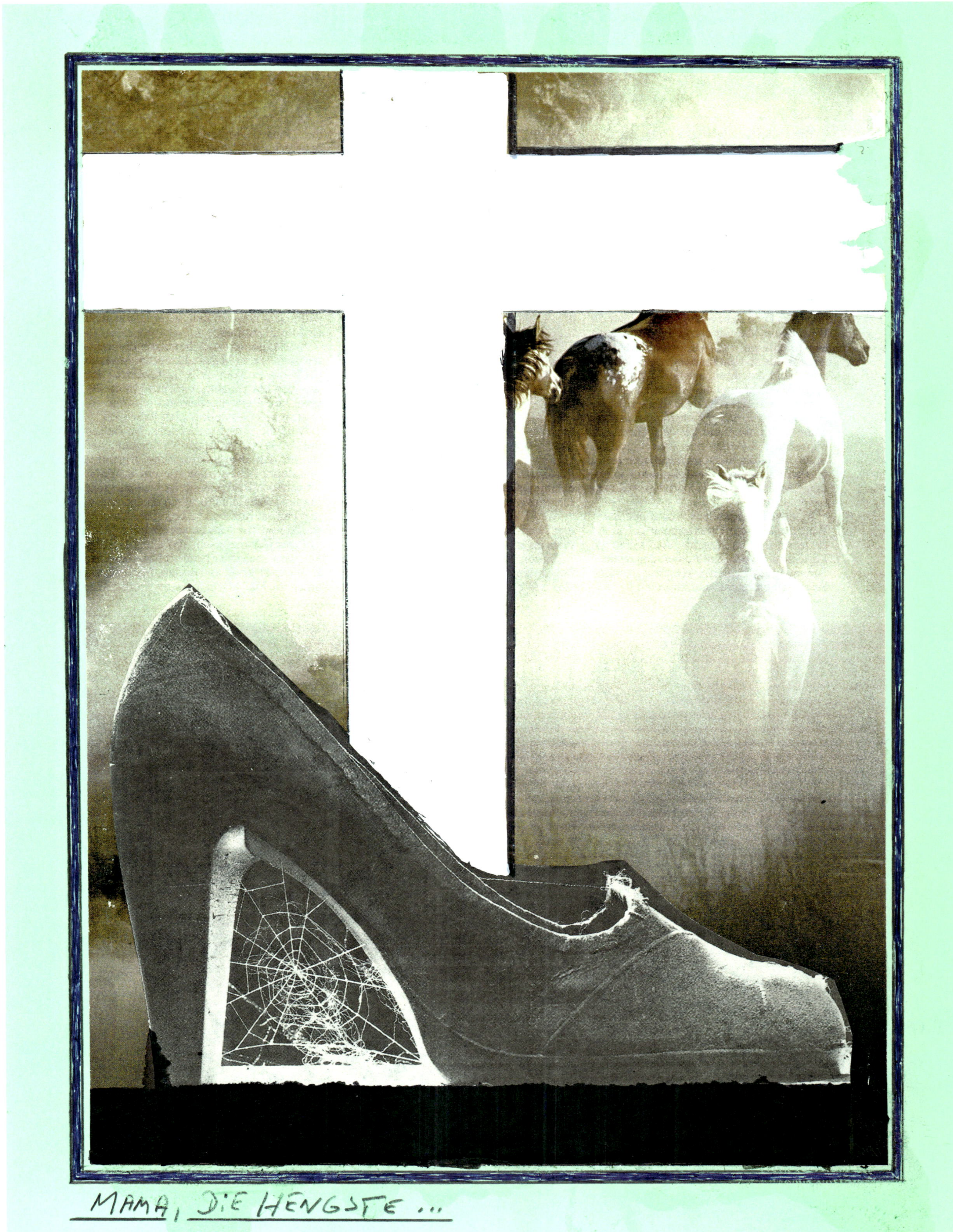

Mummy, the stallions..., 2003

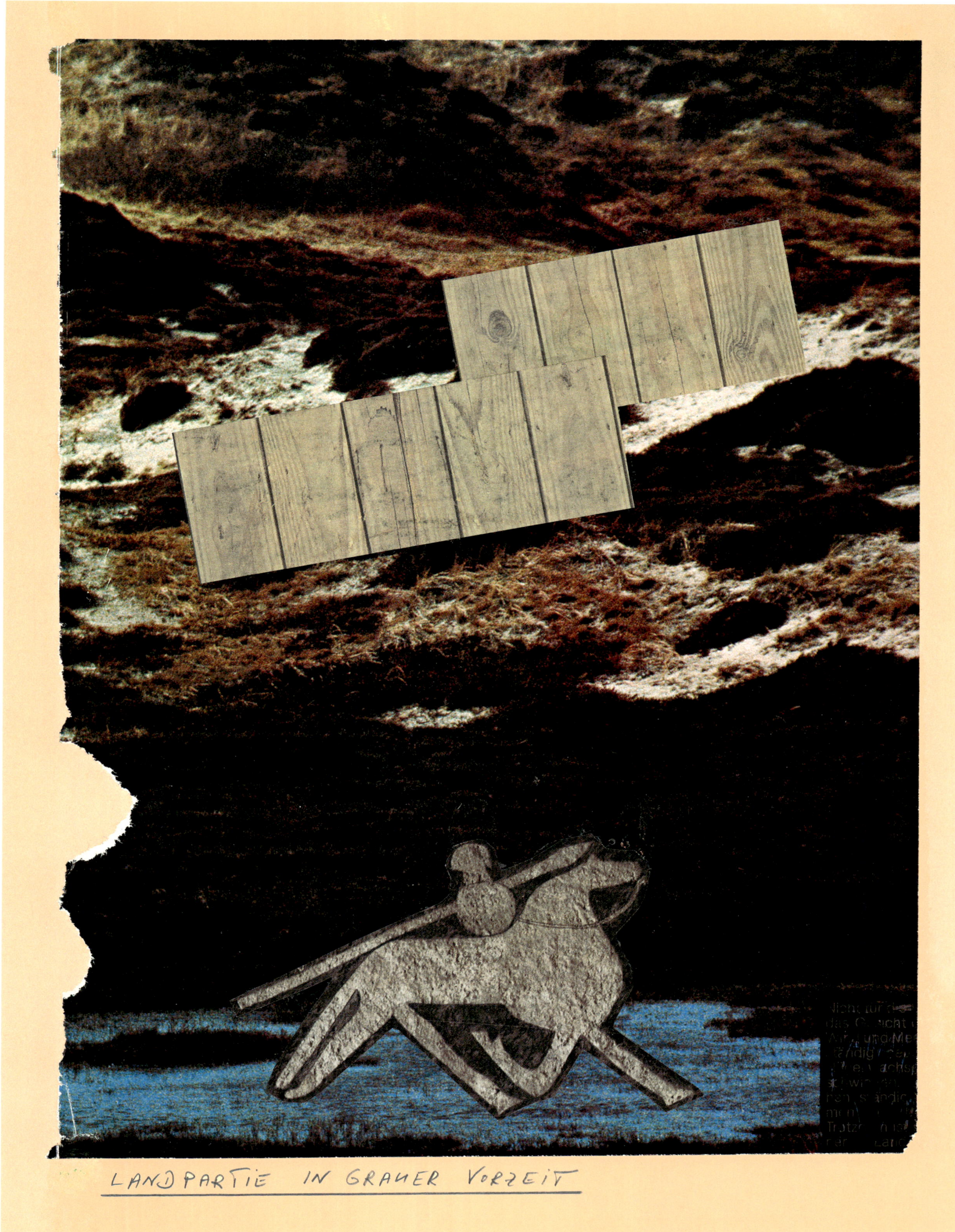

Country outing in the dim and distant past, 2004

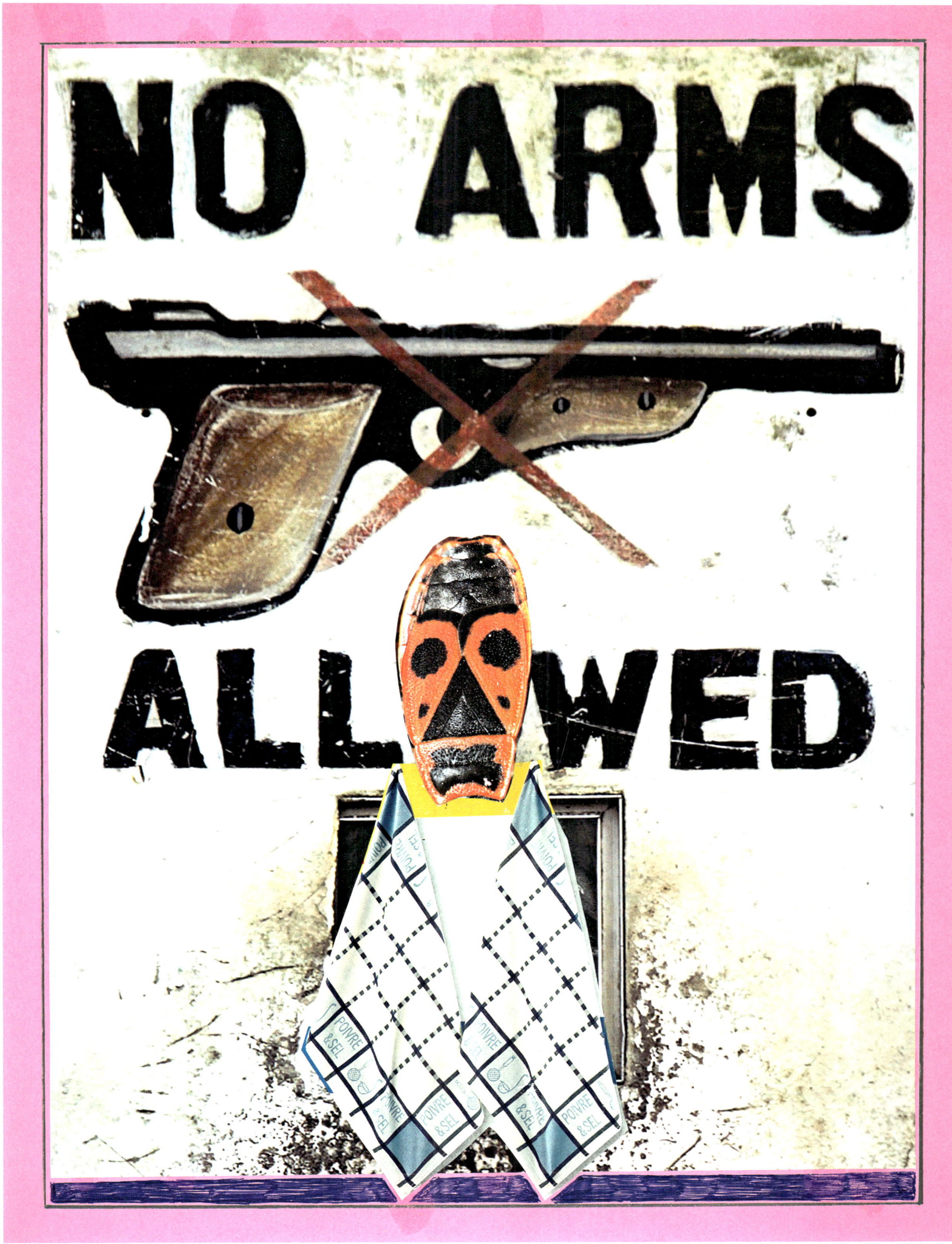

No arms allowed, 2003

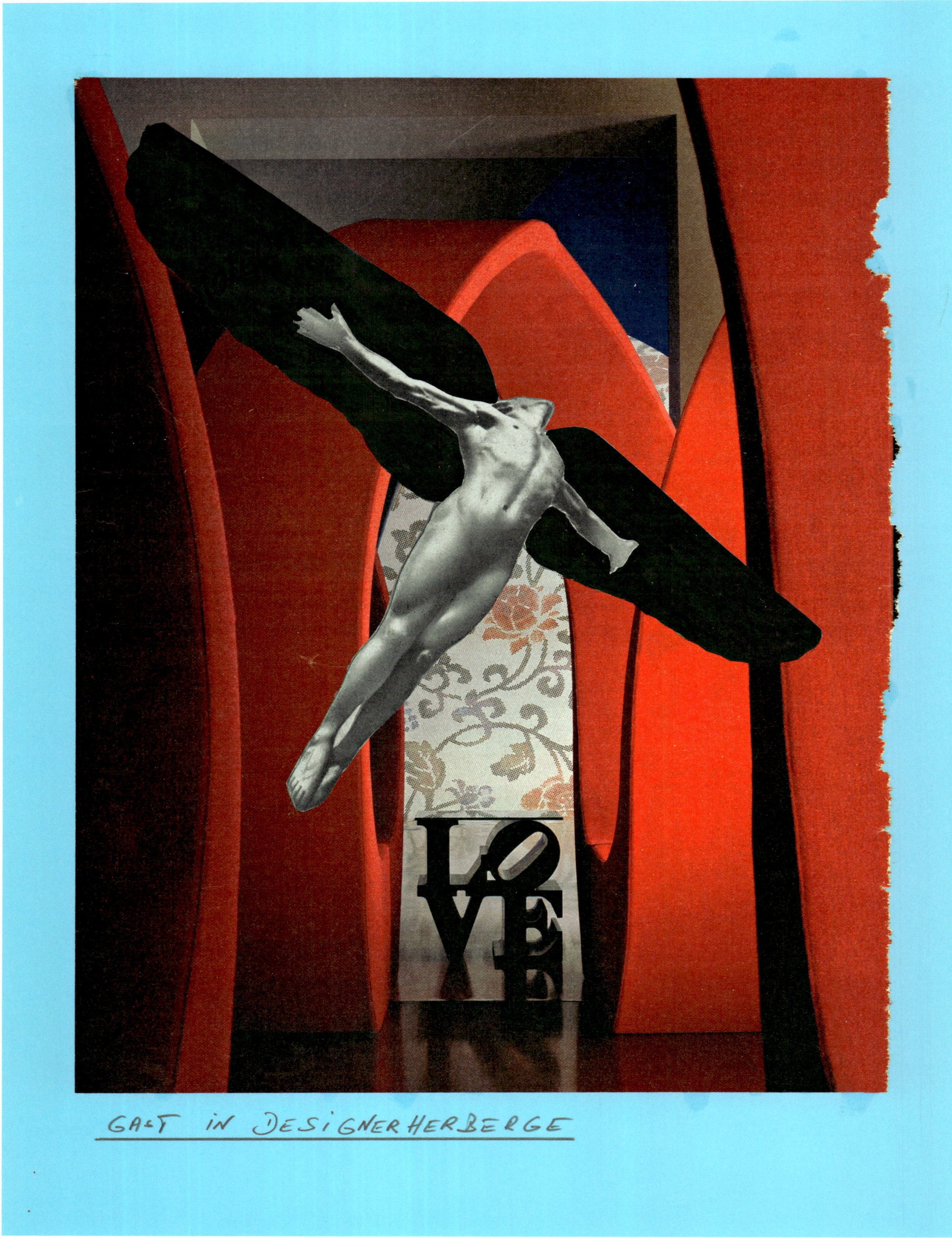

Guest at designer hostelry, 2005

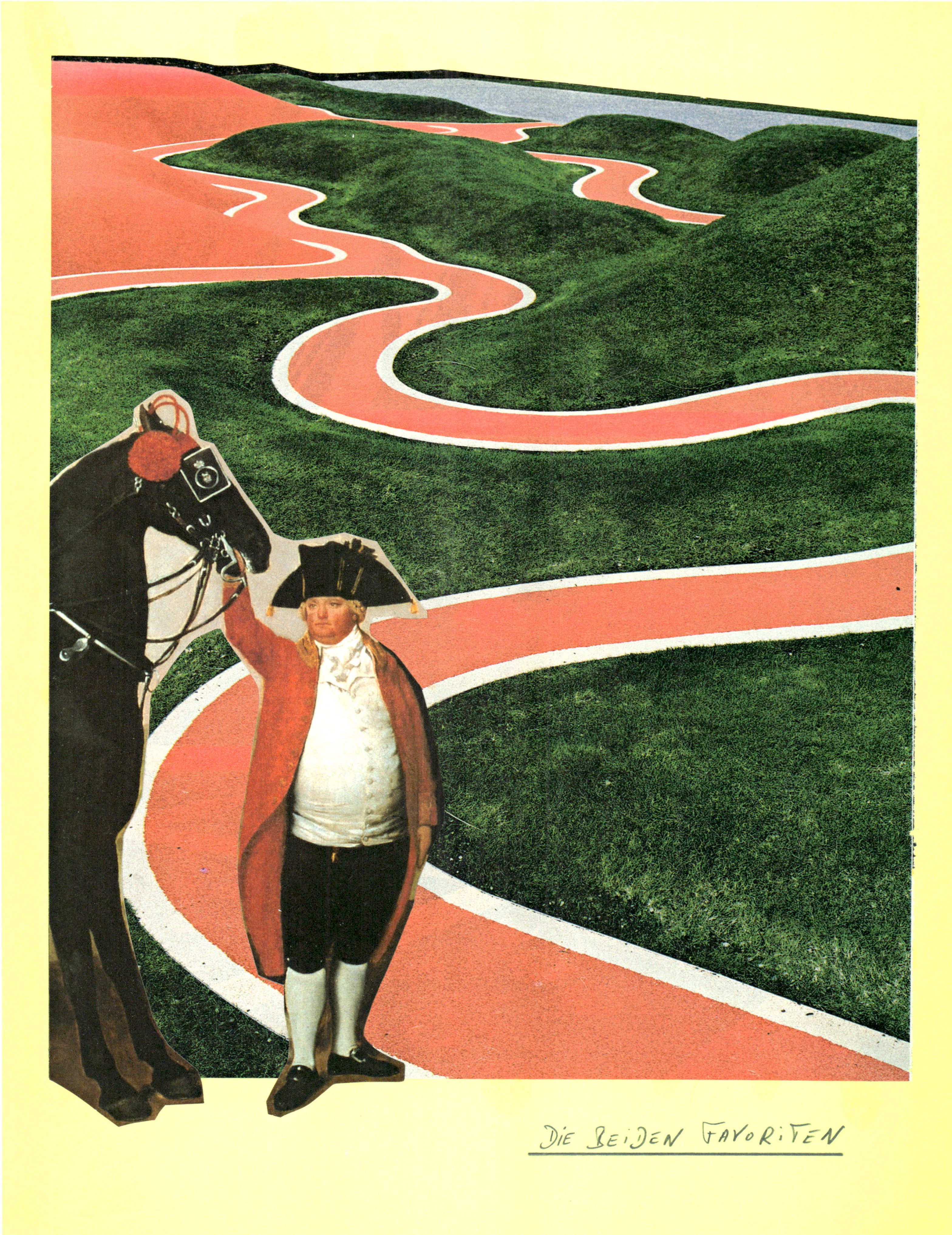

The two favourites, 2005

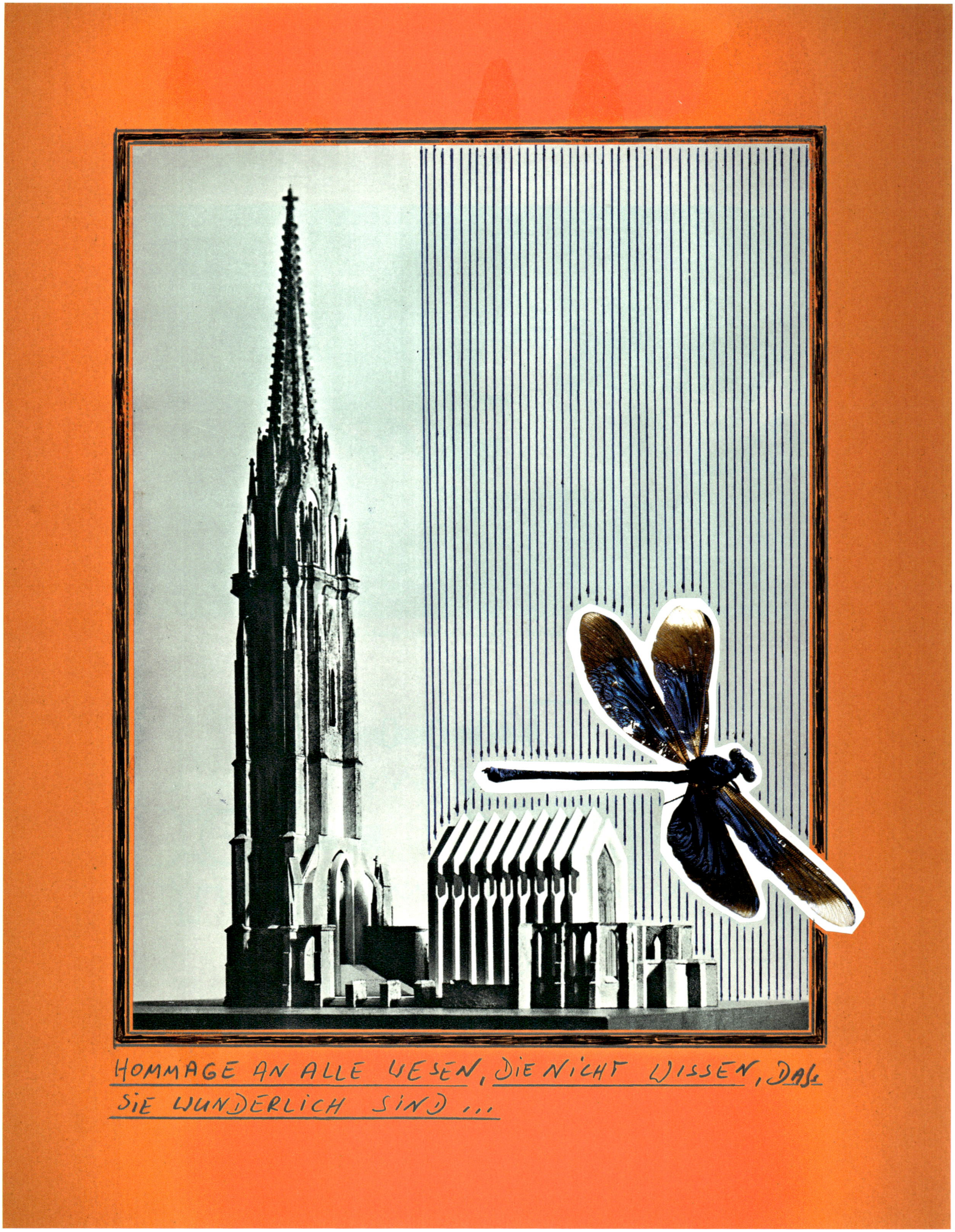

Homage to all creatures that don't know they're odd..., 2004

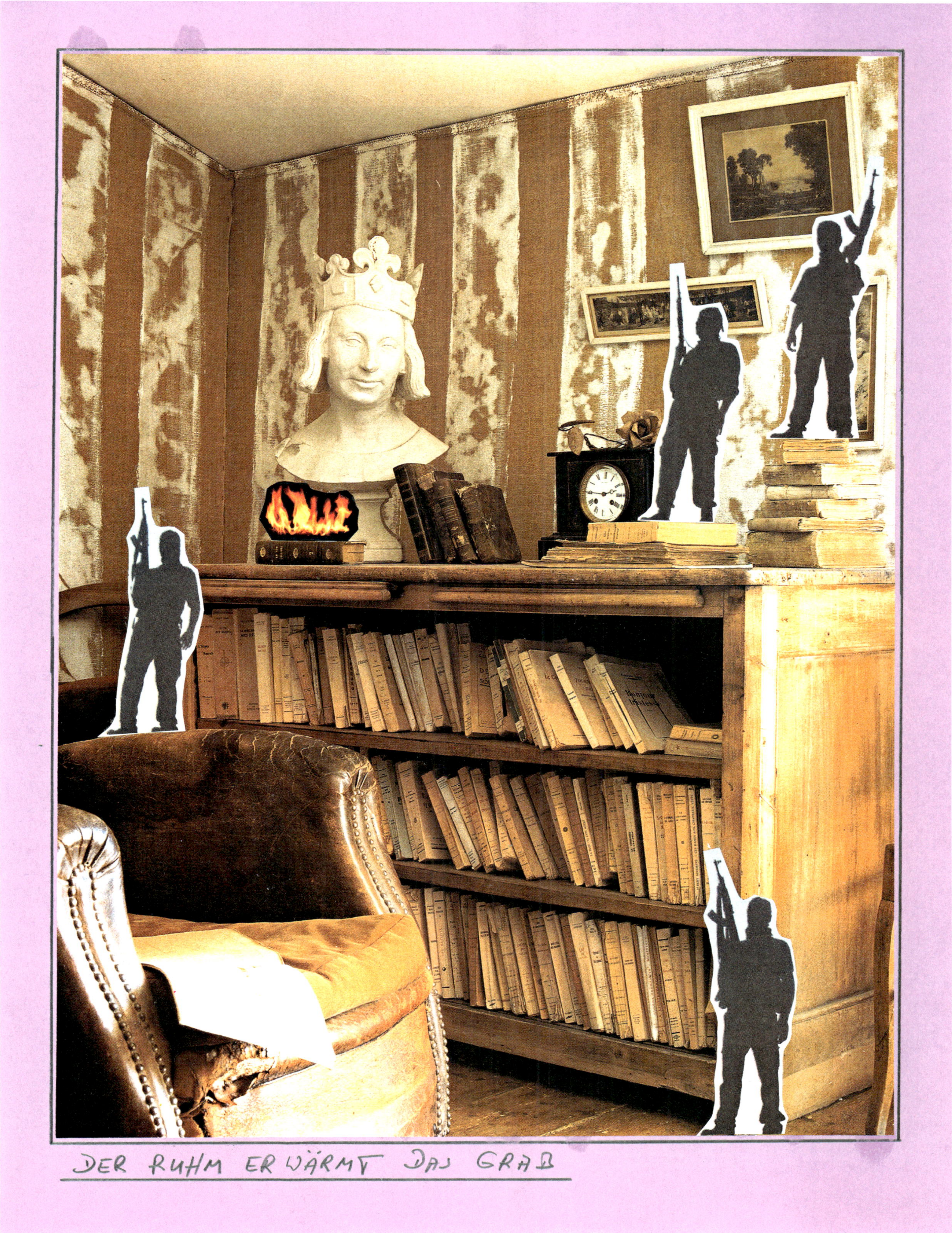

Fame warms the grave, 2004

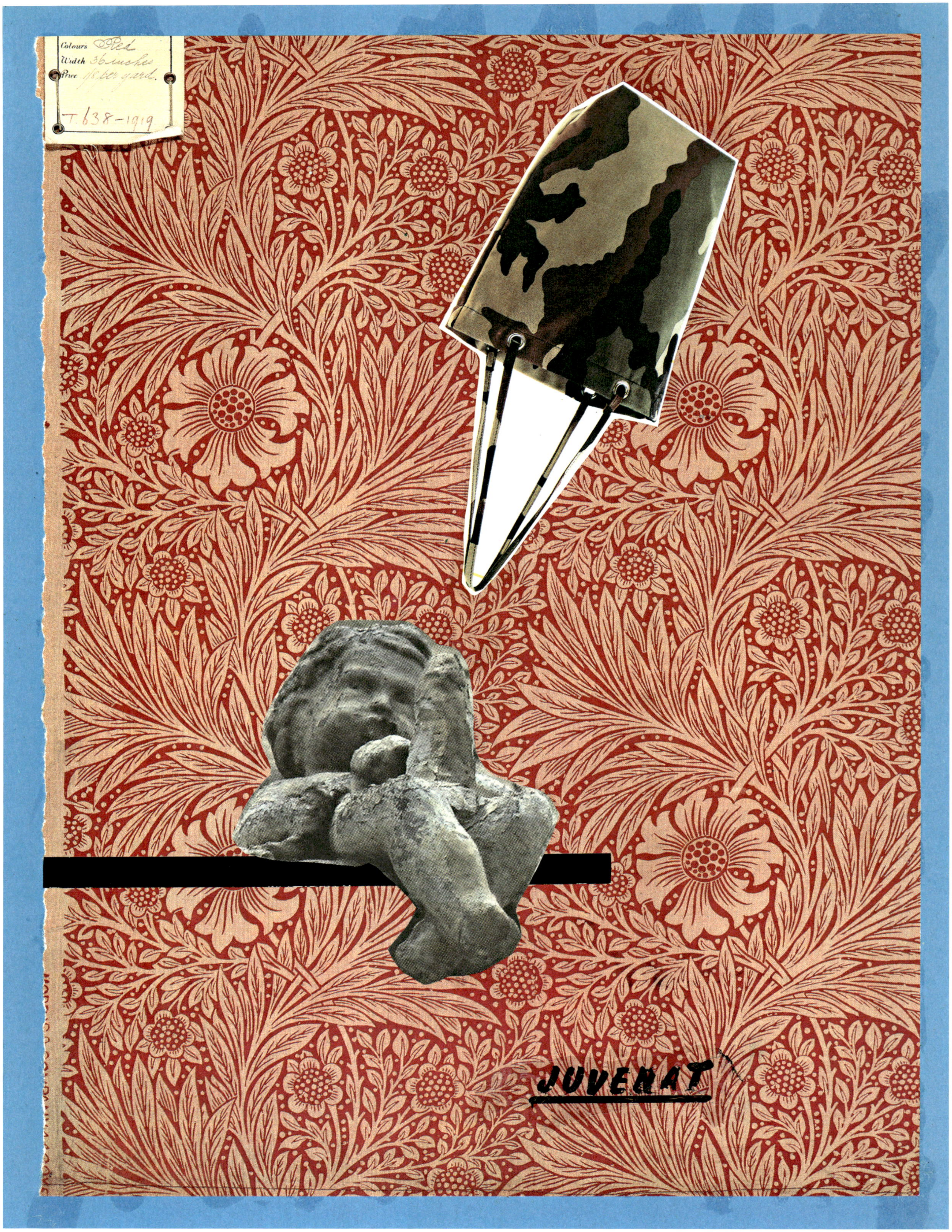

 Juvenescence, 2004

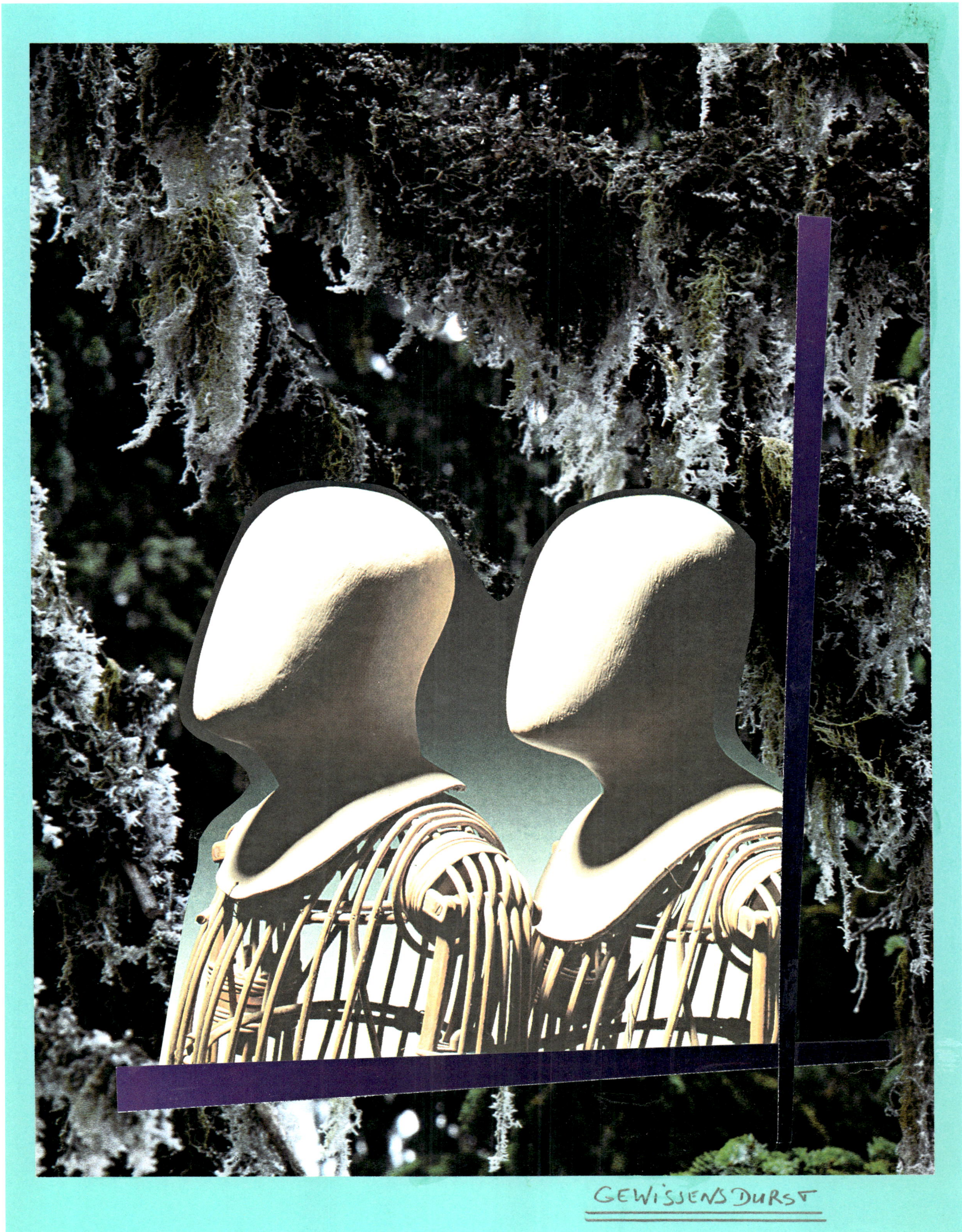

Thirst for conscience, 2004

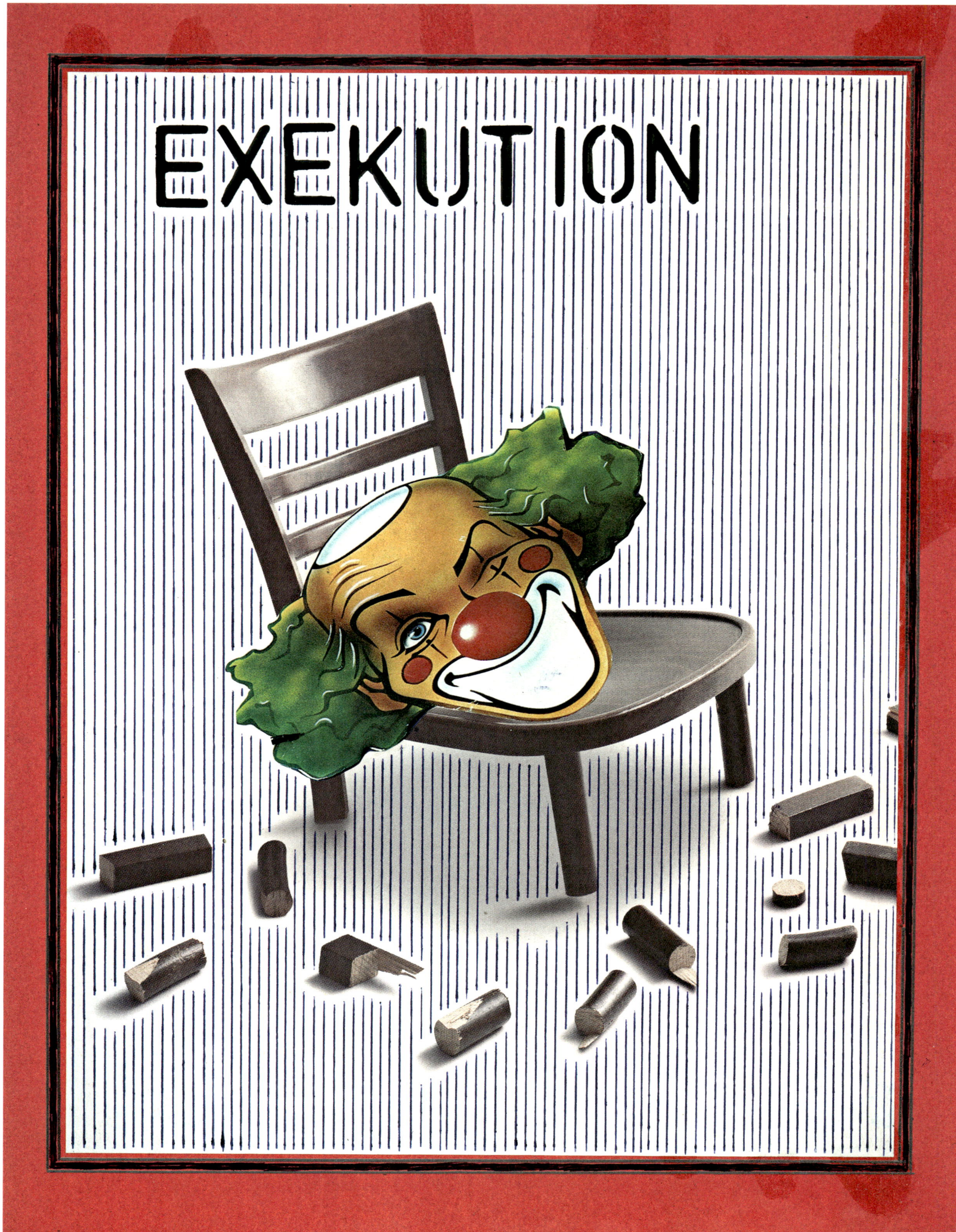

Execution, 2002

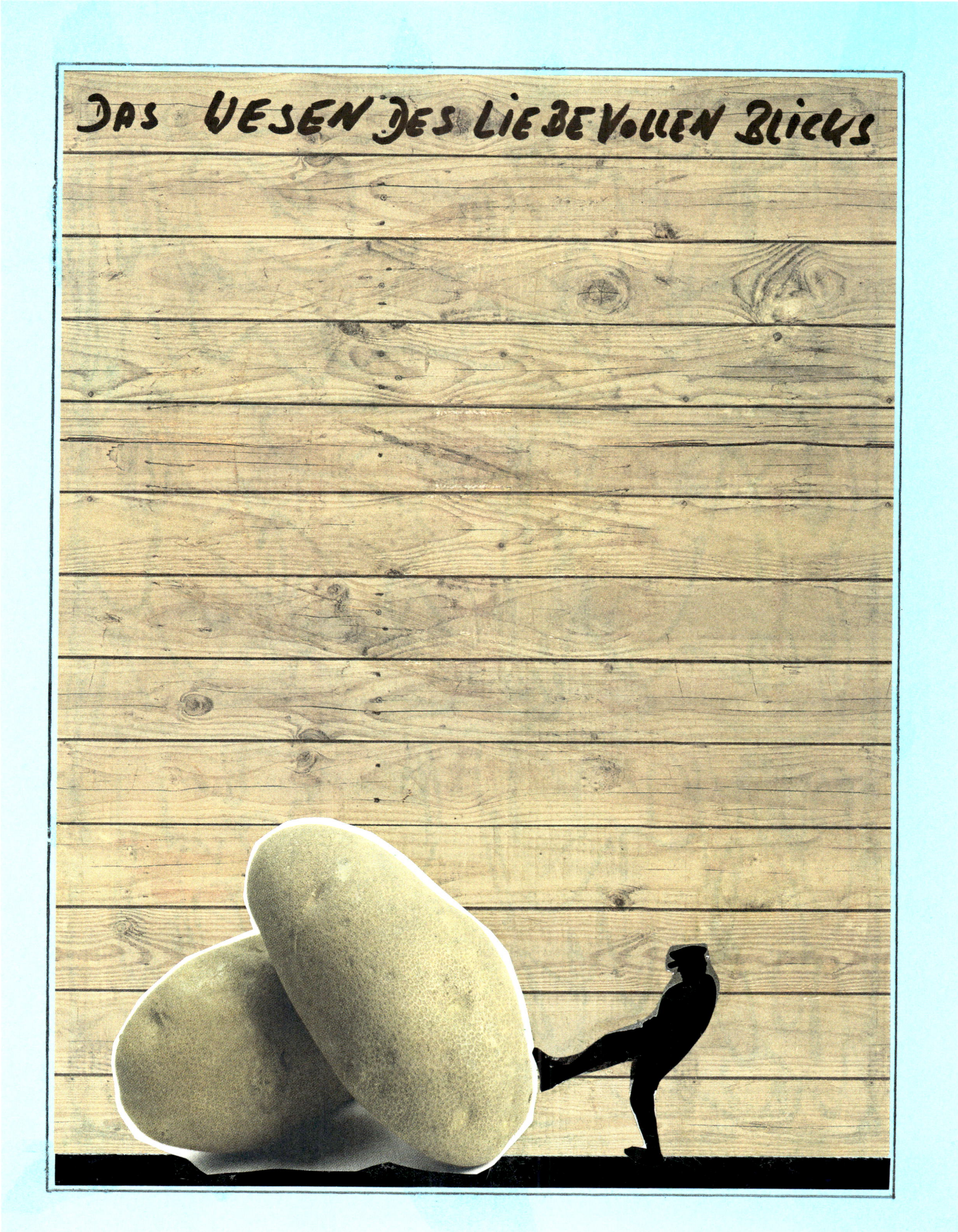

Essence of loving gaze, 2004

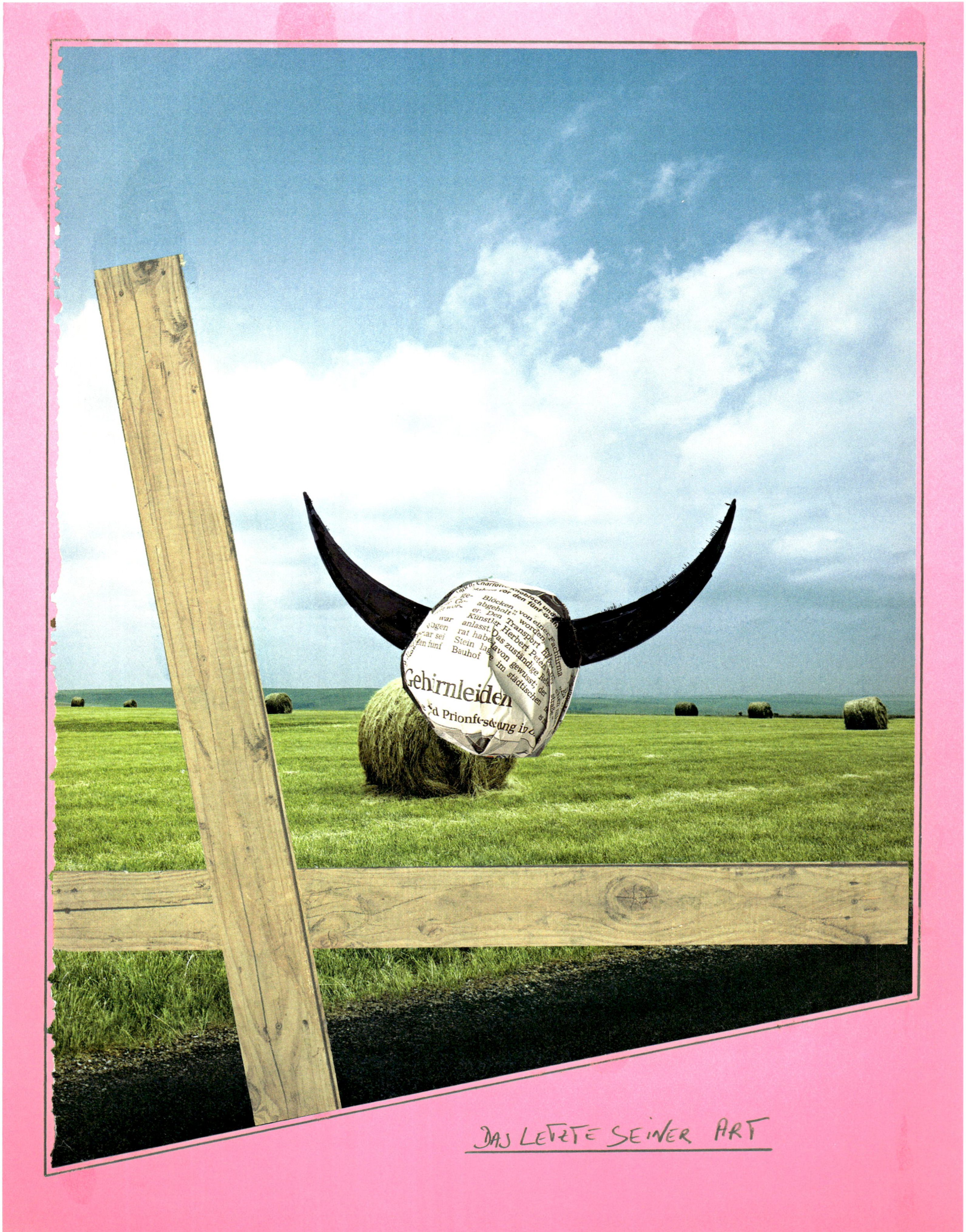

The last of its kind, 2005

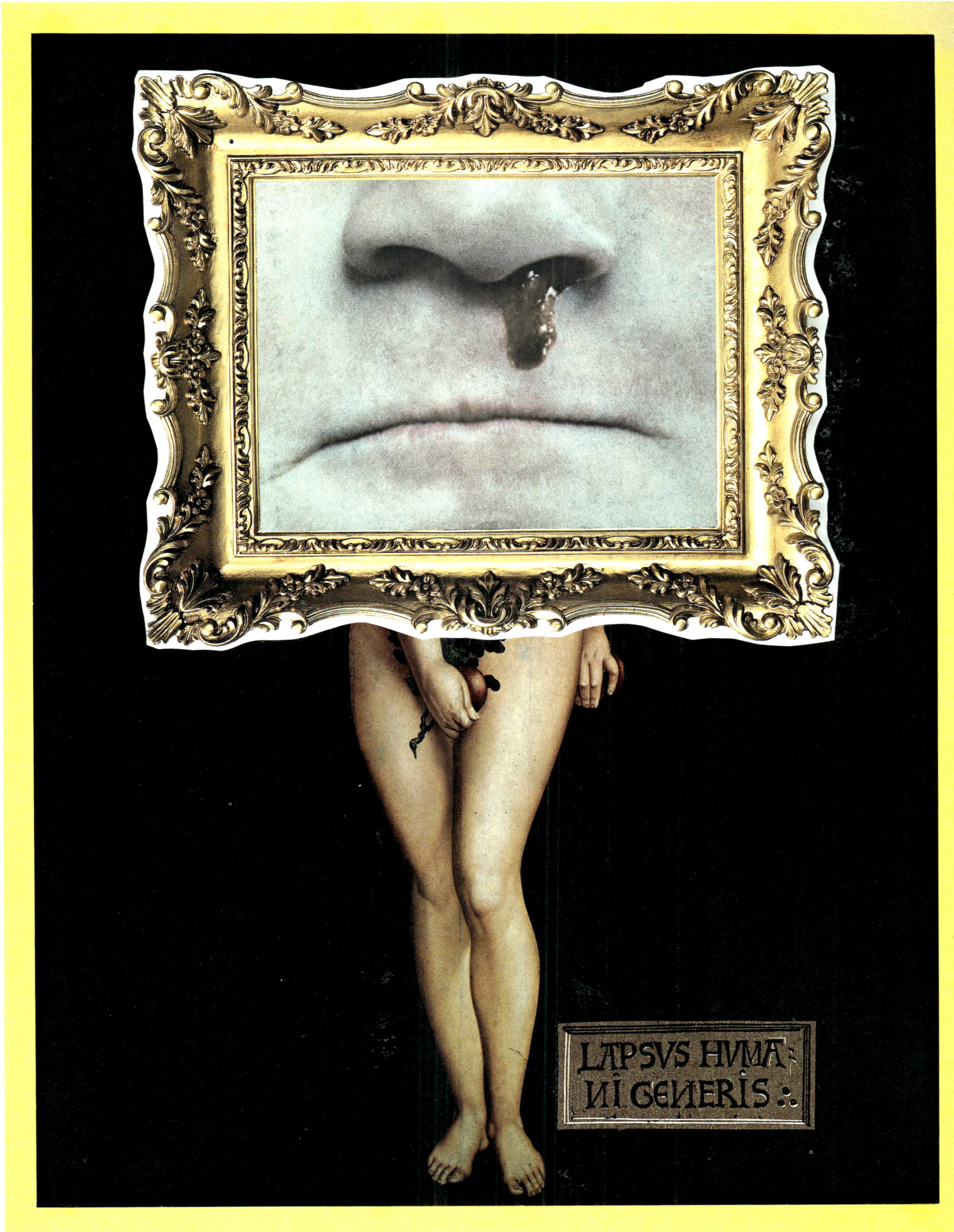

Lapsus Humani Generis, 2003

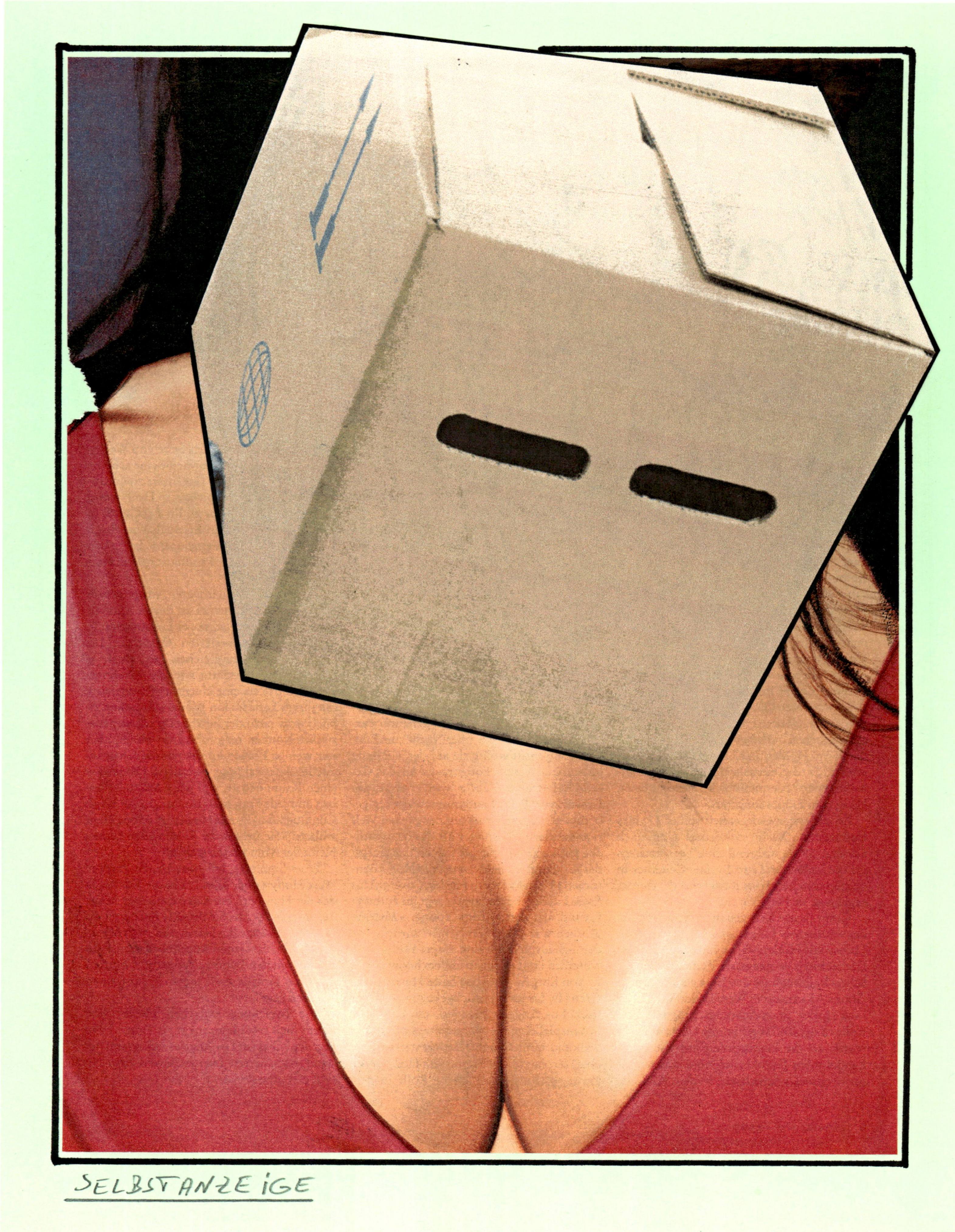

 Self-indictment, 2002

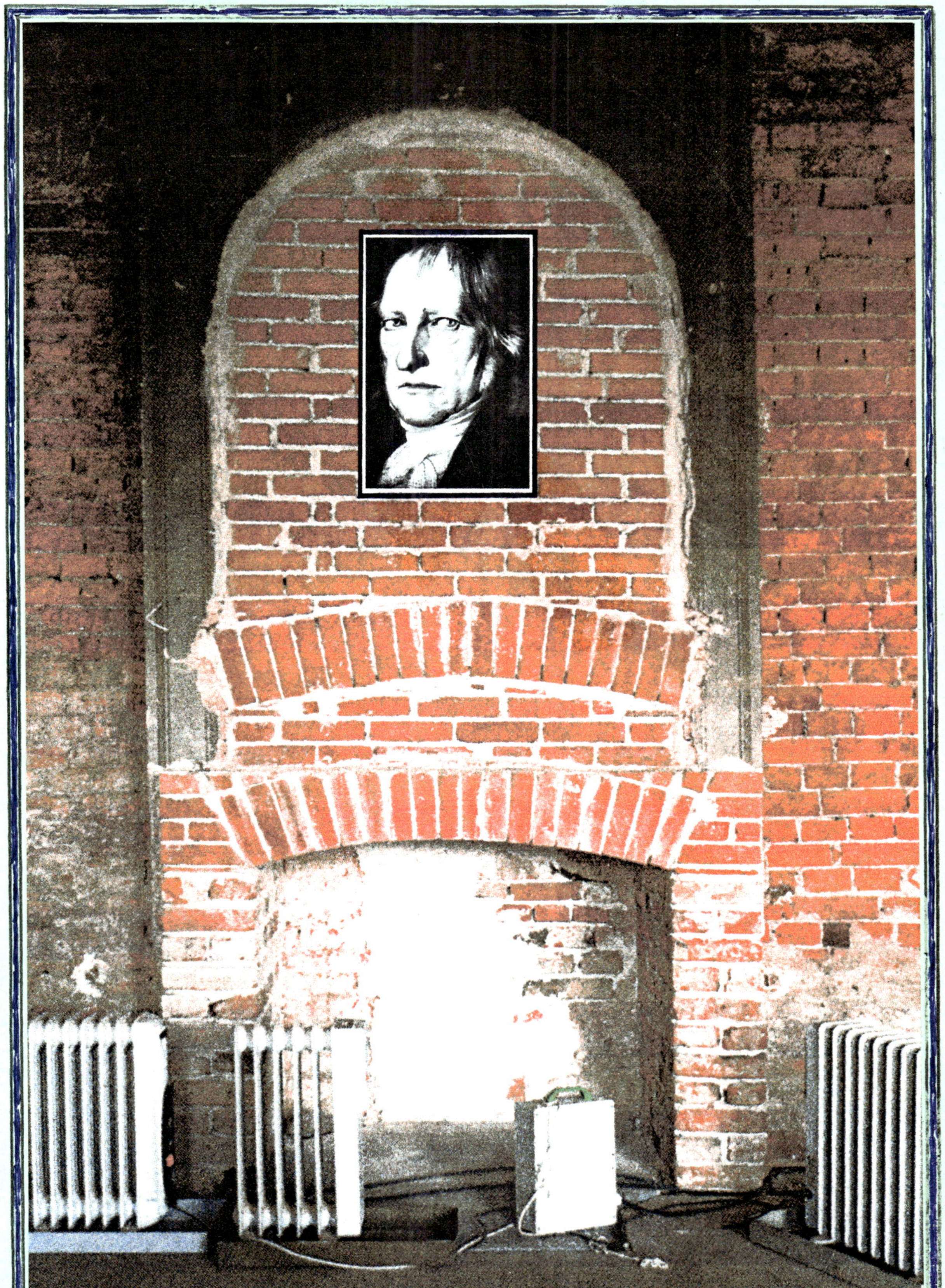

With Hegel the sore throat wasn't so bad..., 2004

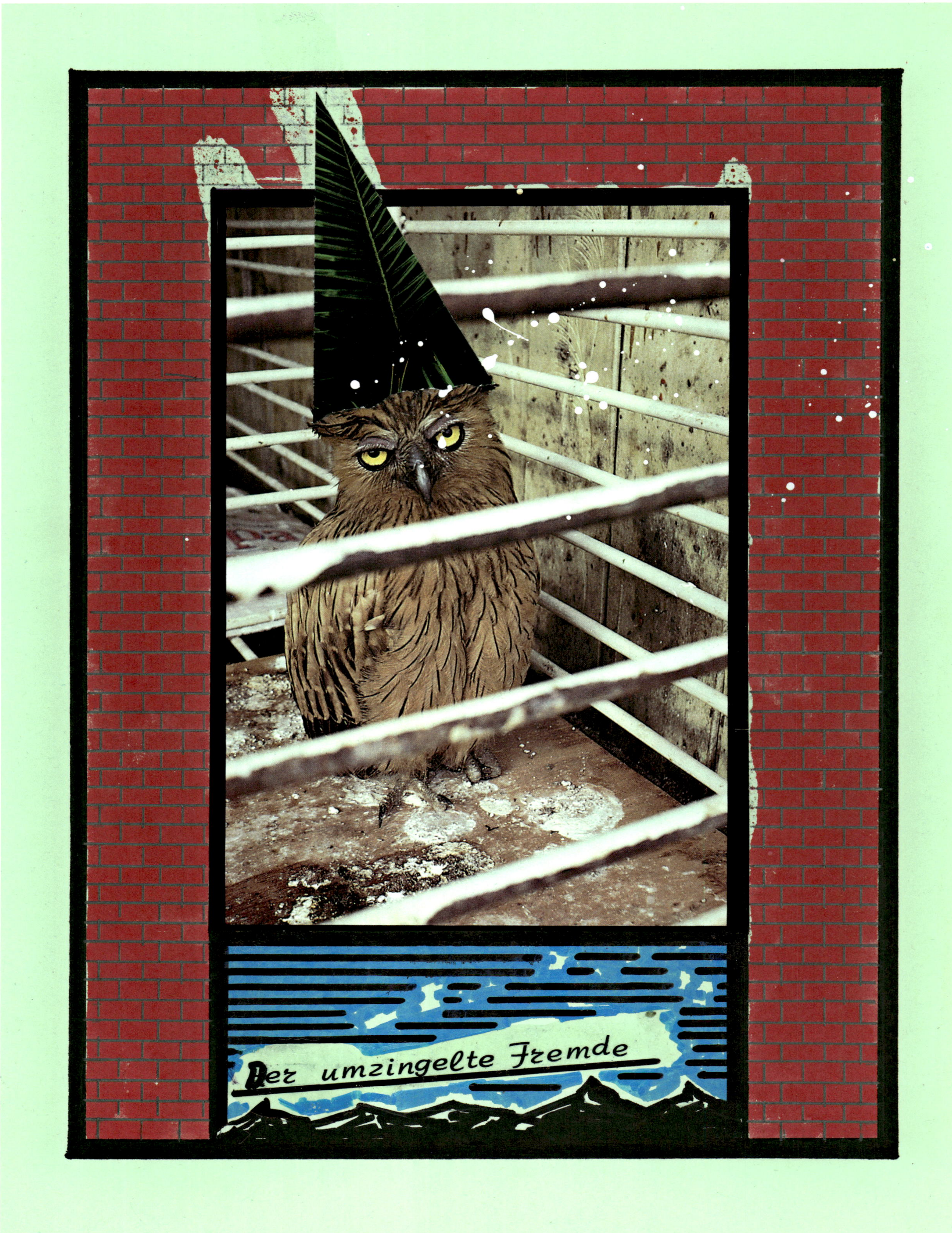

 The beleaguered stranger, 2004

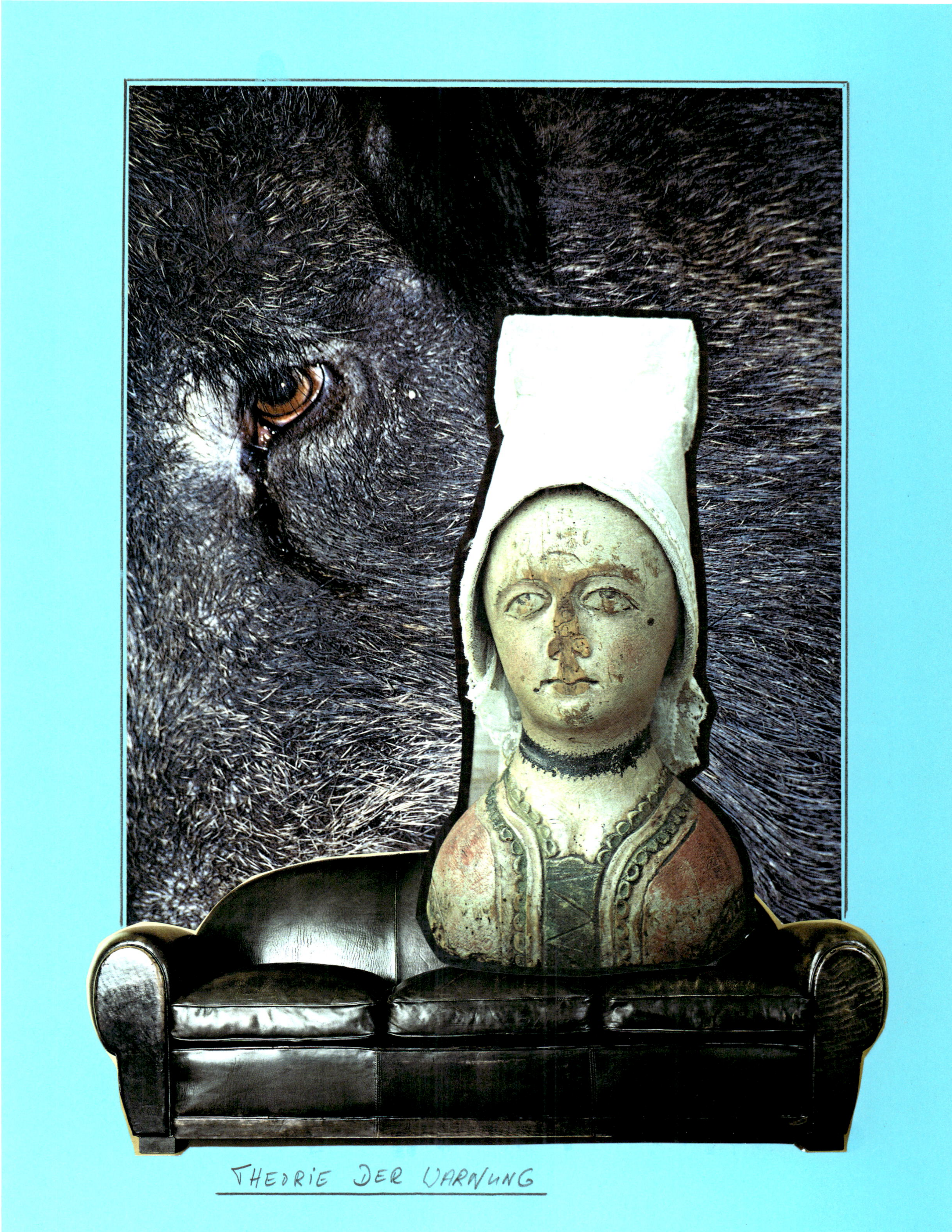

Theory of warning, 2004

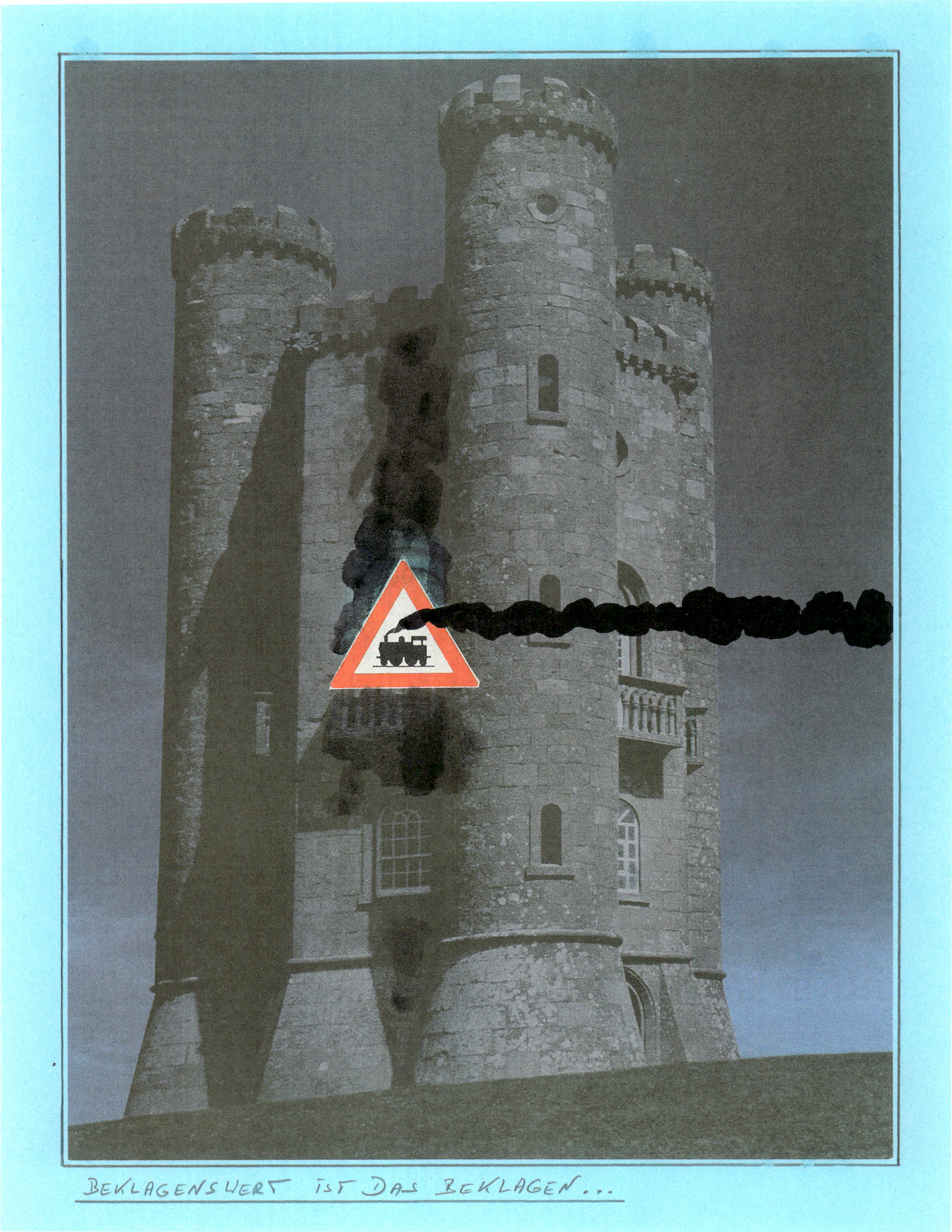

Lamentation is lamentable..., 2005

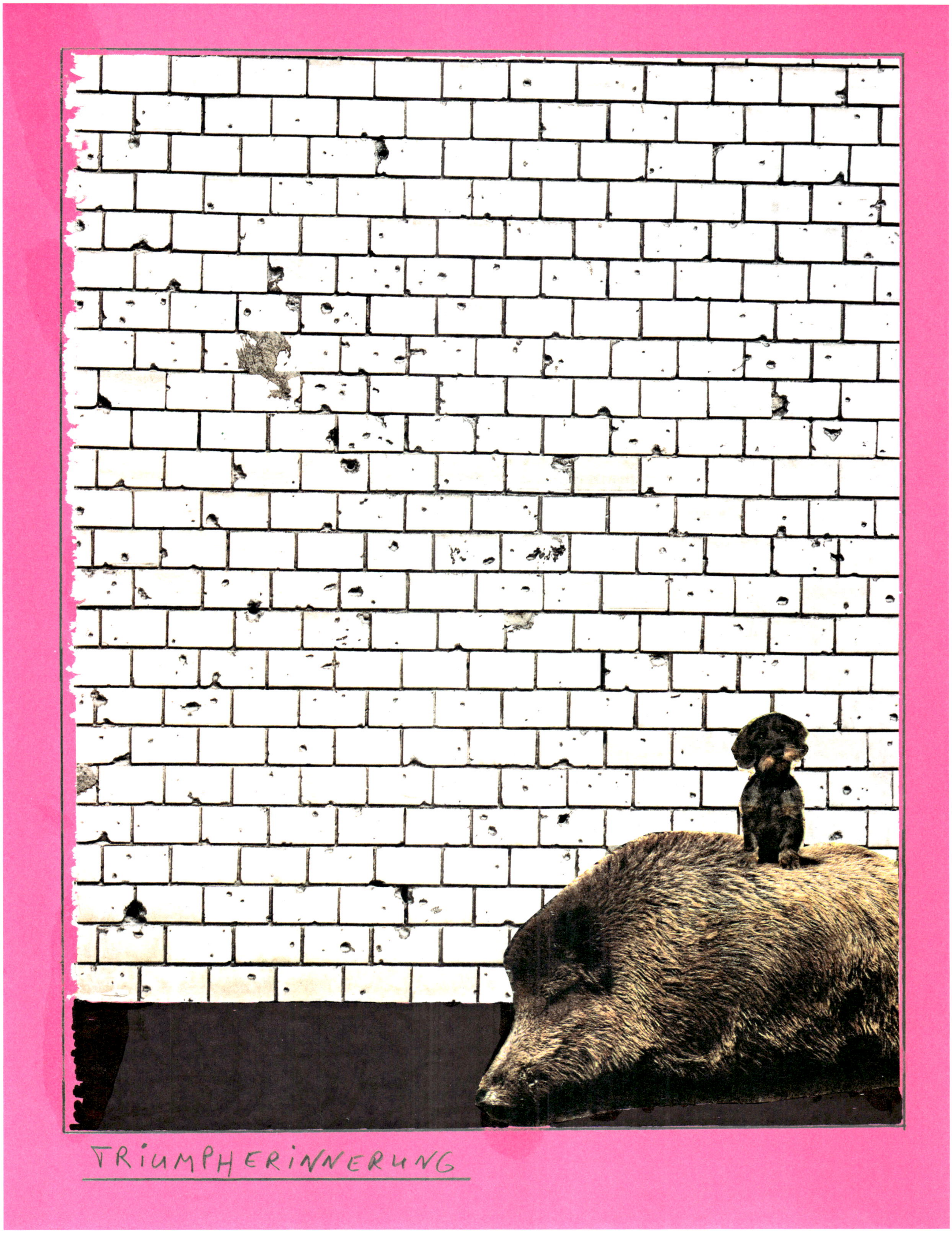

Triumphant memory, 2004

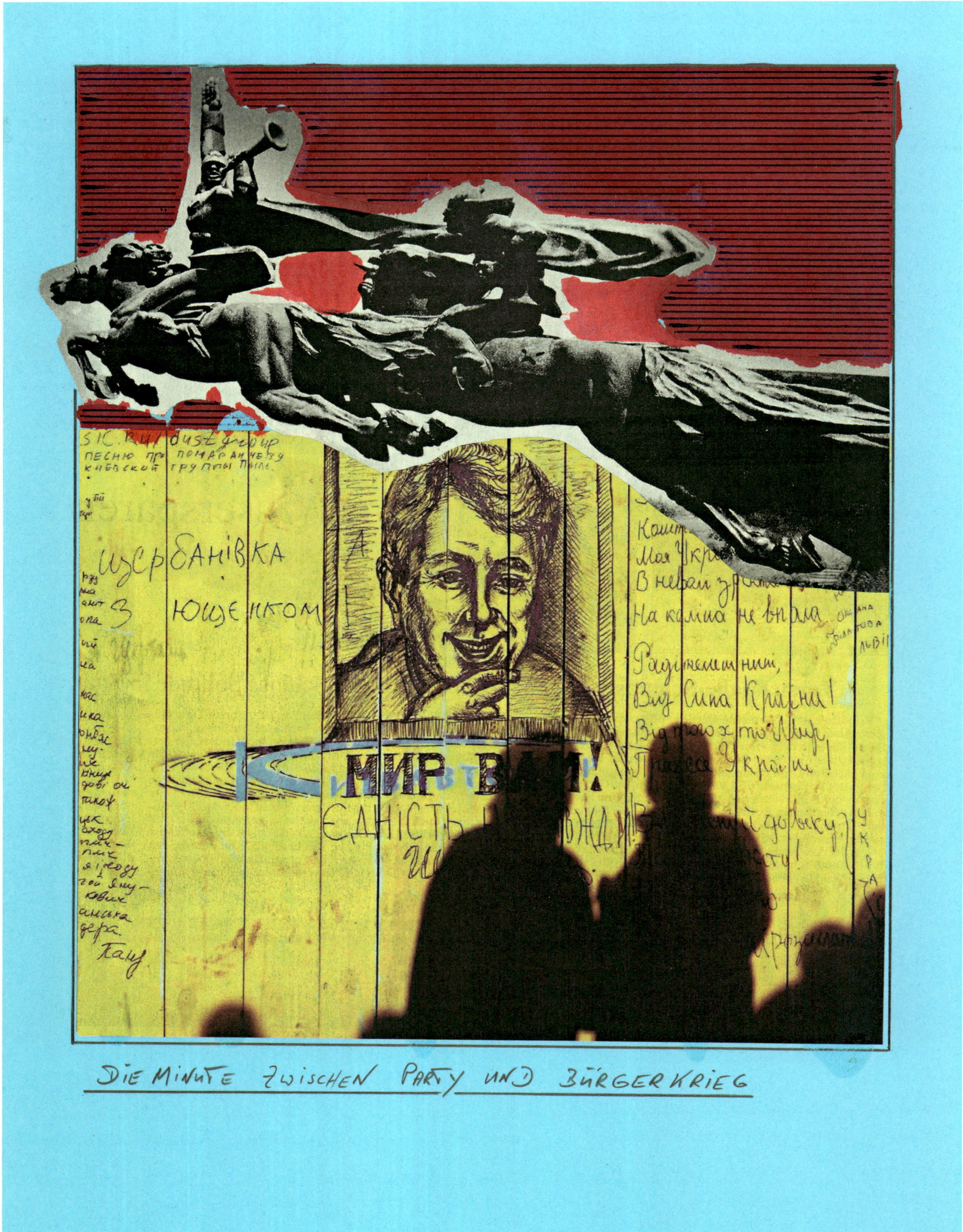

The minute between party and civil war, 2005

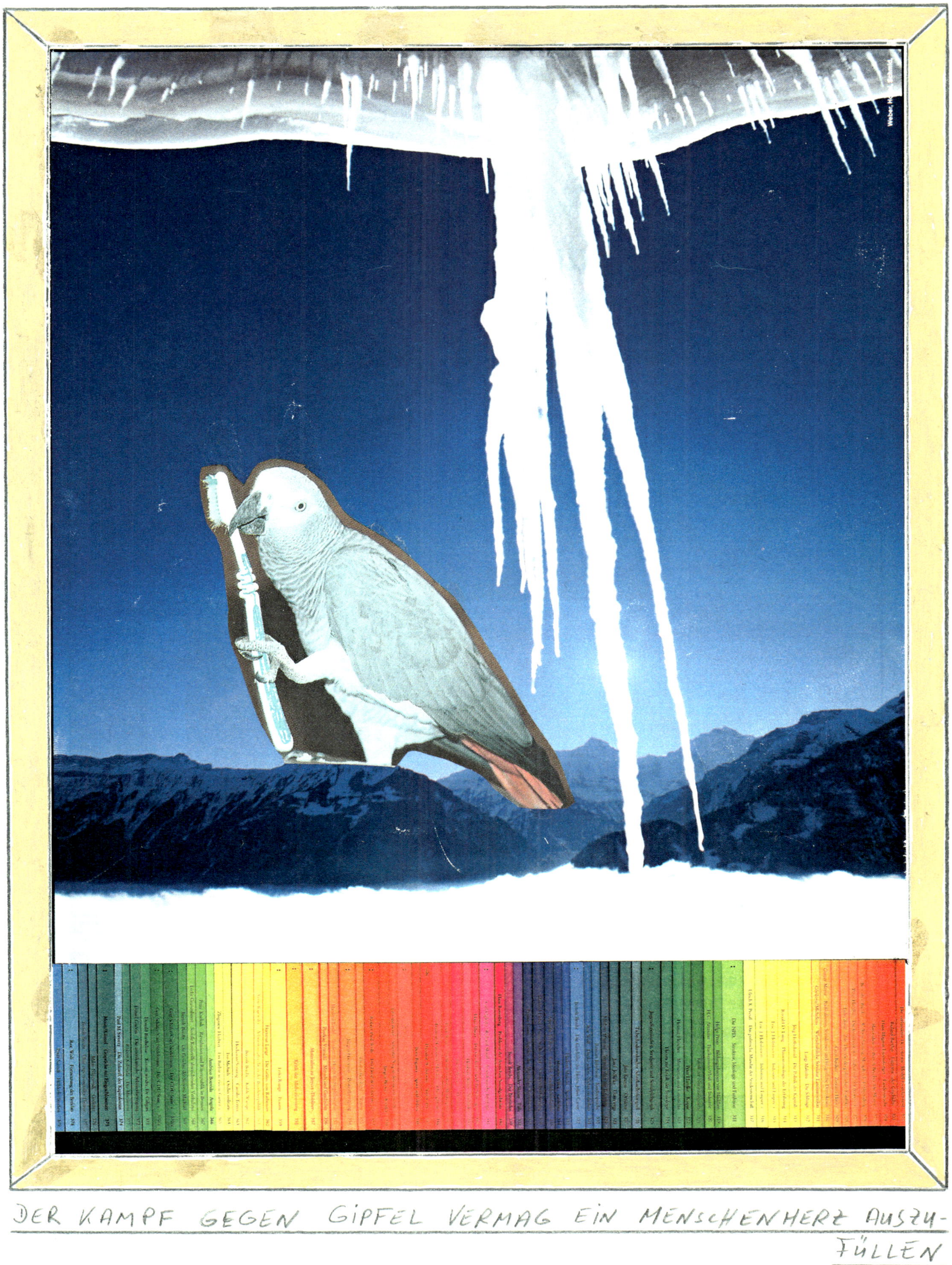

The struggle itself towards the heights is enough to fill a man's heart, 2003

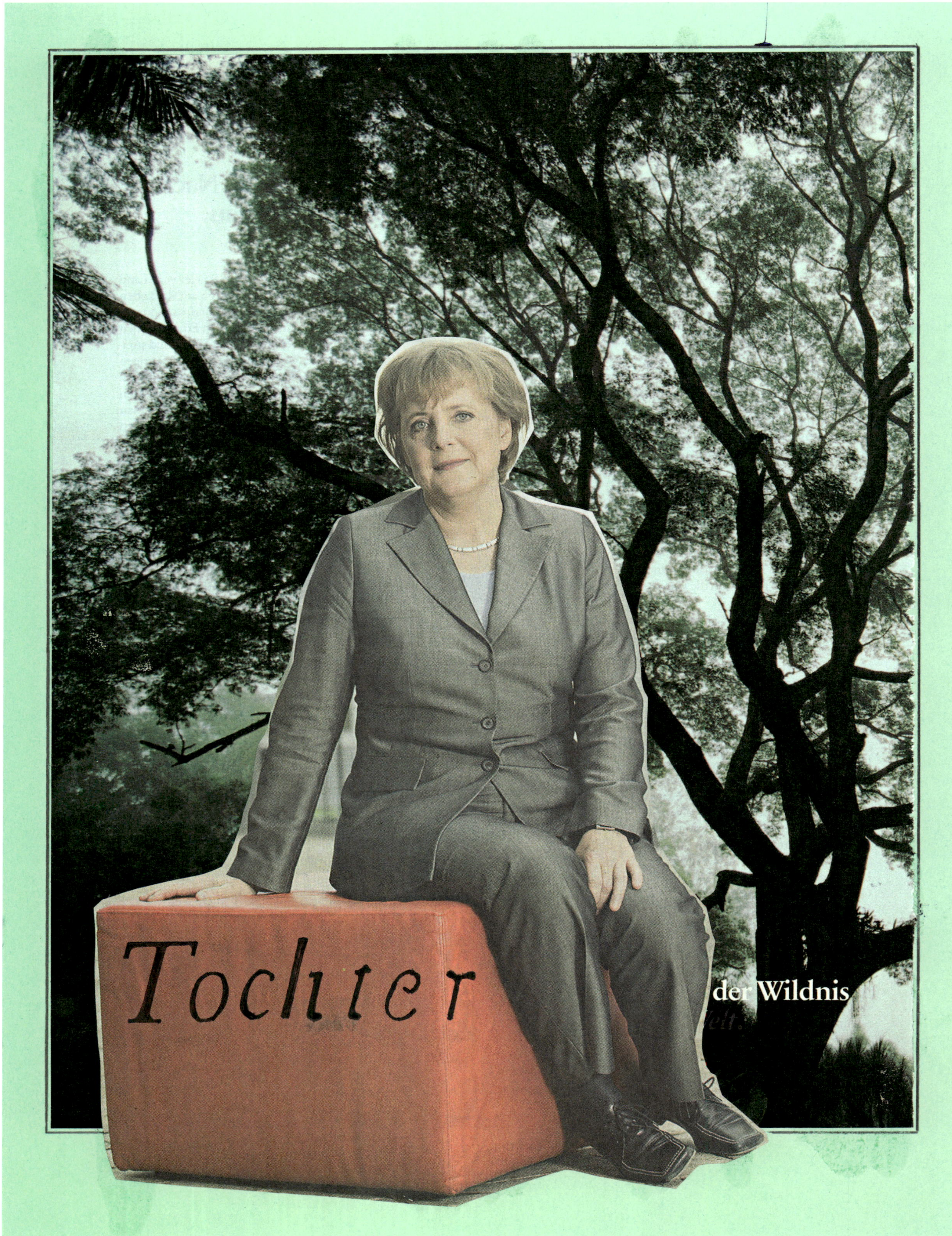

 Daughter of the wilderness, 2005

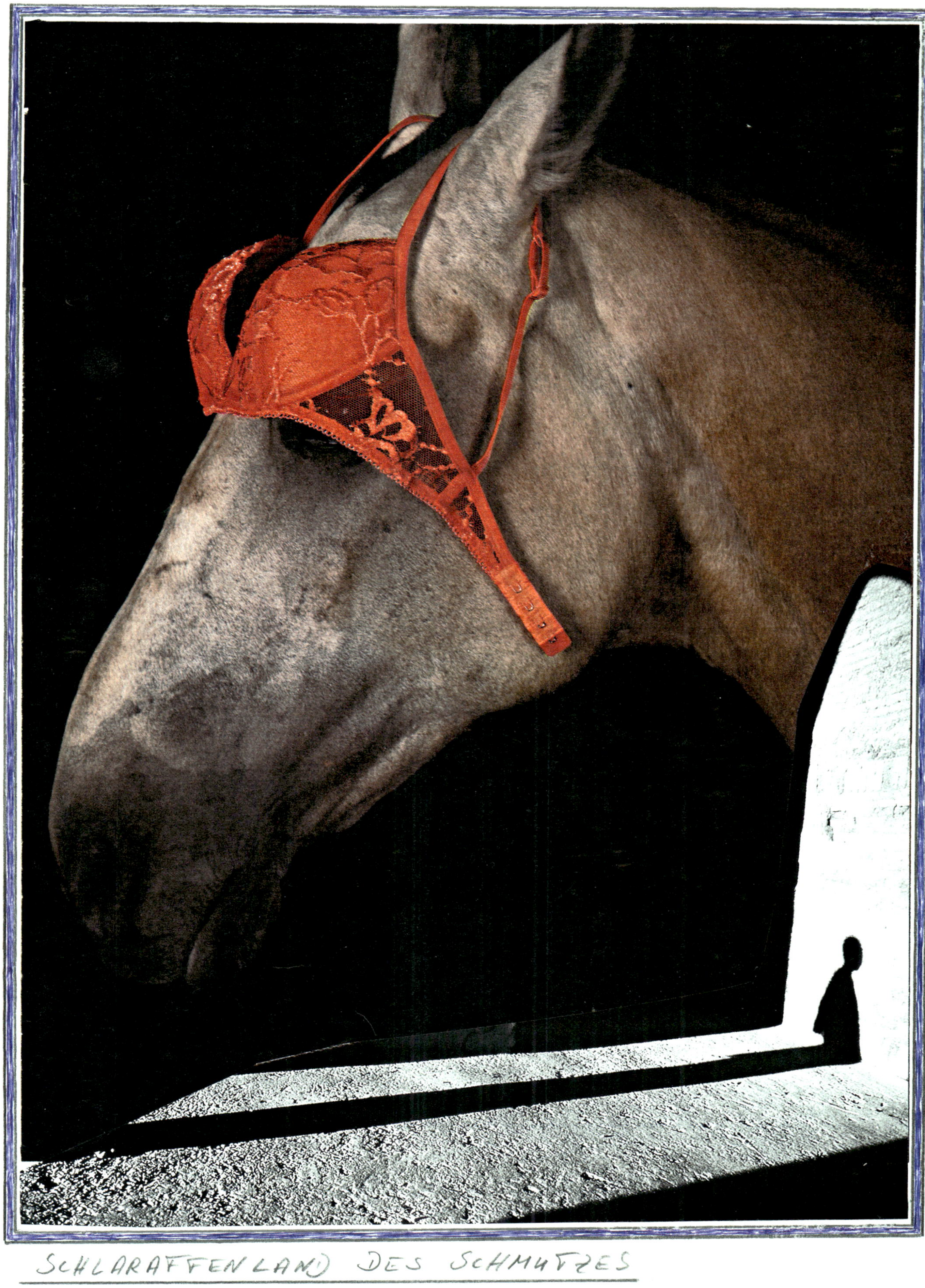

Cockaigne of filth, 2004

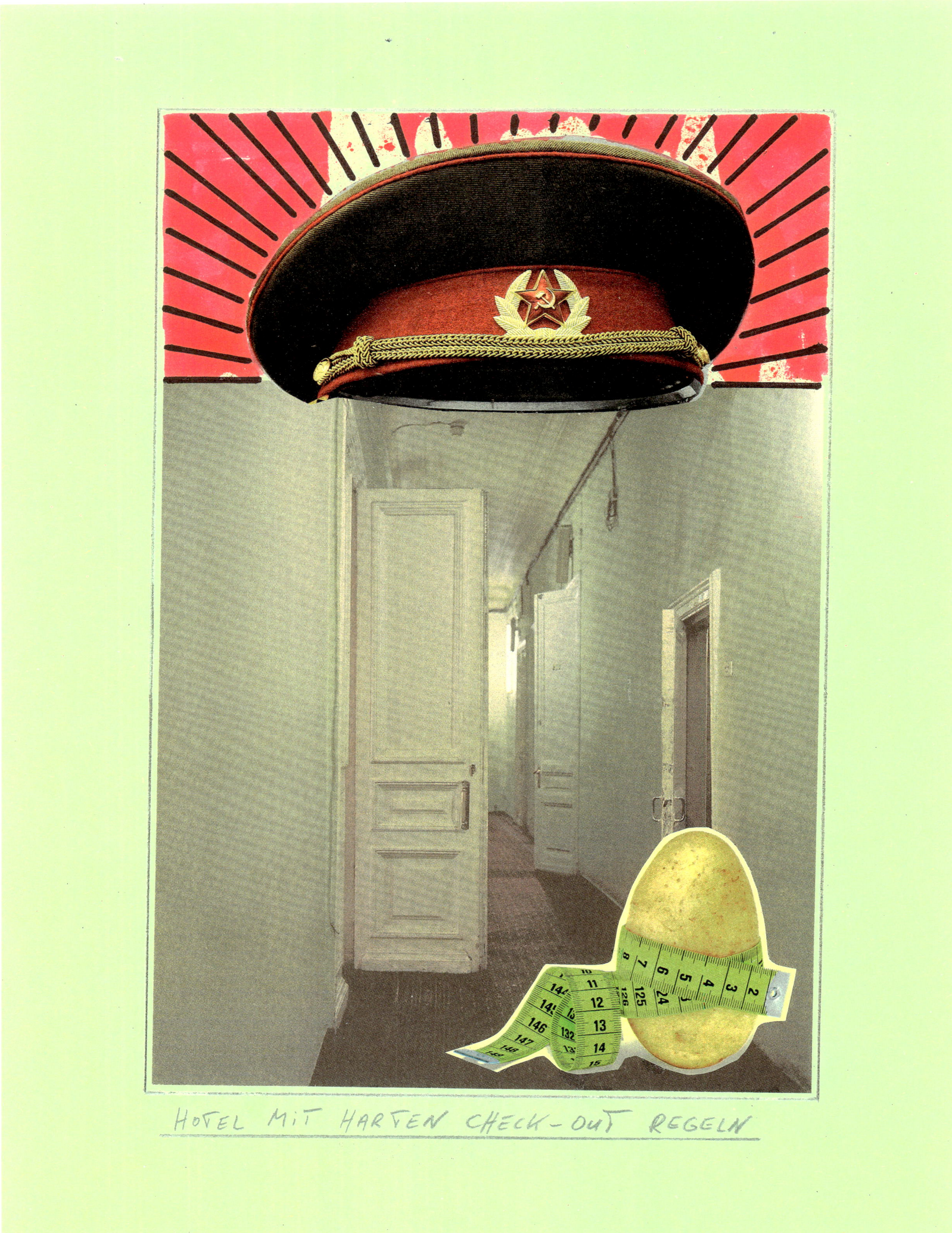

 Hotel with tough check-out rules, 2007

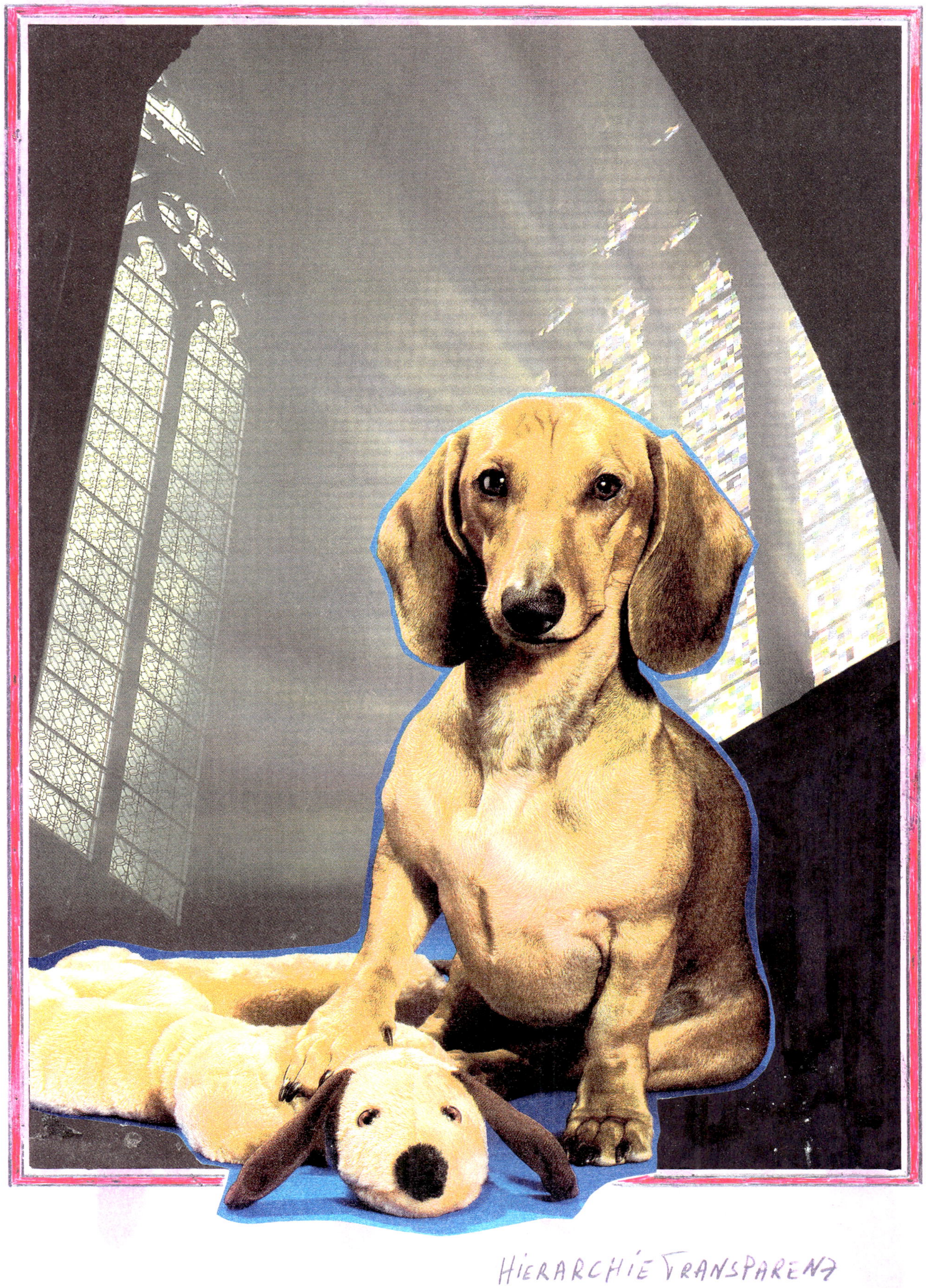

Transparent hierarchy, 2007

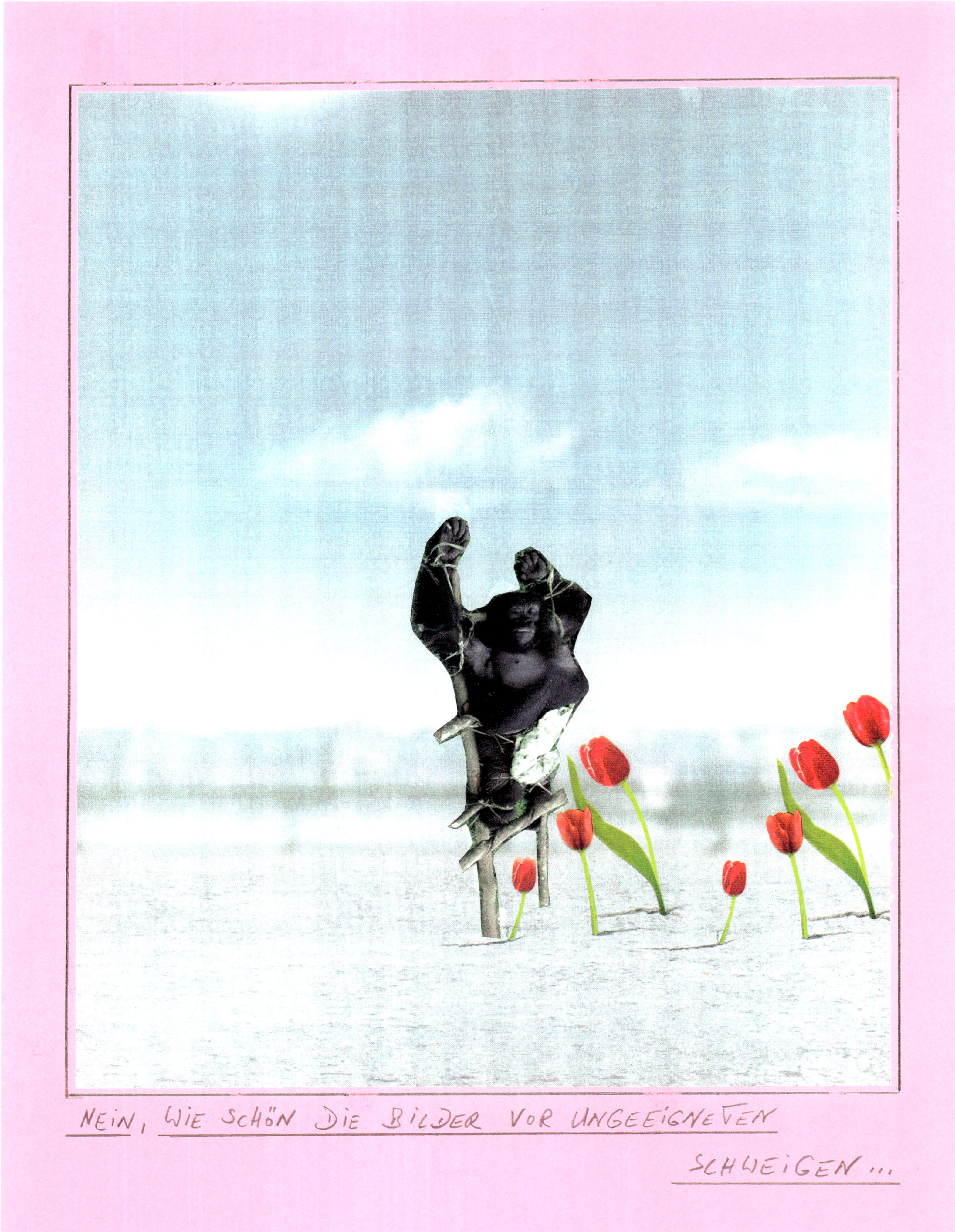

How nicely pictures keep stumm in front of those unsuited..., 2007–2008

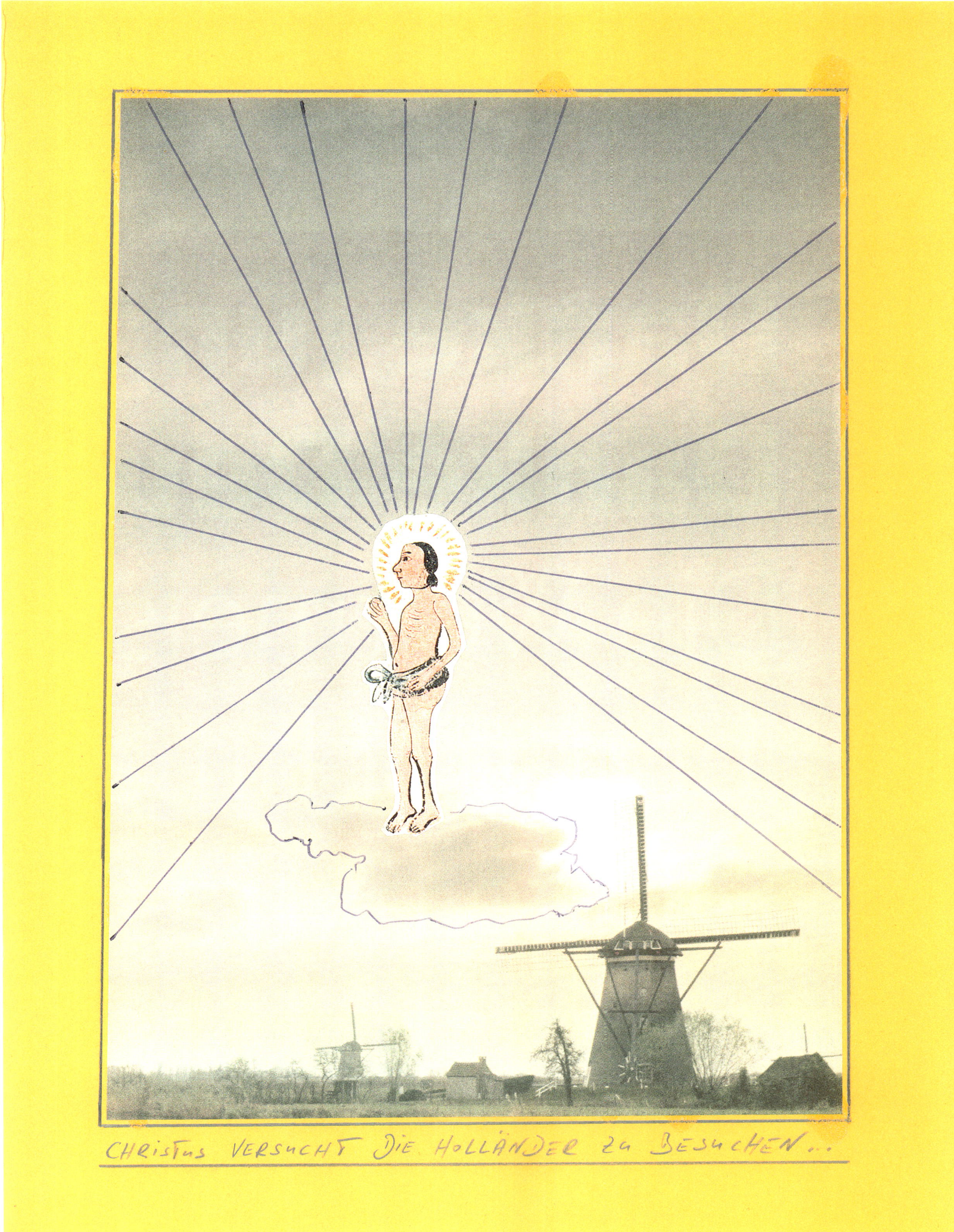

Christ attempts to visit the Dutch..., 2007

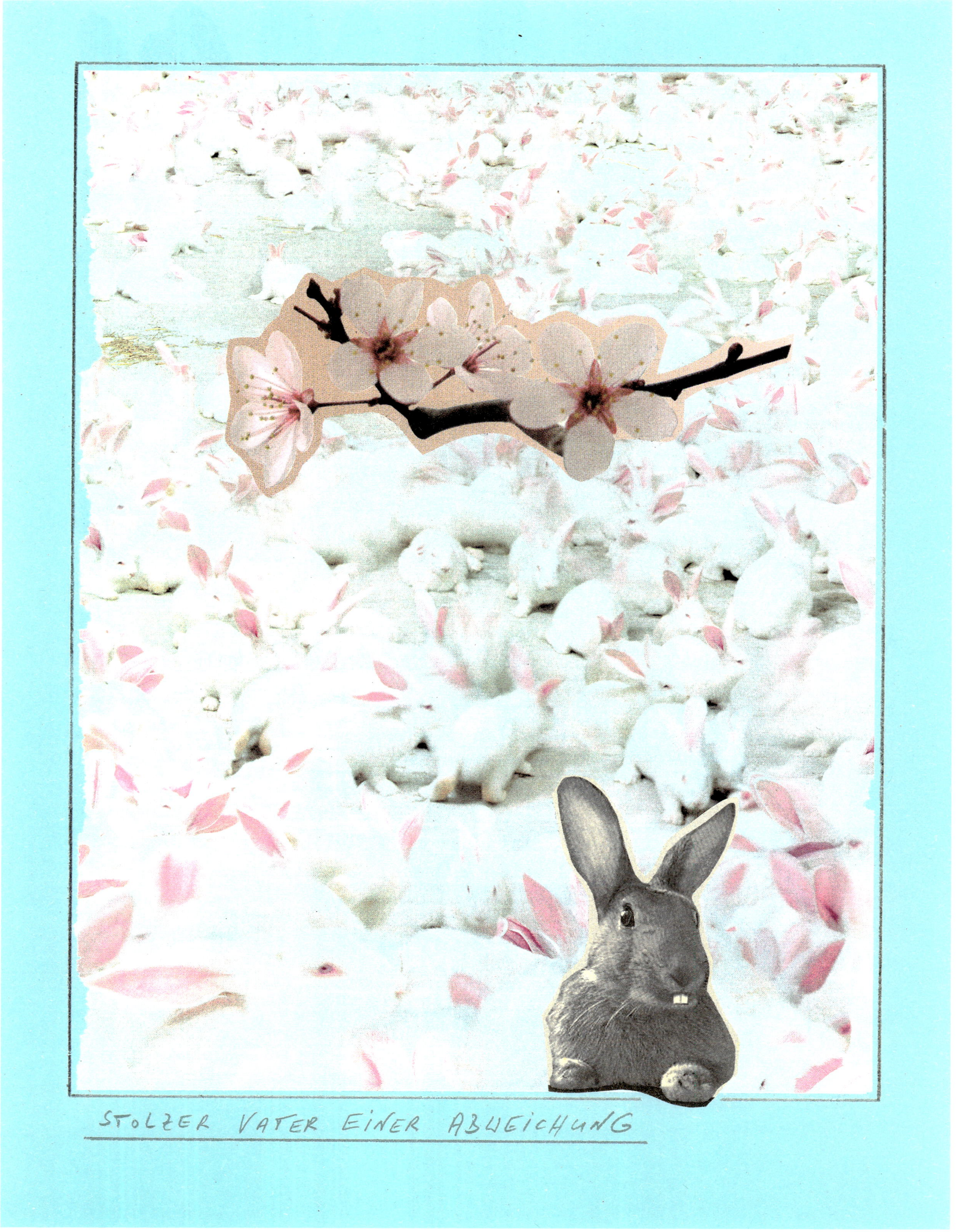

 Proud father of an aberration, 2007

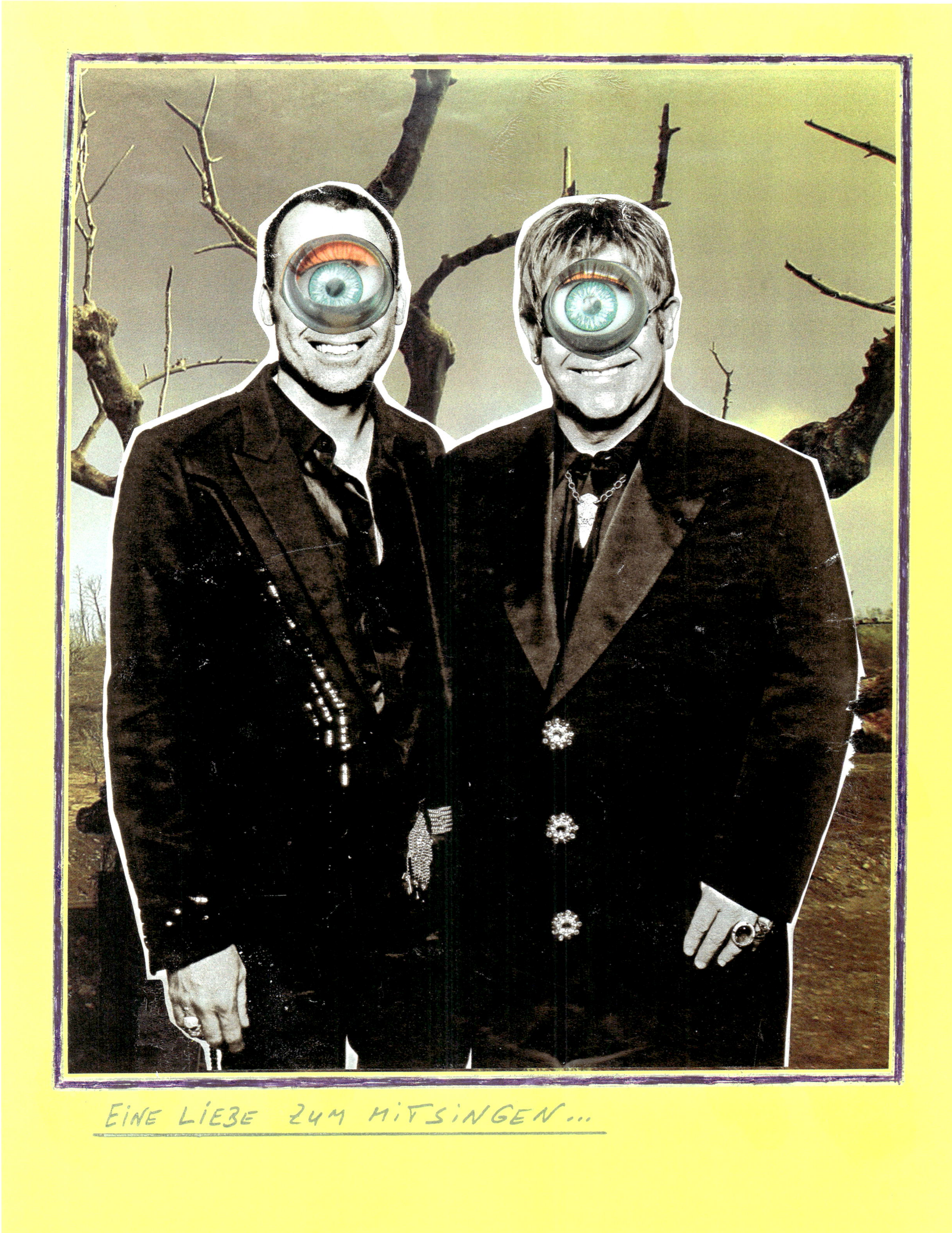

A love to sing along to, 2007

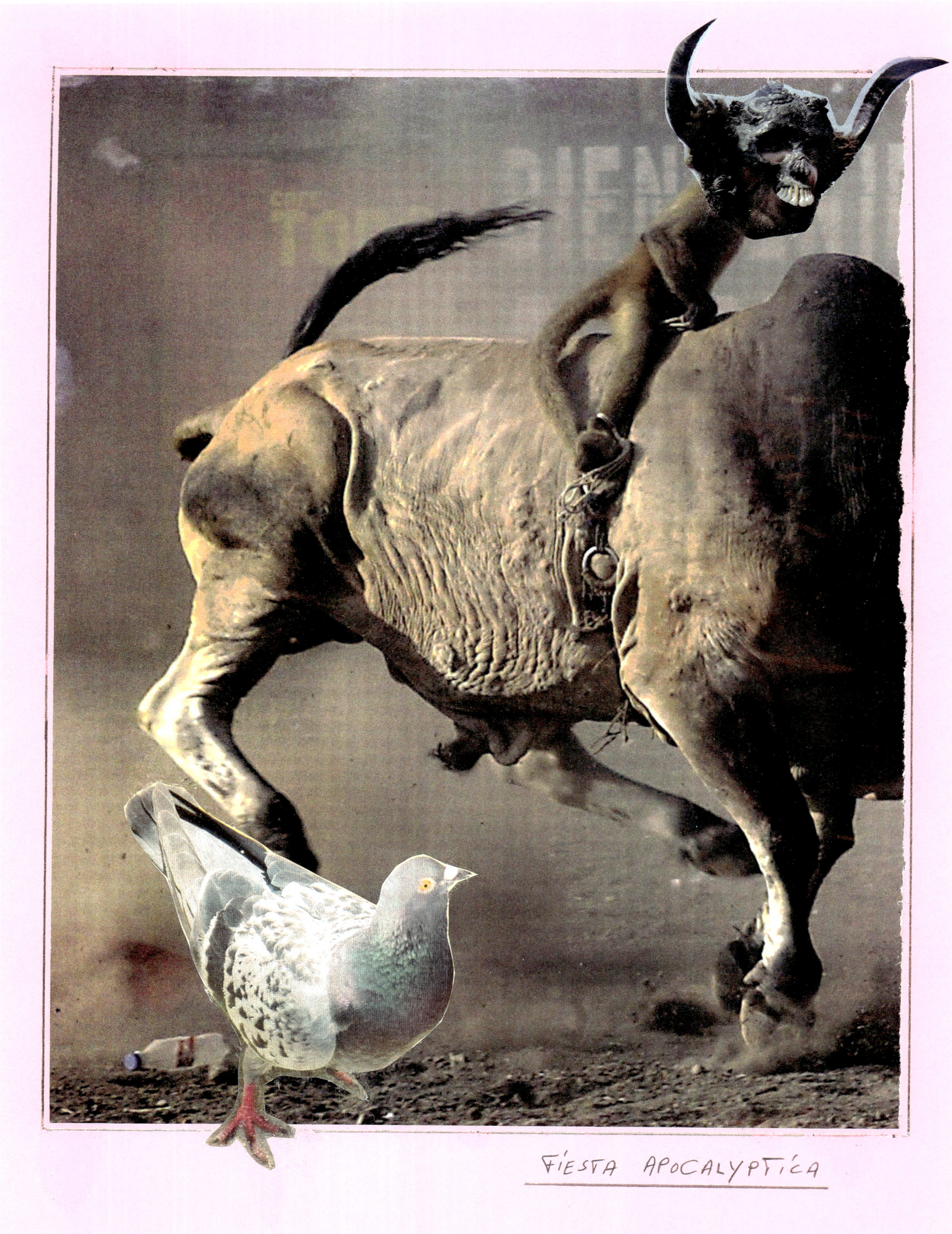

Fiesta Apokalyptica, 2007

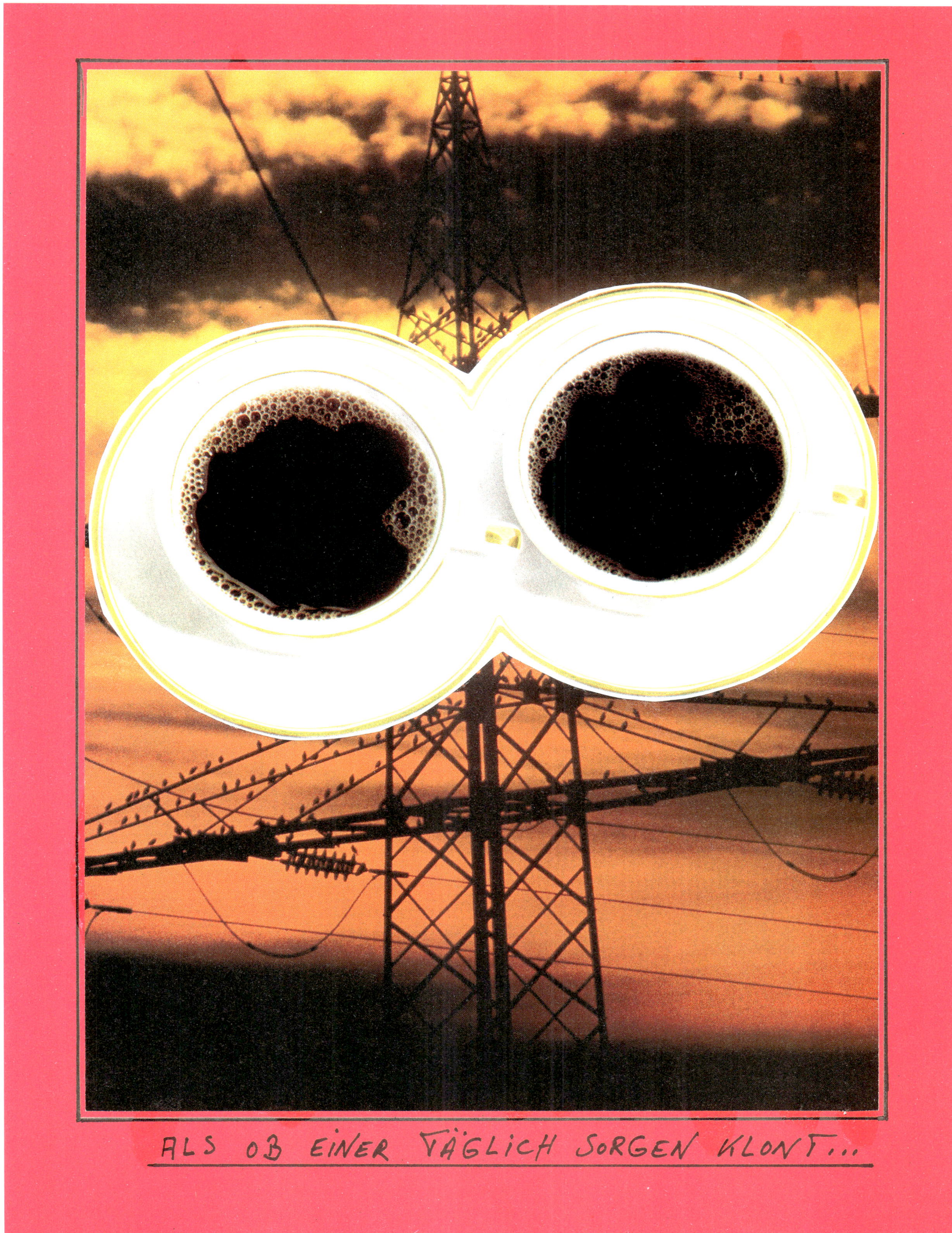

Like someone's cloning worries every day..., 2008

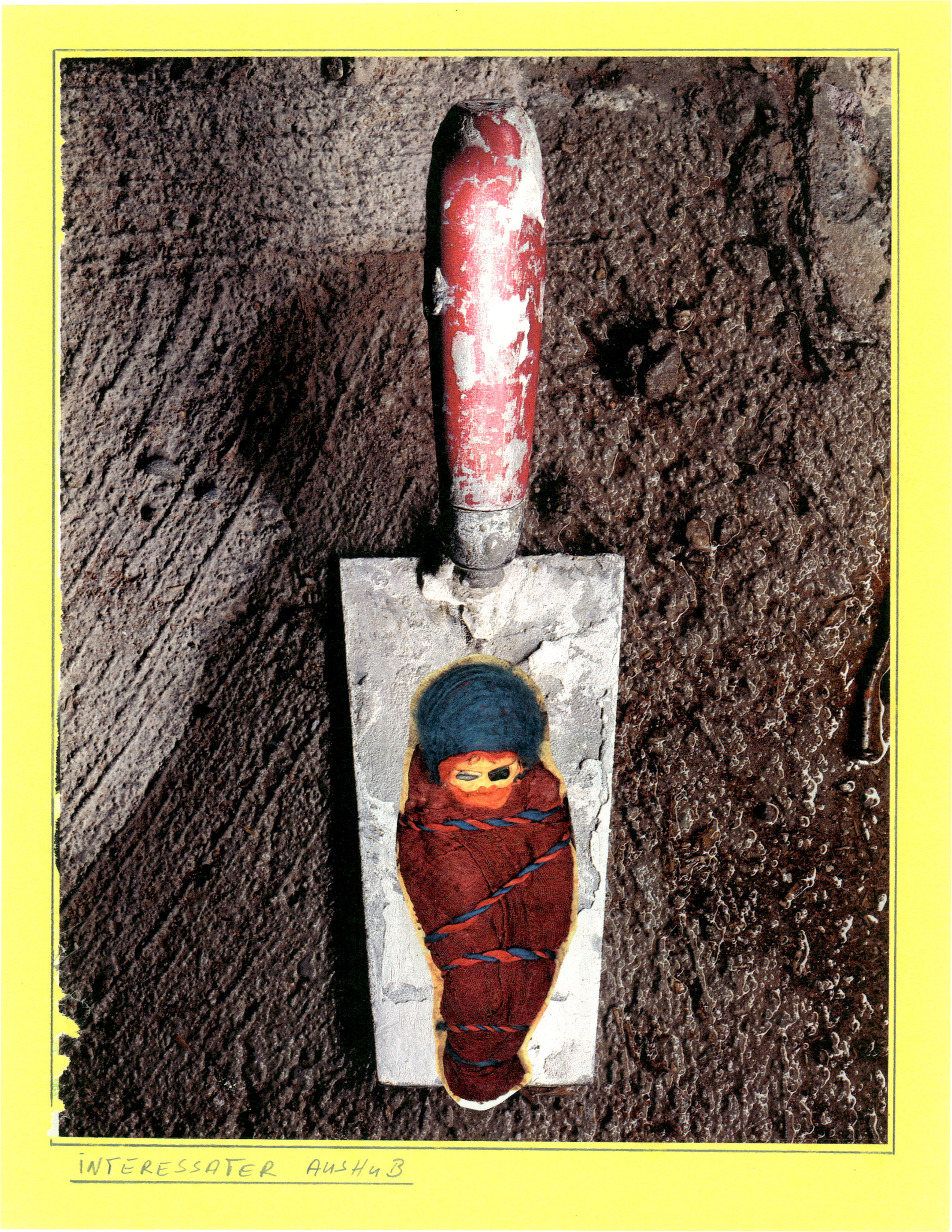

Interesting excavation, 2006

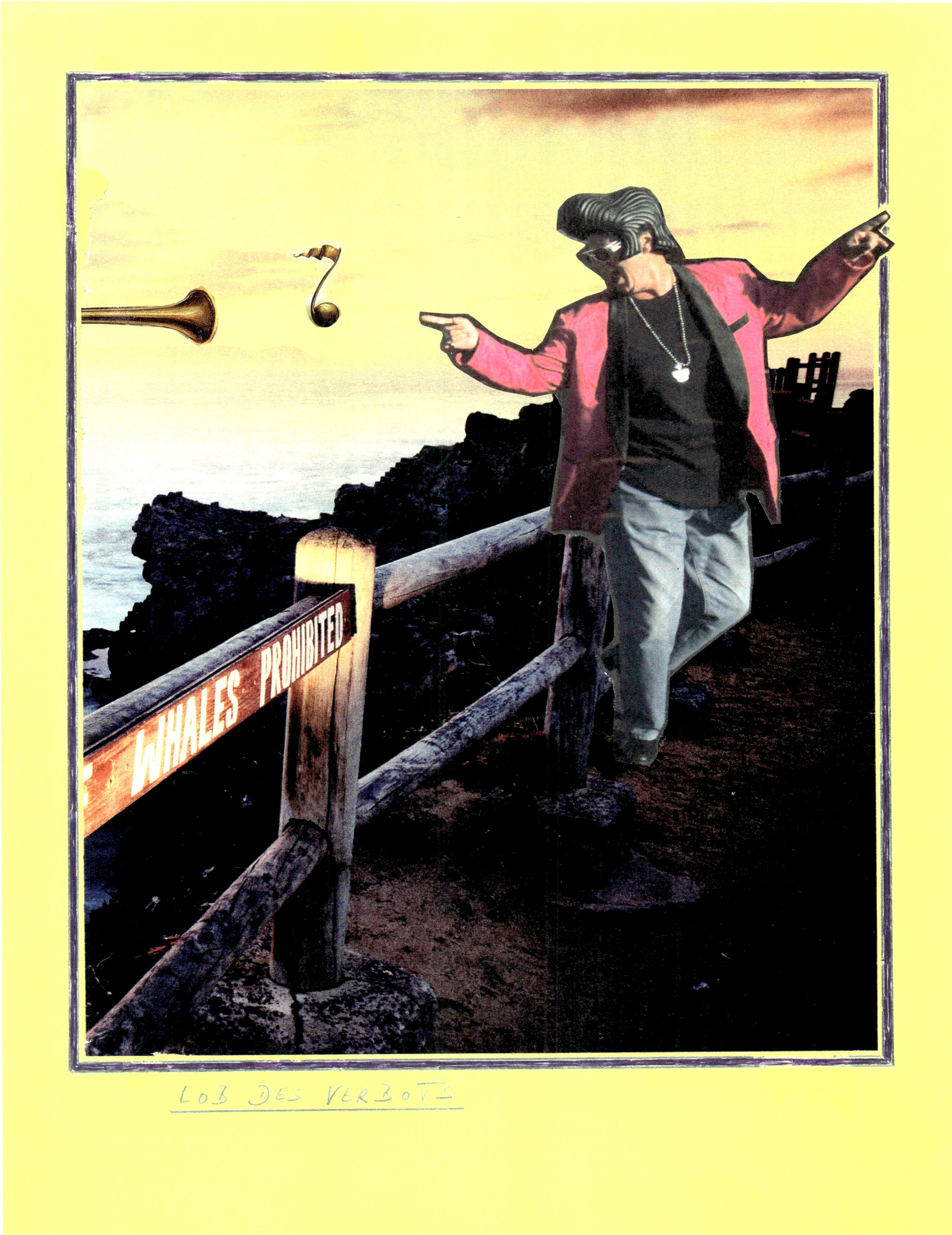

In praise of forbidding, 2007

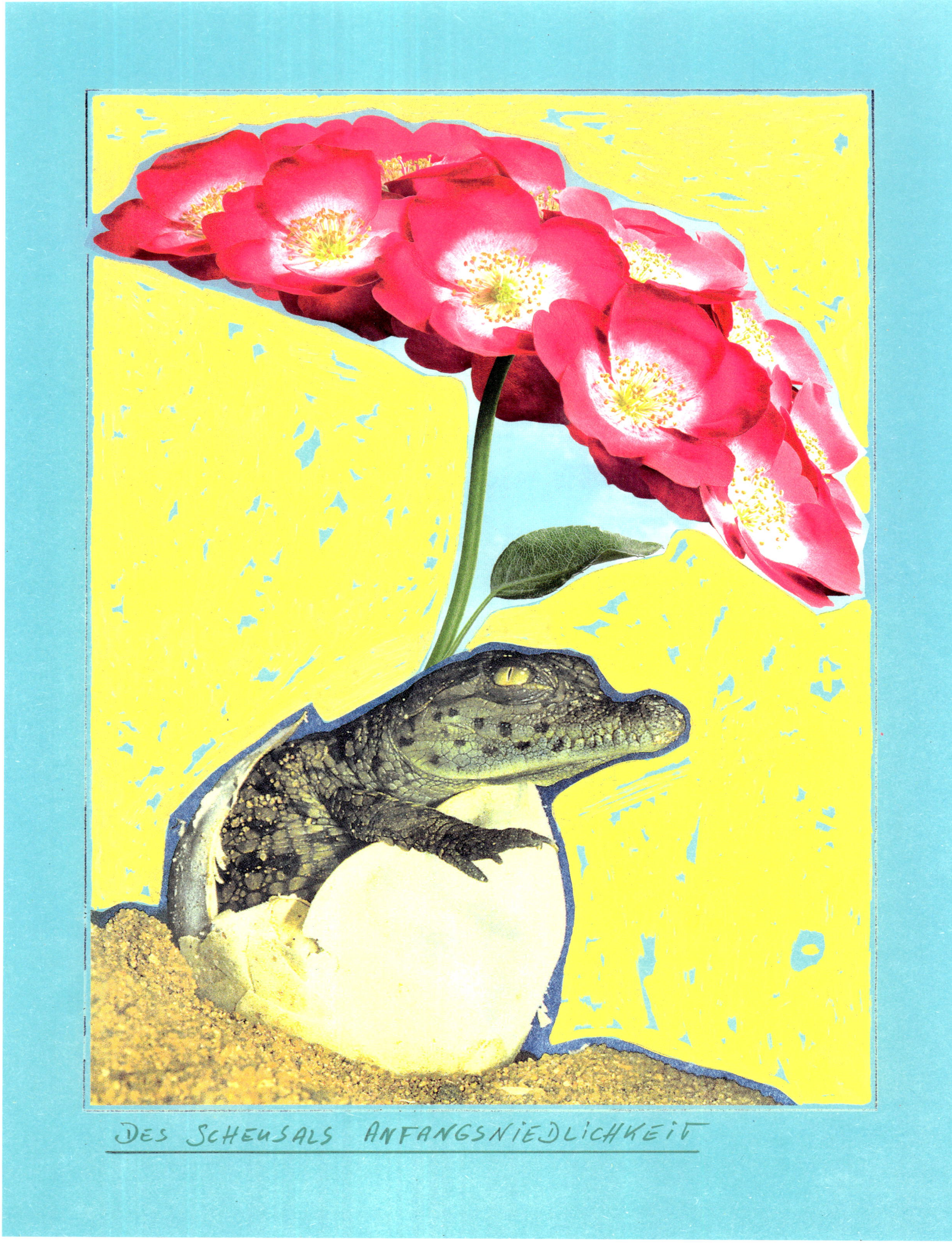

 The monster's early cuteness, 2007–2008

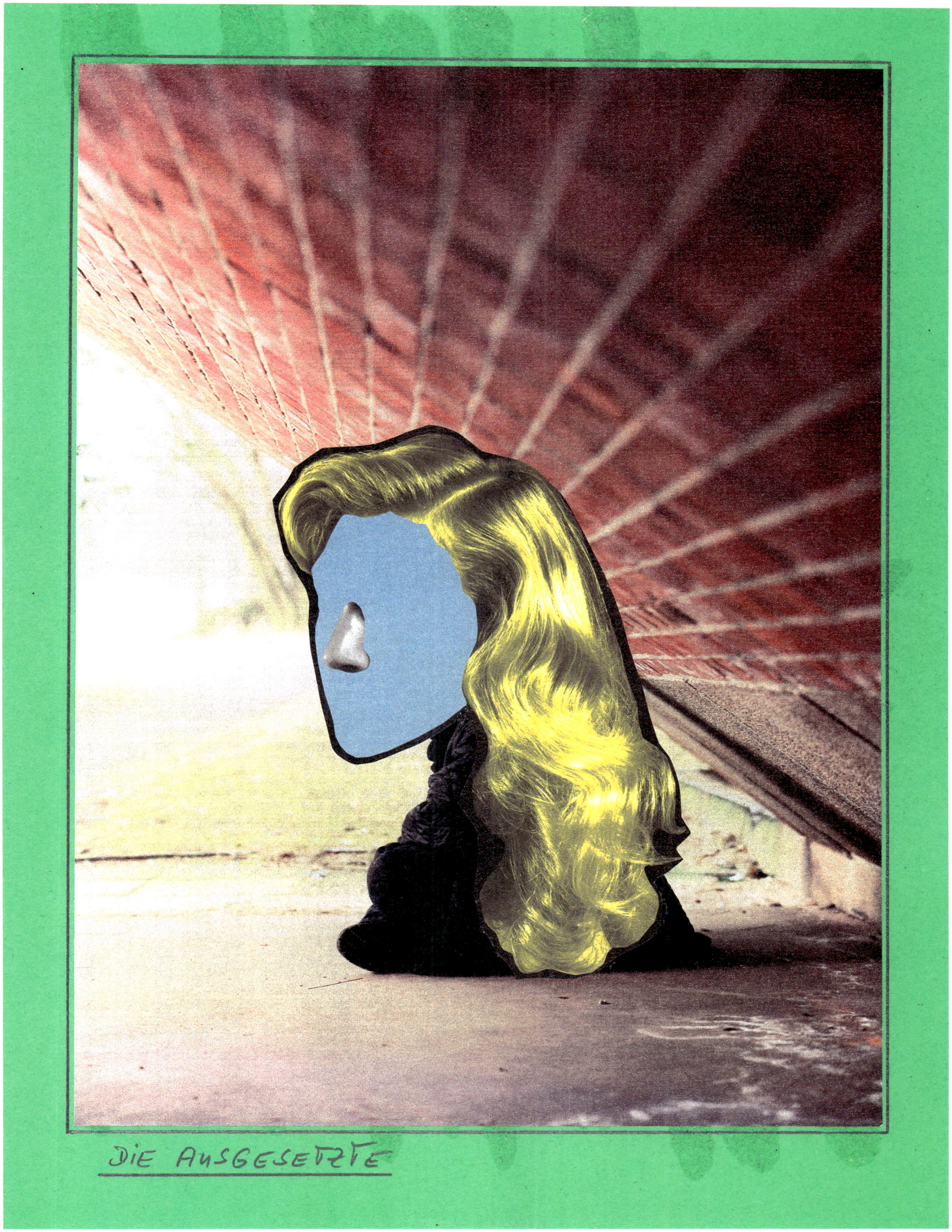

Abandoned, 2008

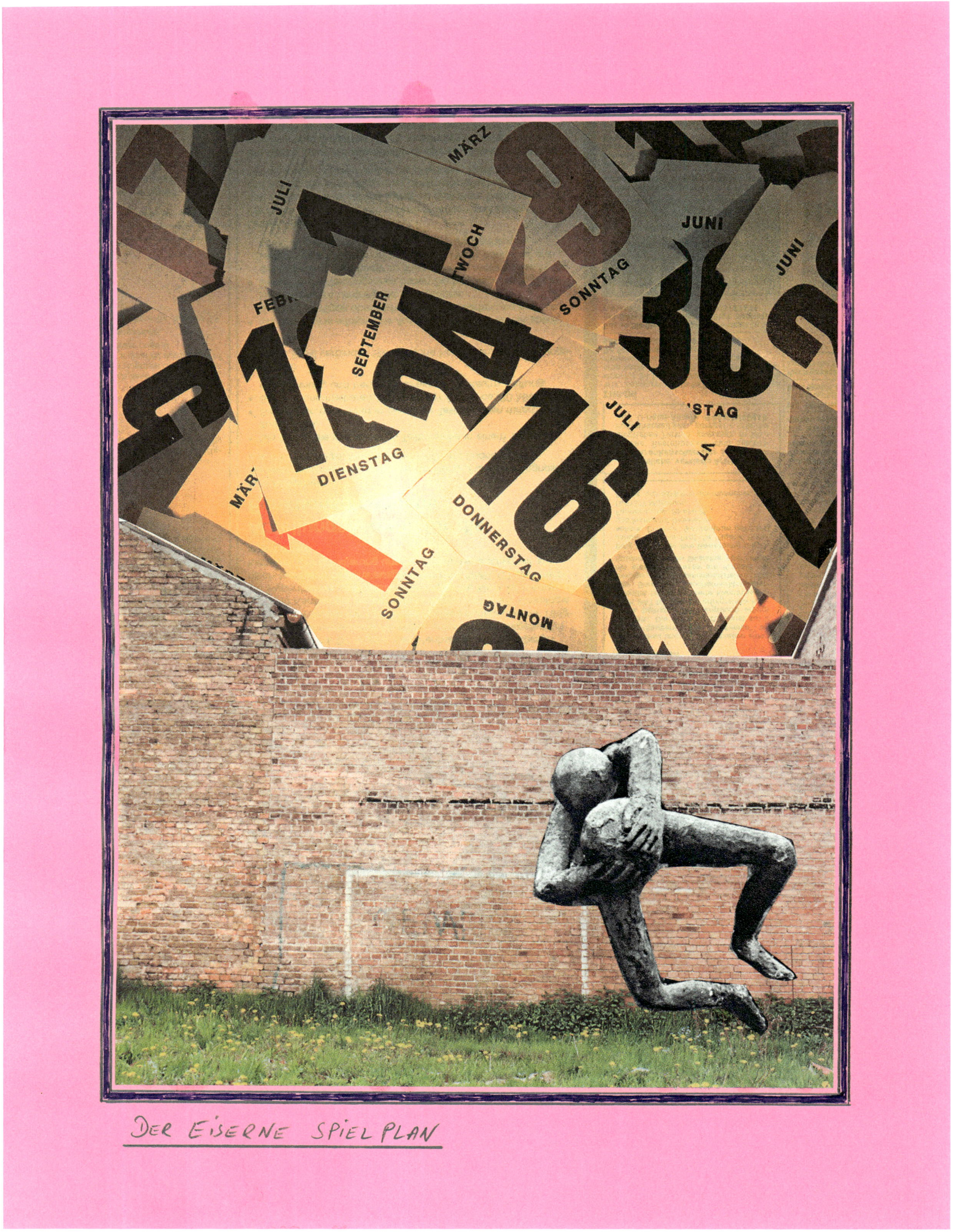

The iron fixtures schedule, 2008

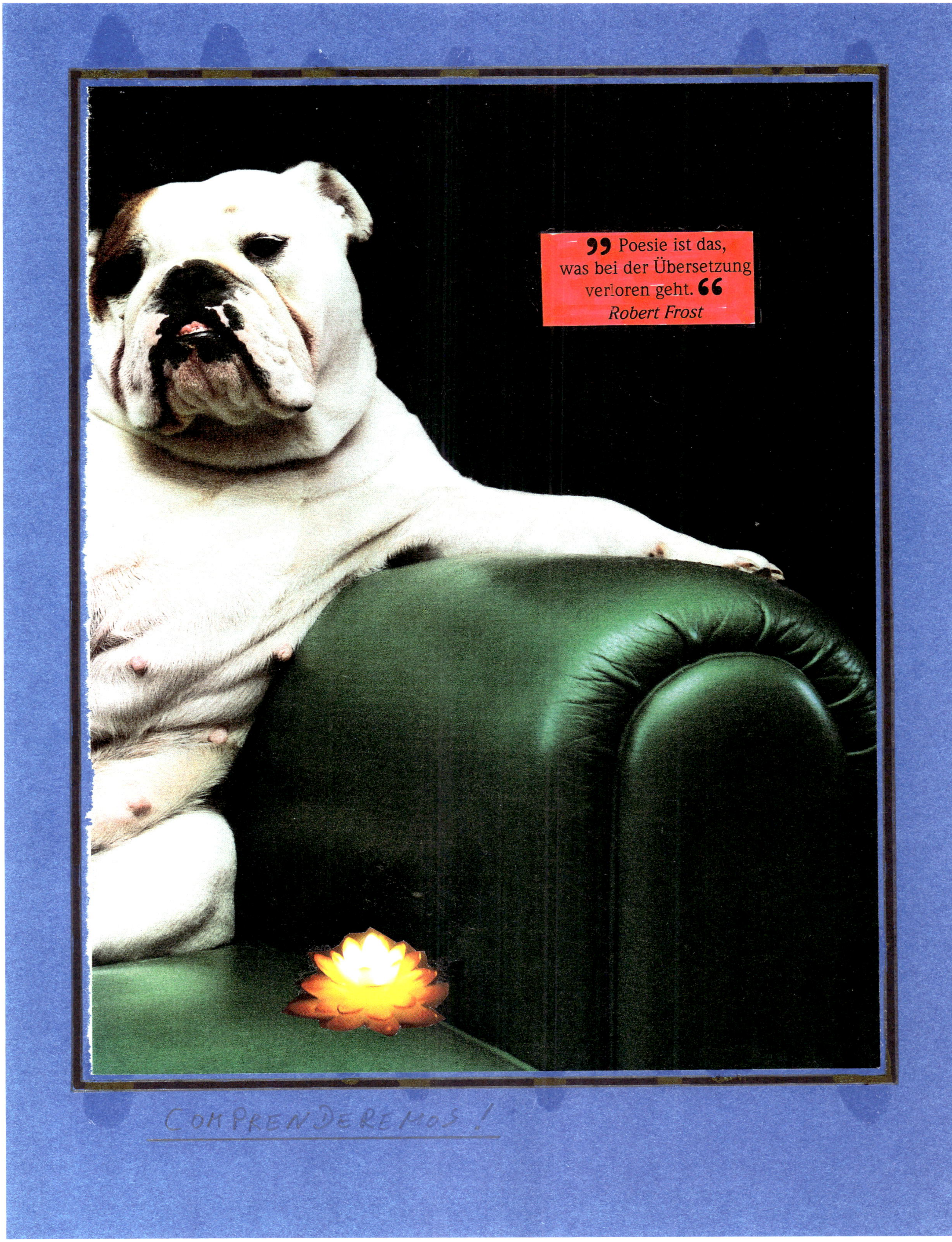

Comprenderemos! (Poetry is what gets lost in translation), 2008

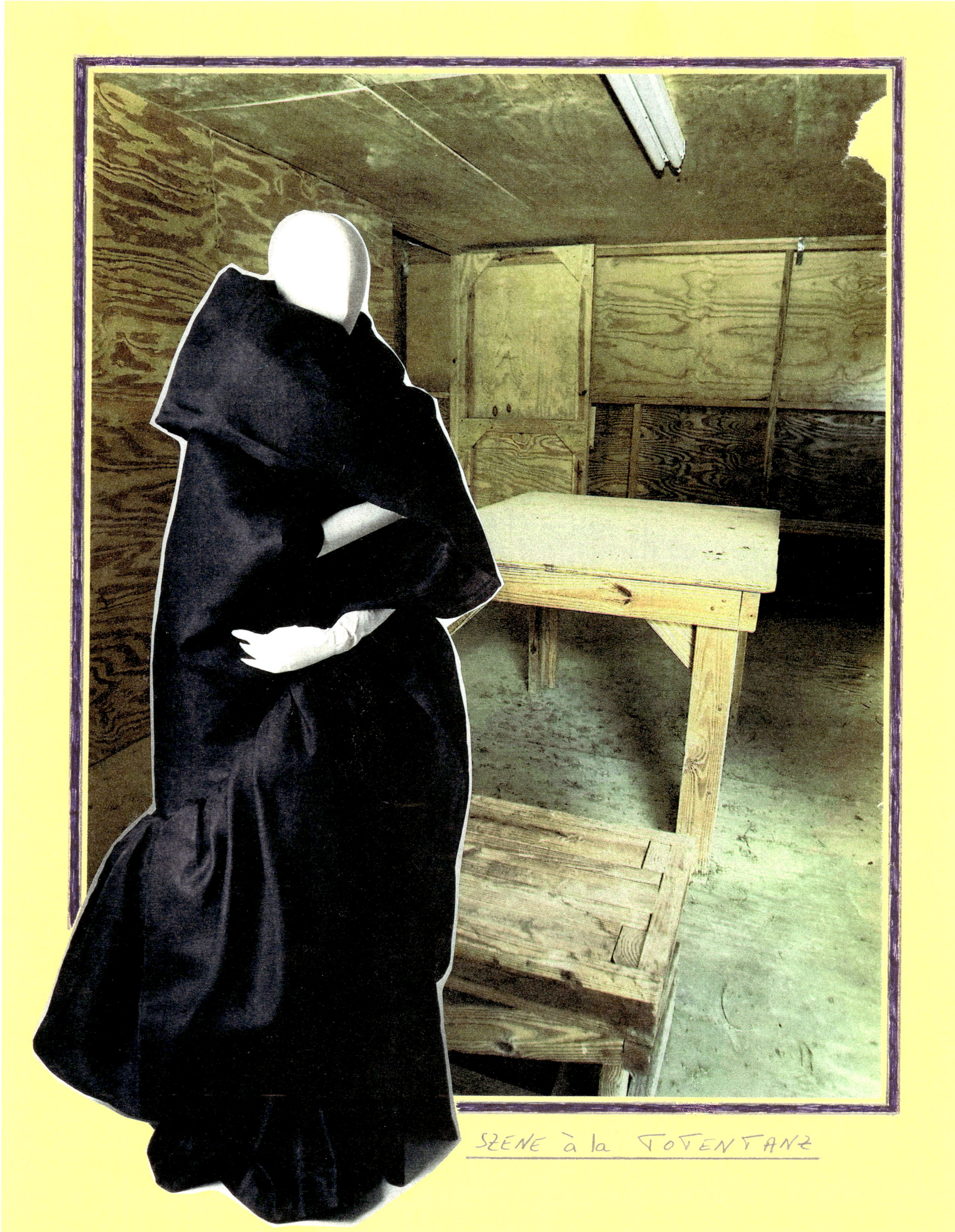

Scene à la Dance of Death, 2007

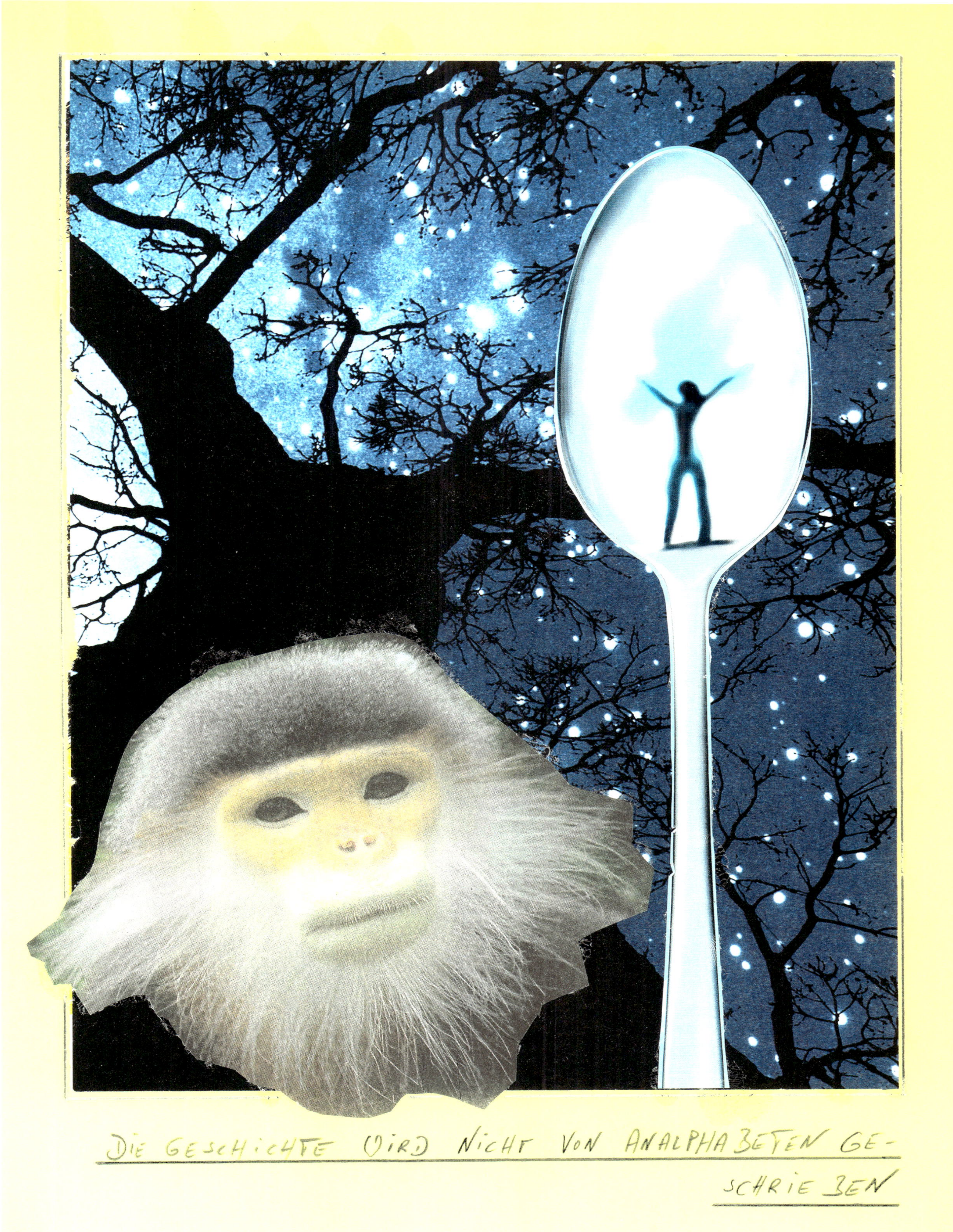

History is not written by the illiterate, 2008

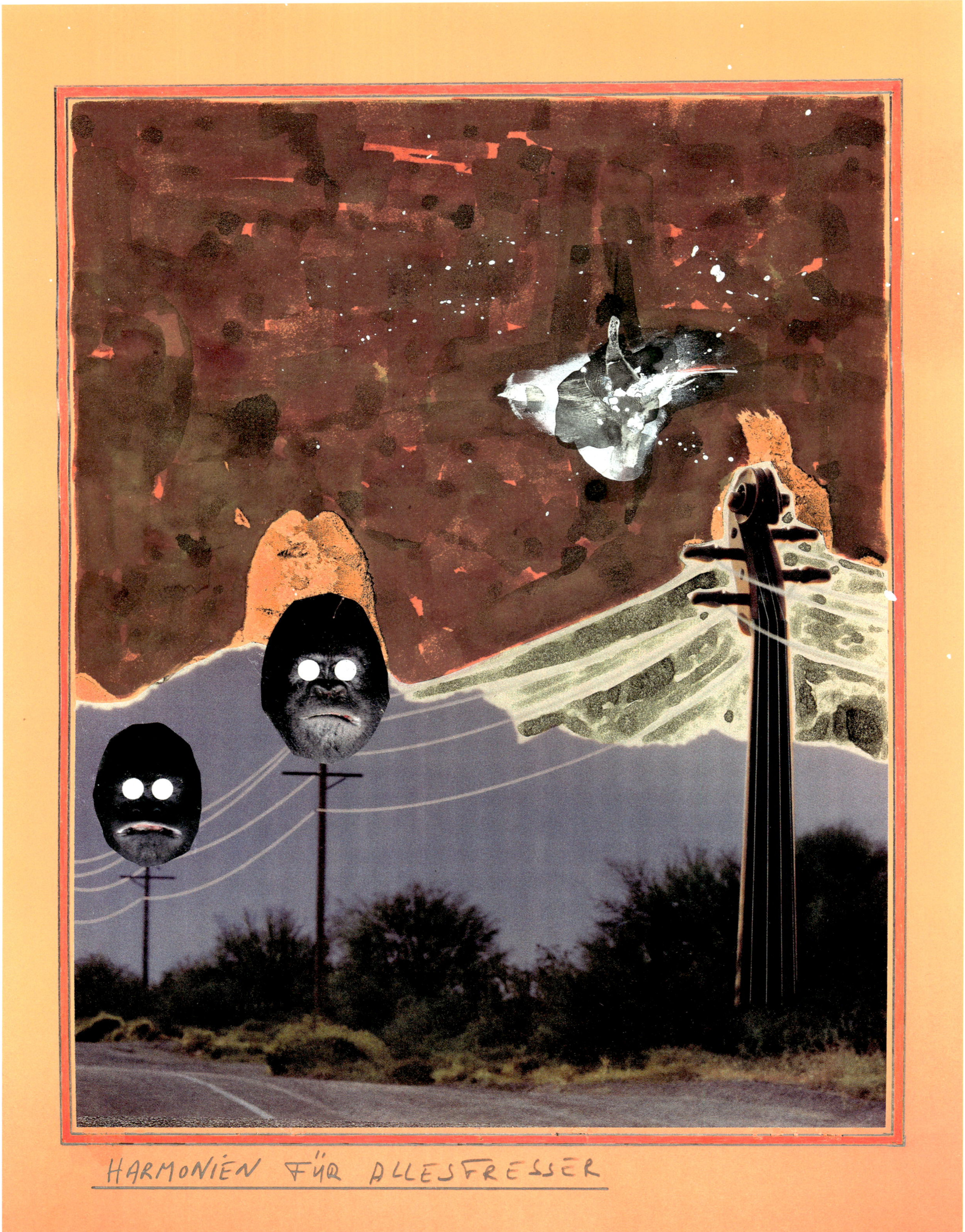

 Harmonies for omnivores, 2008

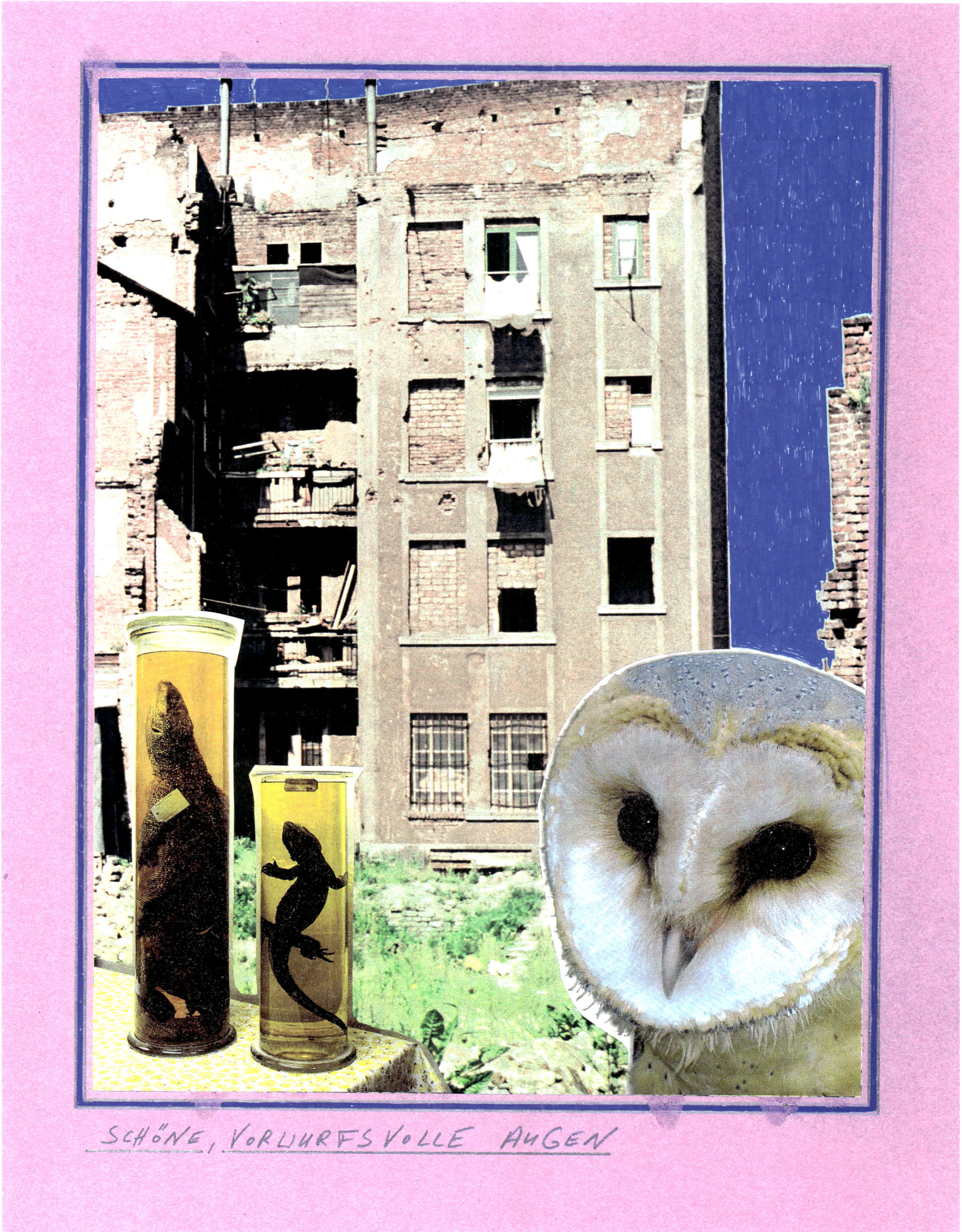

Beautiful, reproachful eyes, 2008

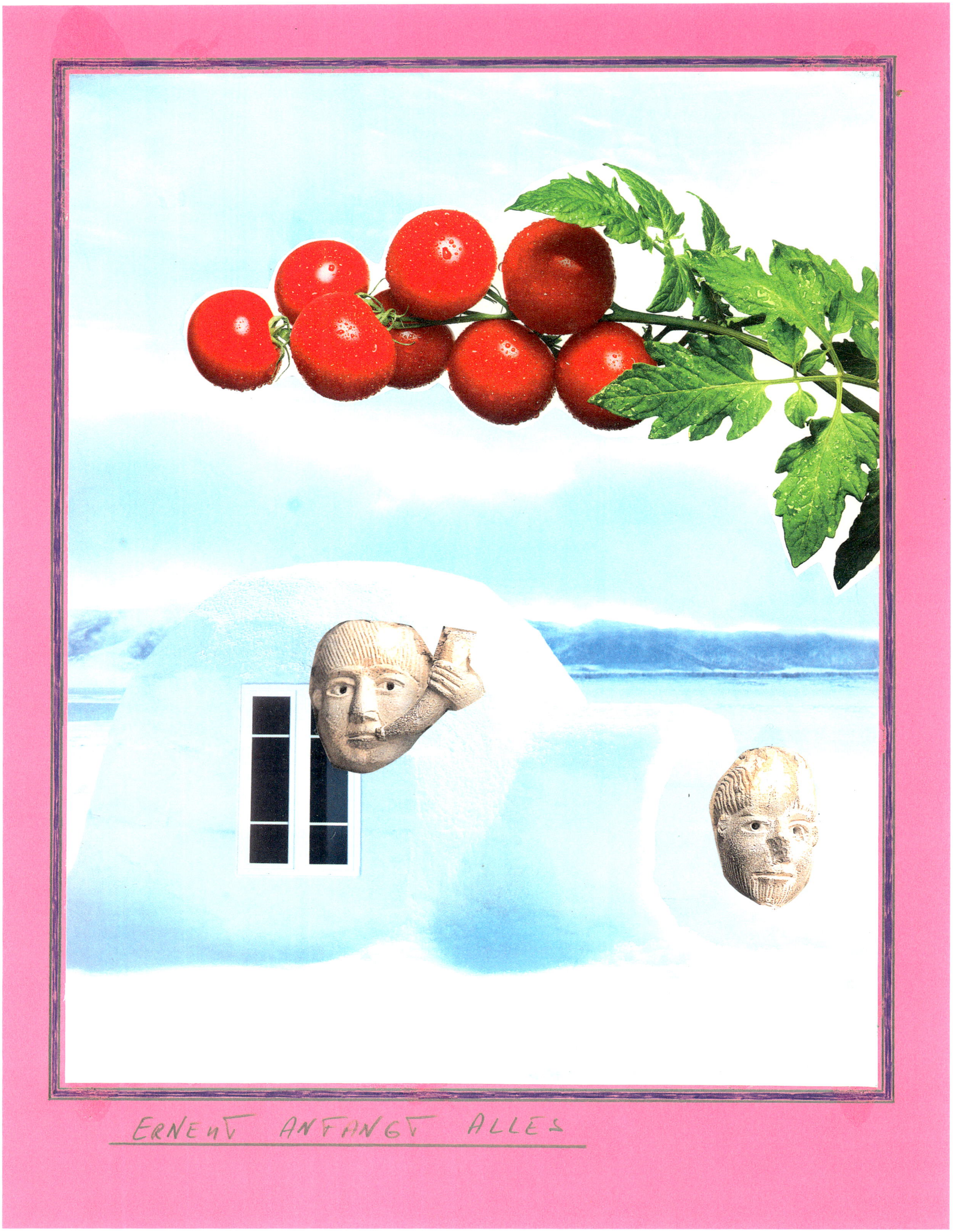

 Anew begins everything..., 2003

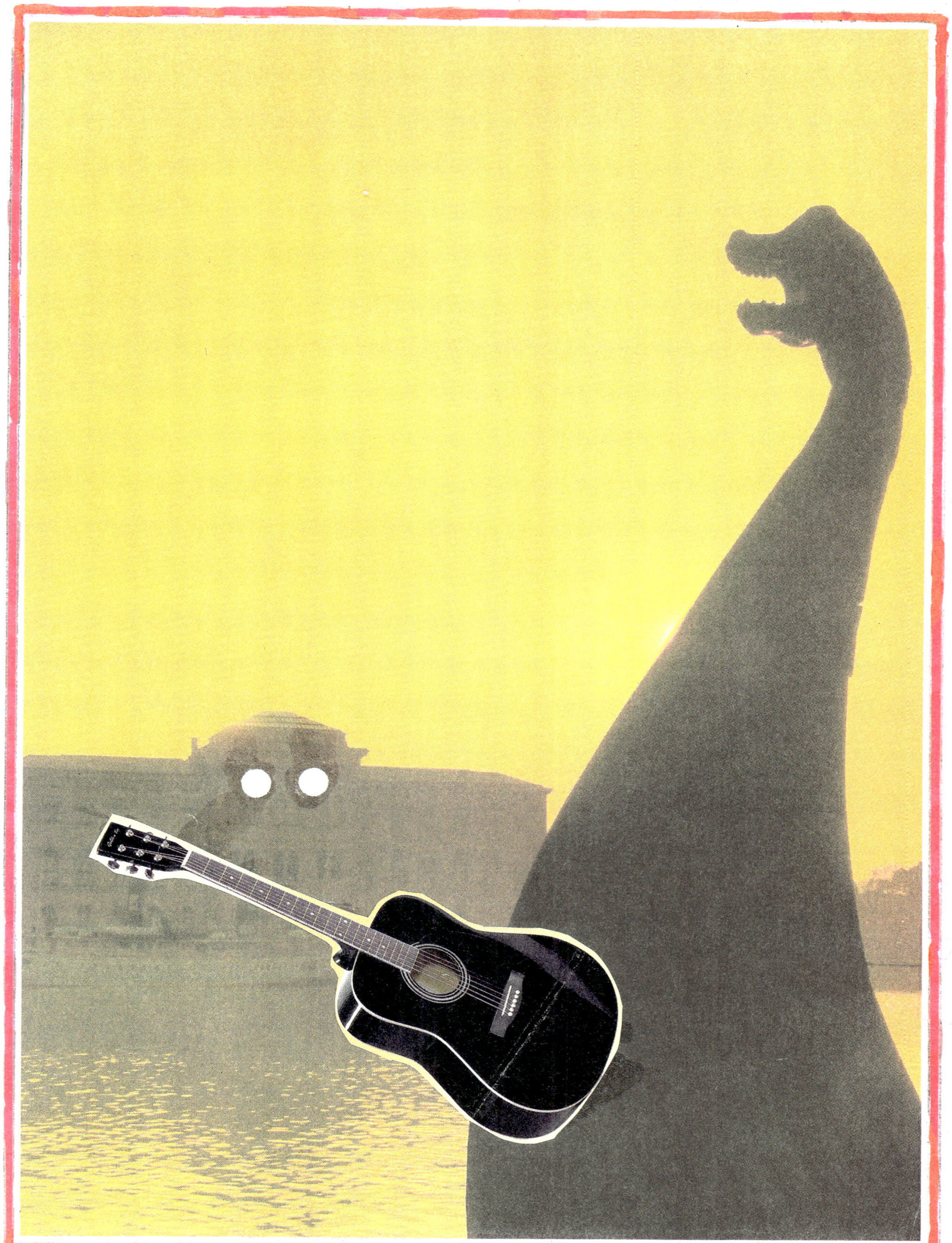

MELODIEN DER OHNMACHT

Melodies of impotence, 2008

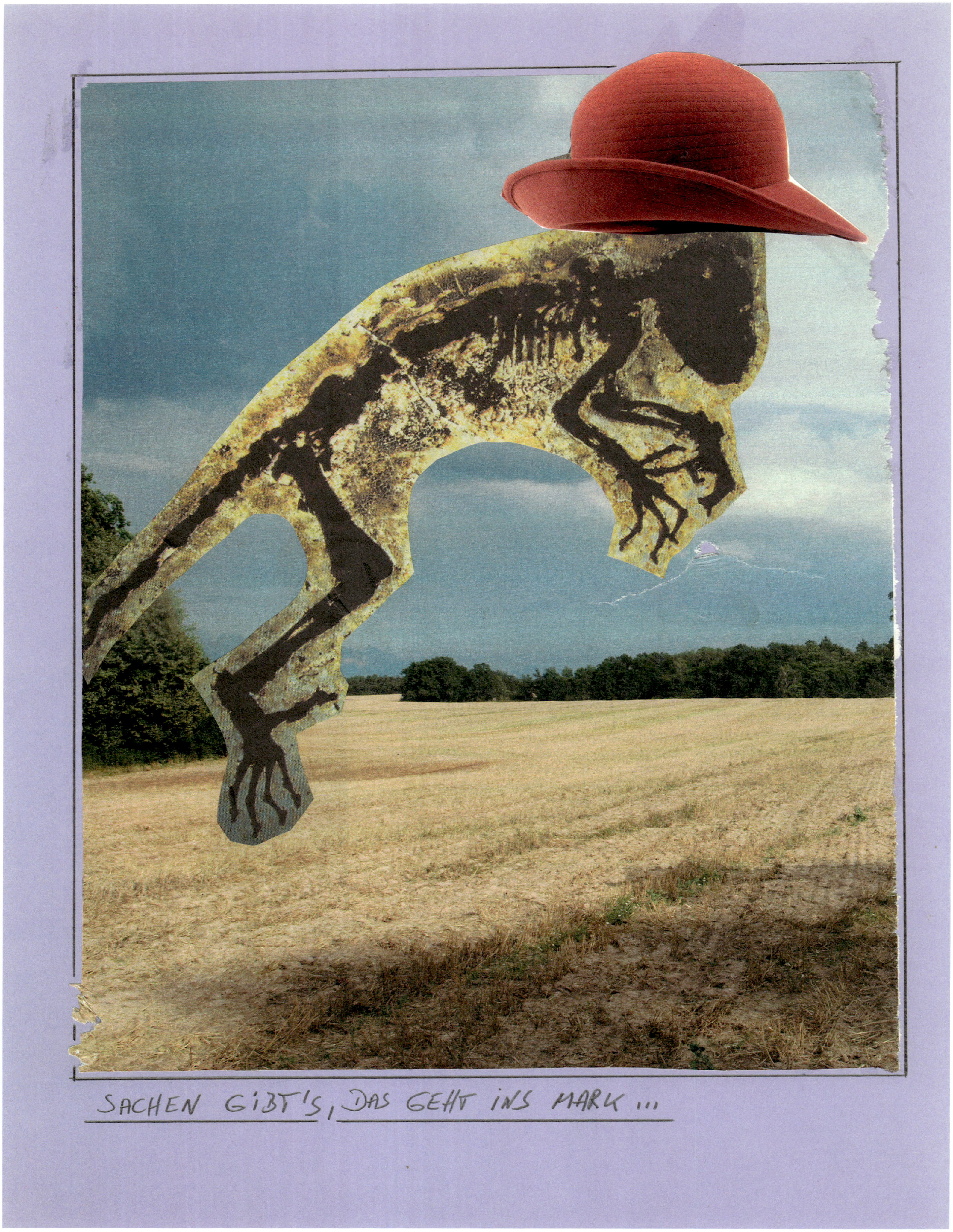

Some things cut to the quick, 2009

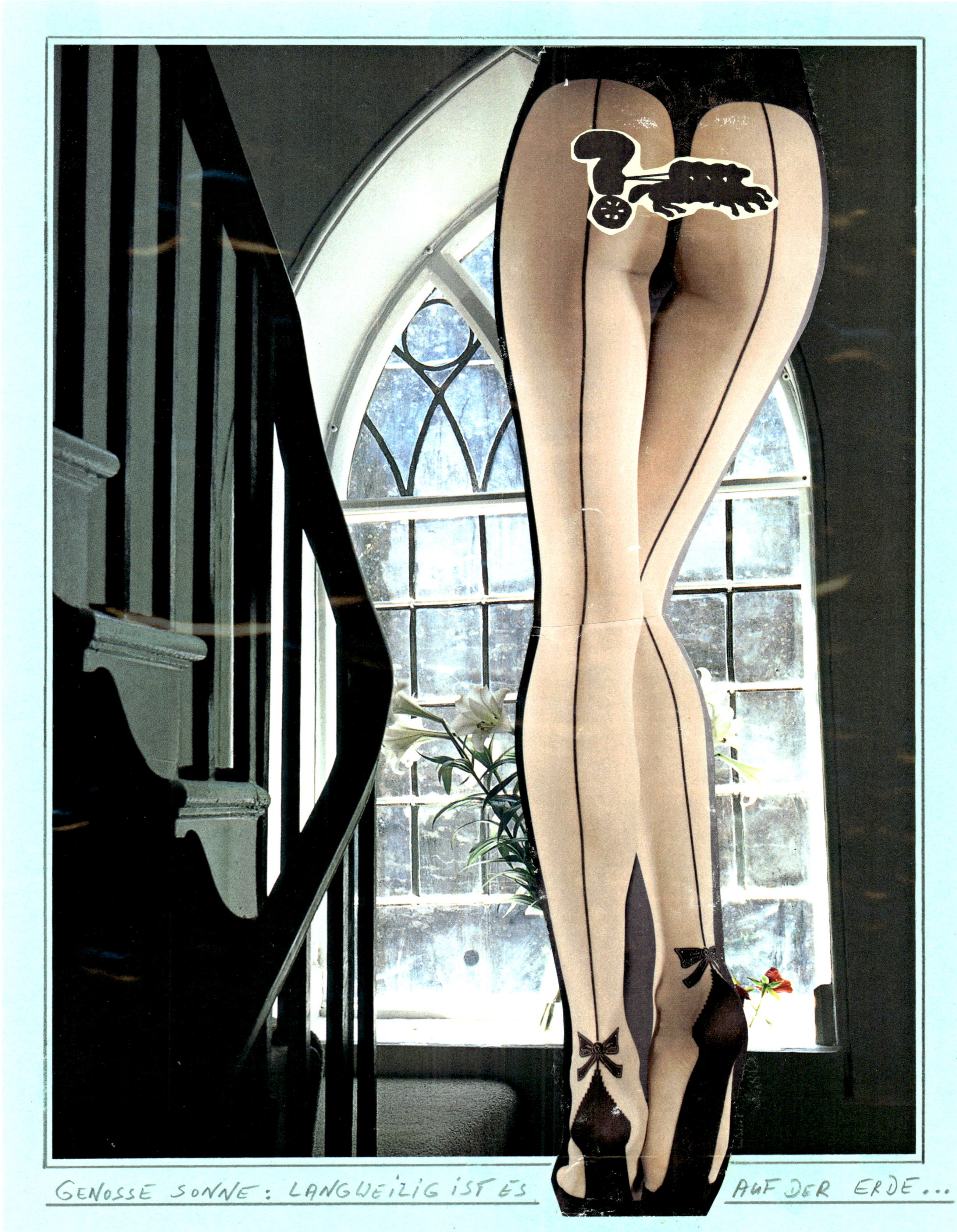

Comrade Sun: tedium reigns on Earth, 2009

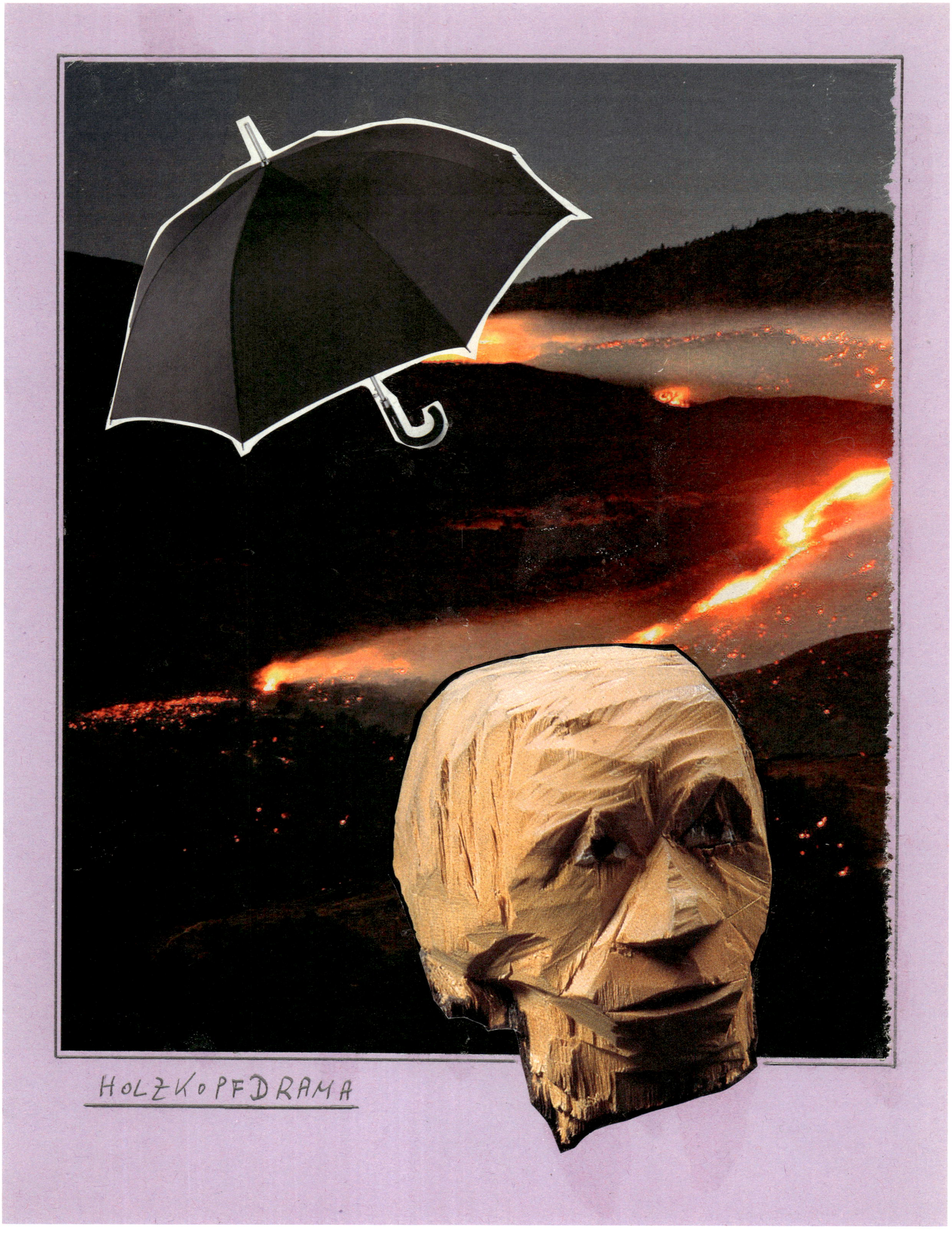

Numbskull drama, 2009

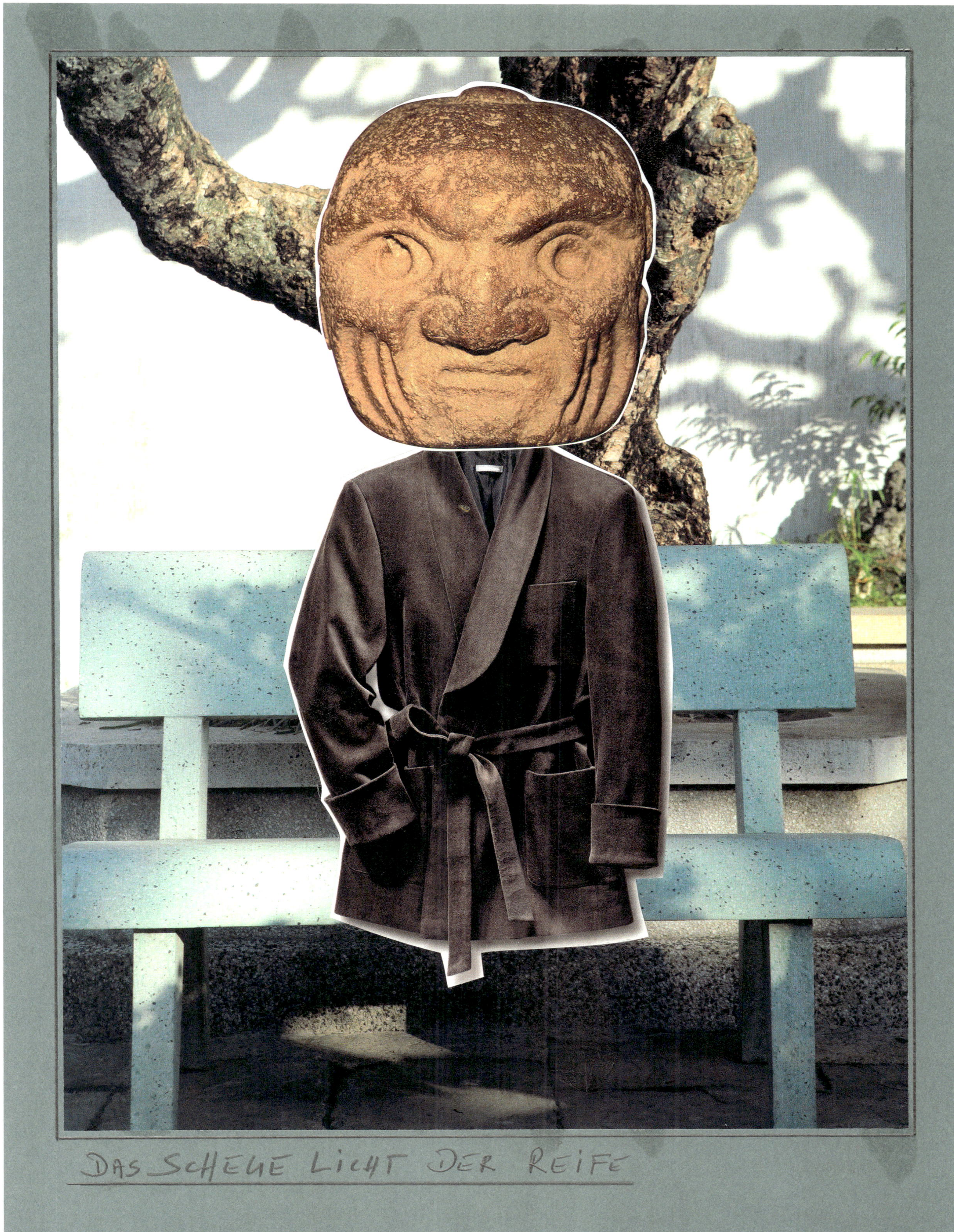

The shy light of maturity, 2008

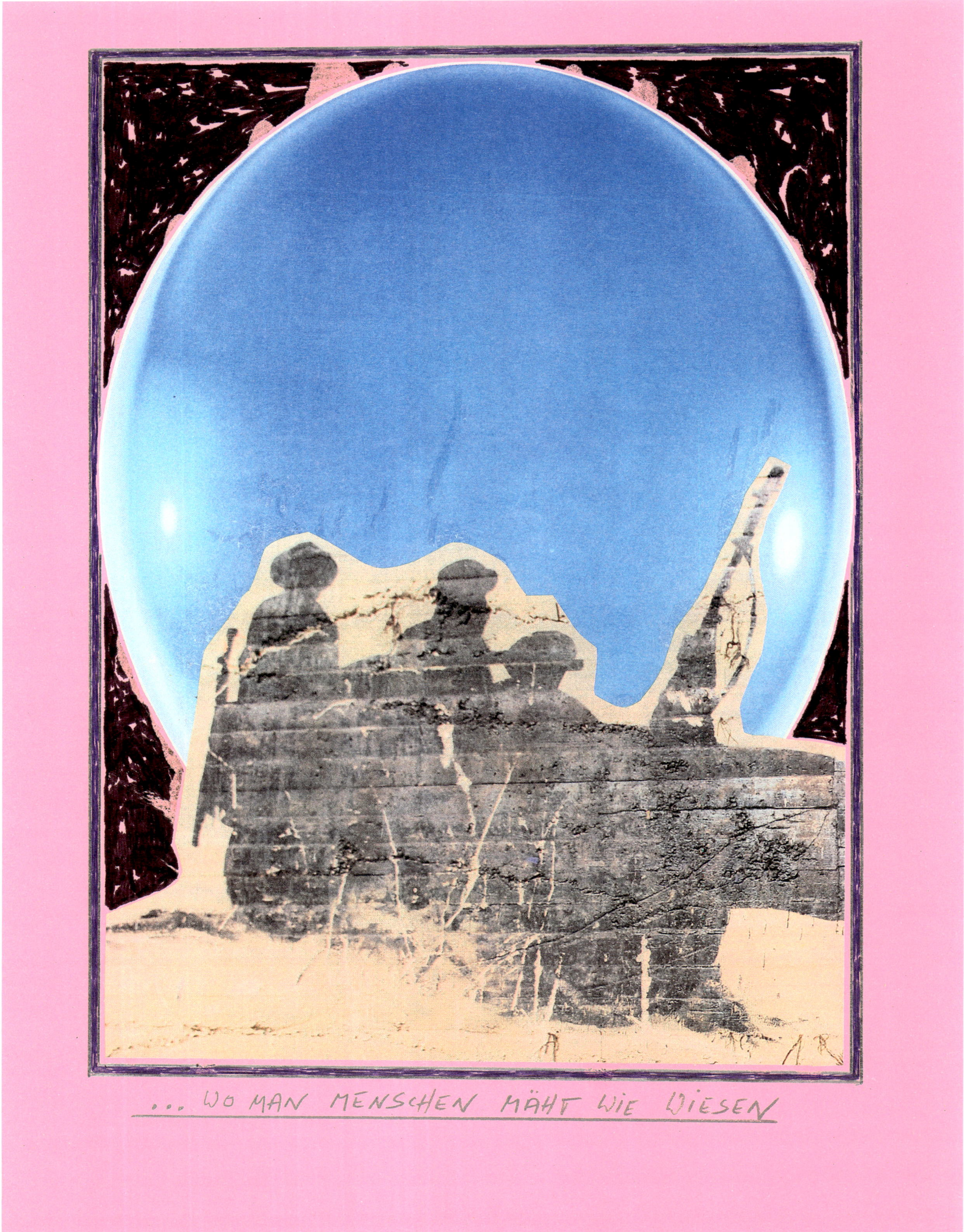

 ... where people are mown like meadows, 2008

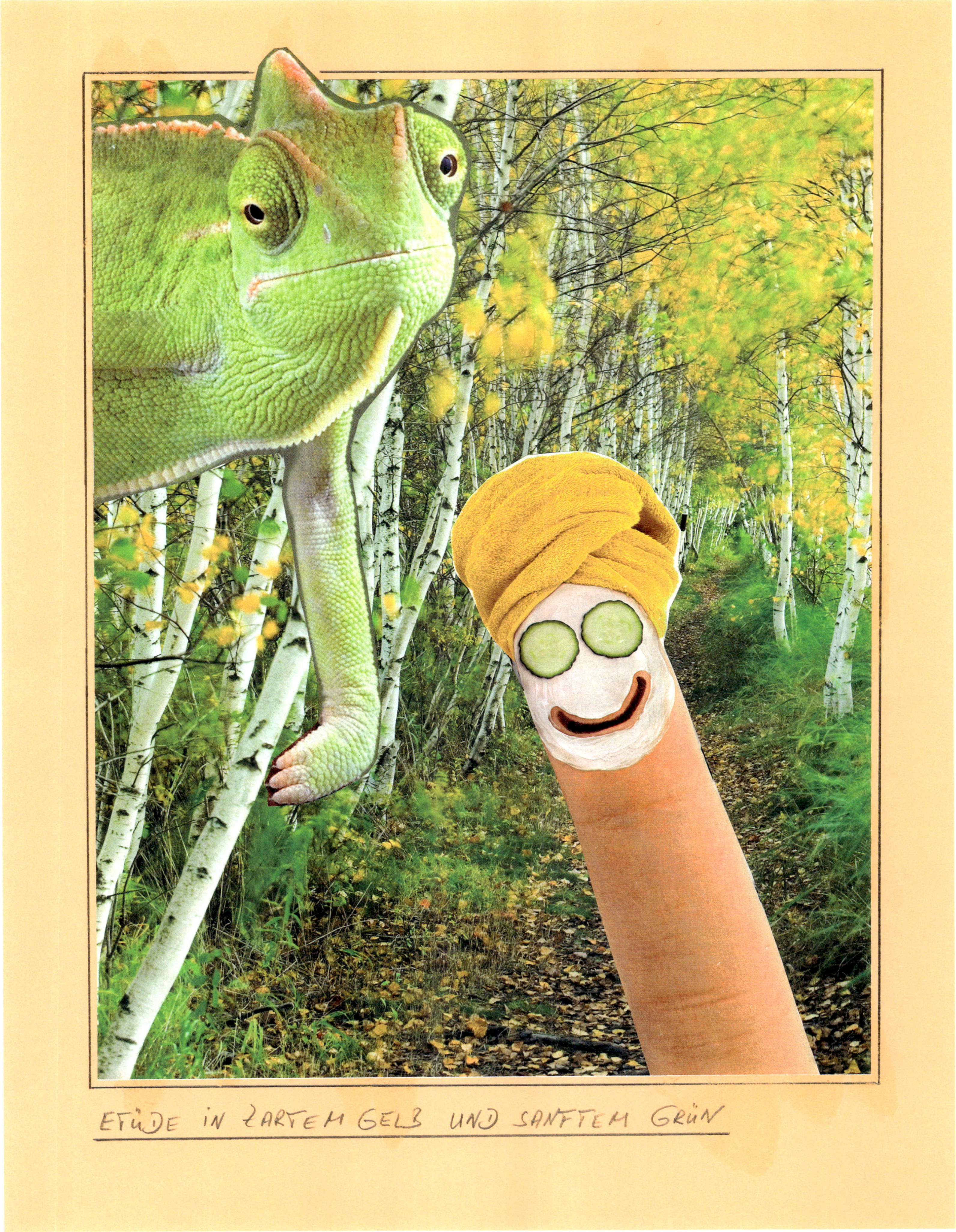

Study in gentle yellow and soft green, 2009

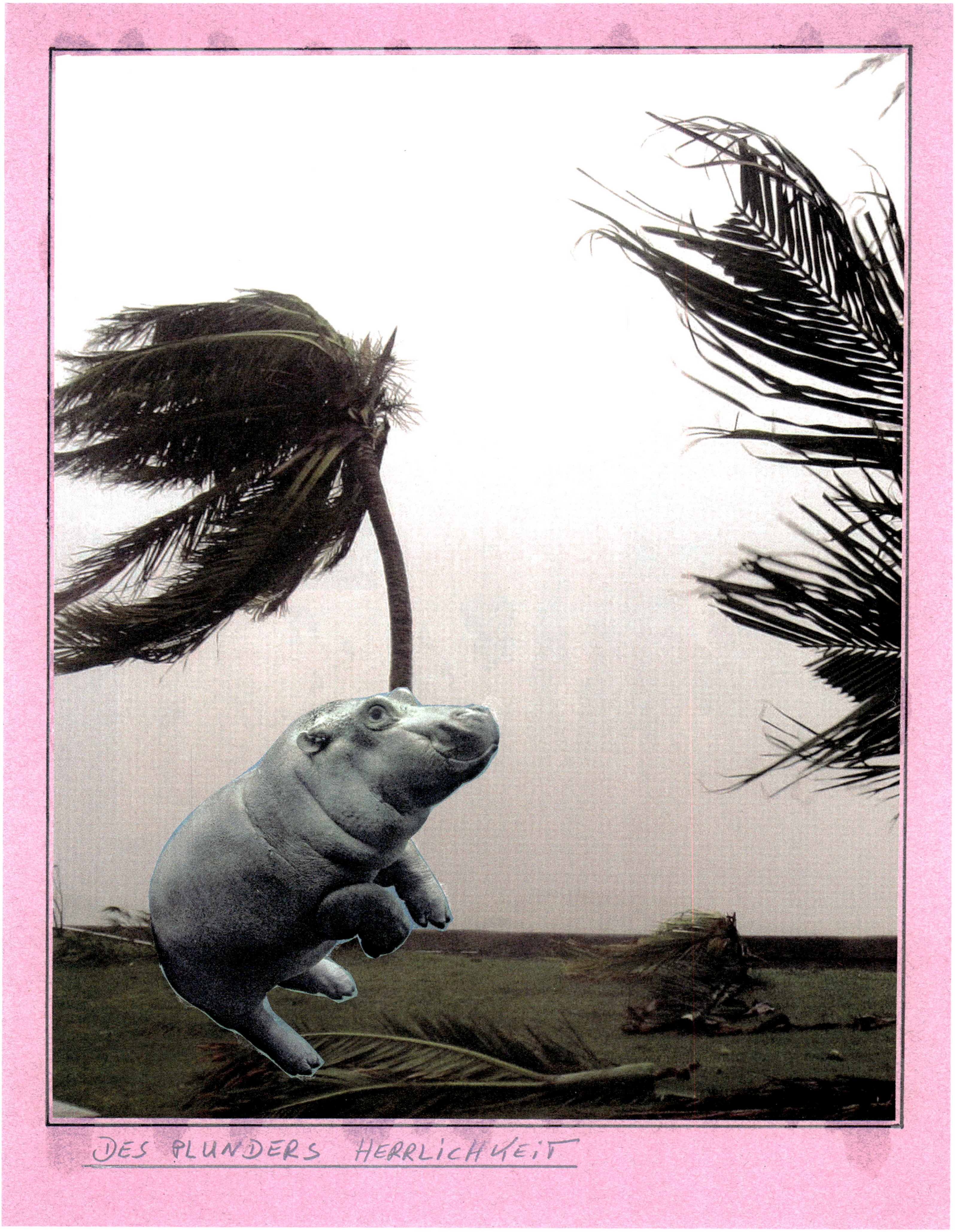

The splendour of trumpery, 2008

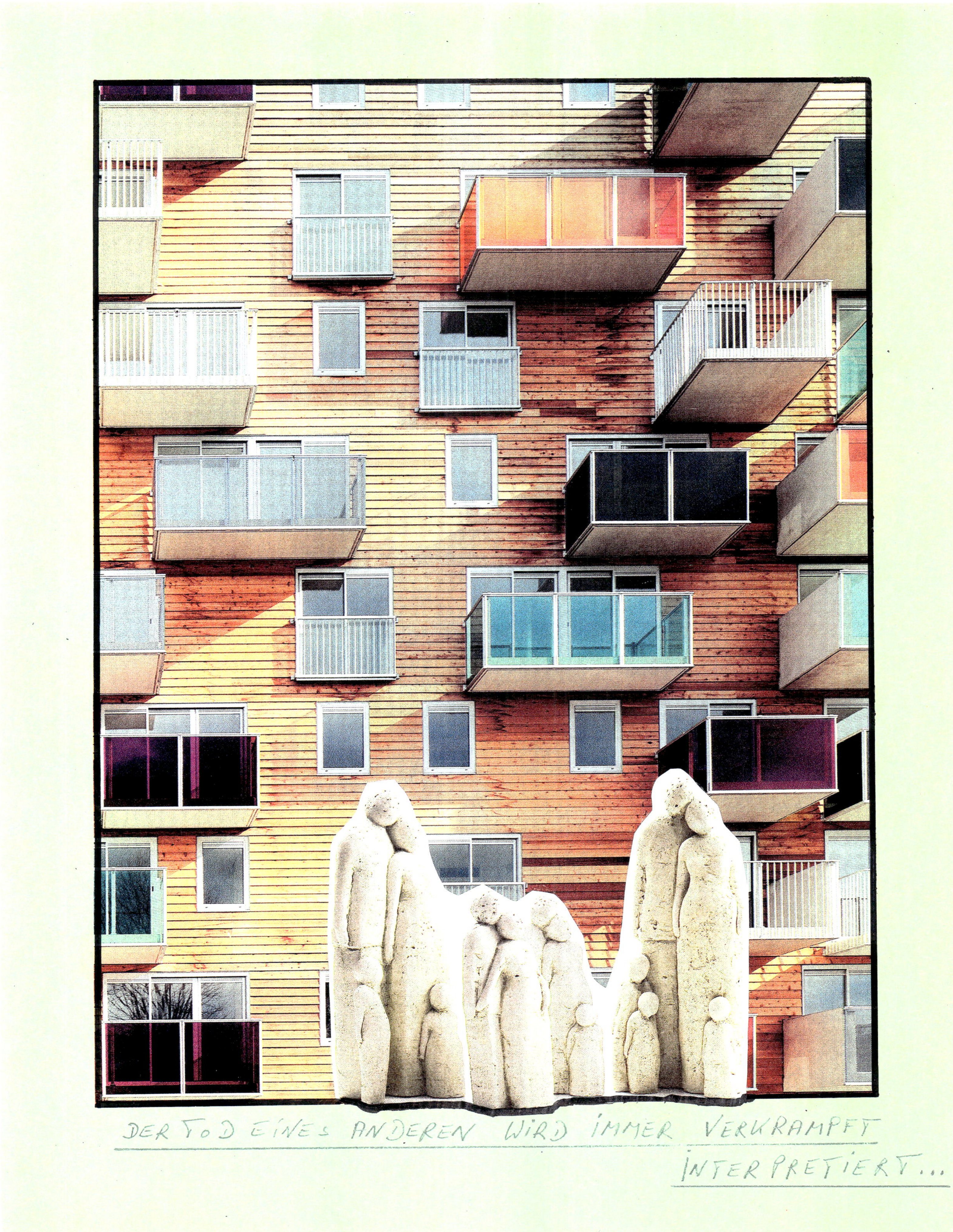

The death of another always receives an uptight interpretation..., 2008

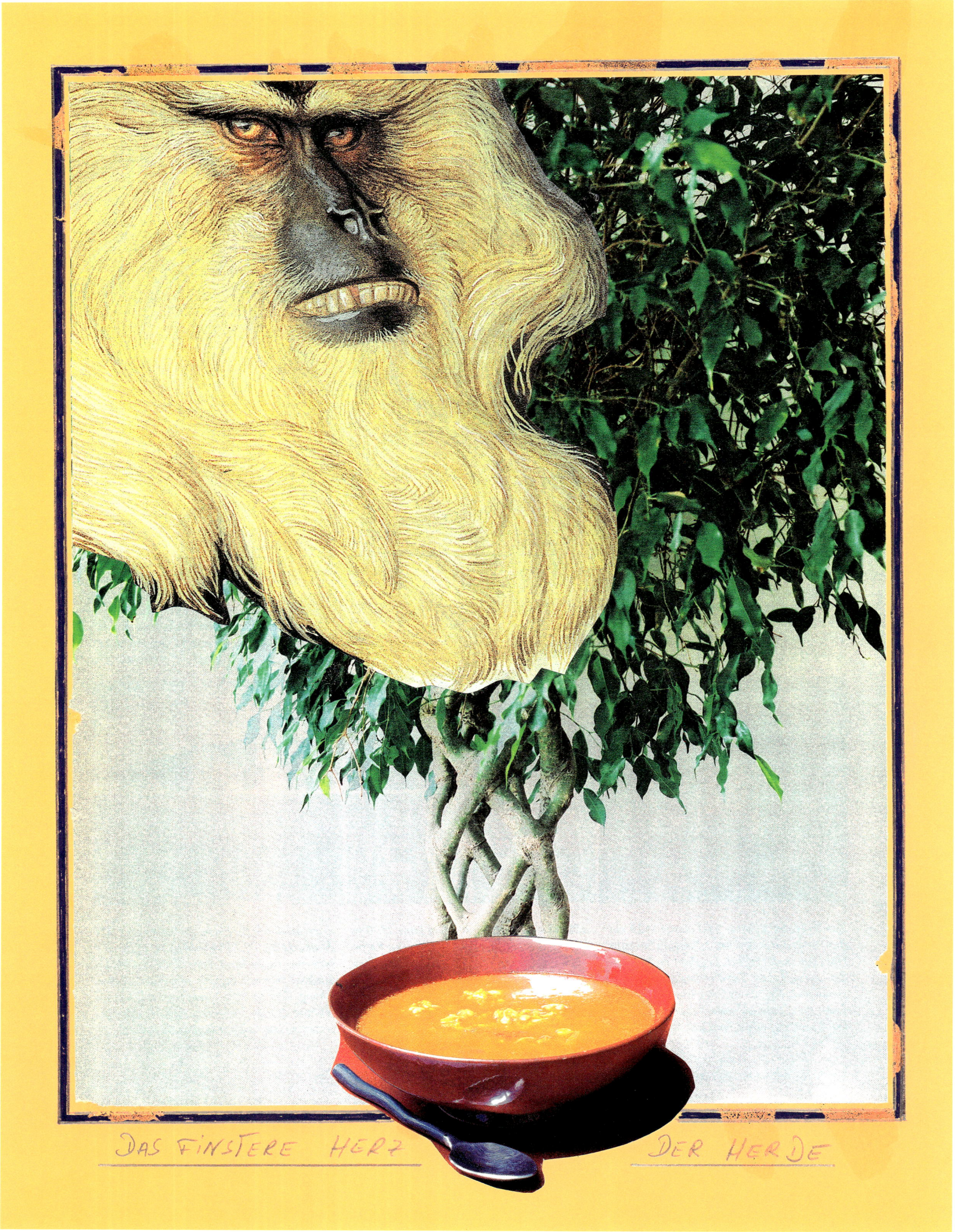

 The dark heart of the herd, 2007

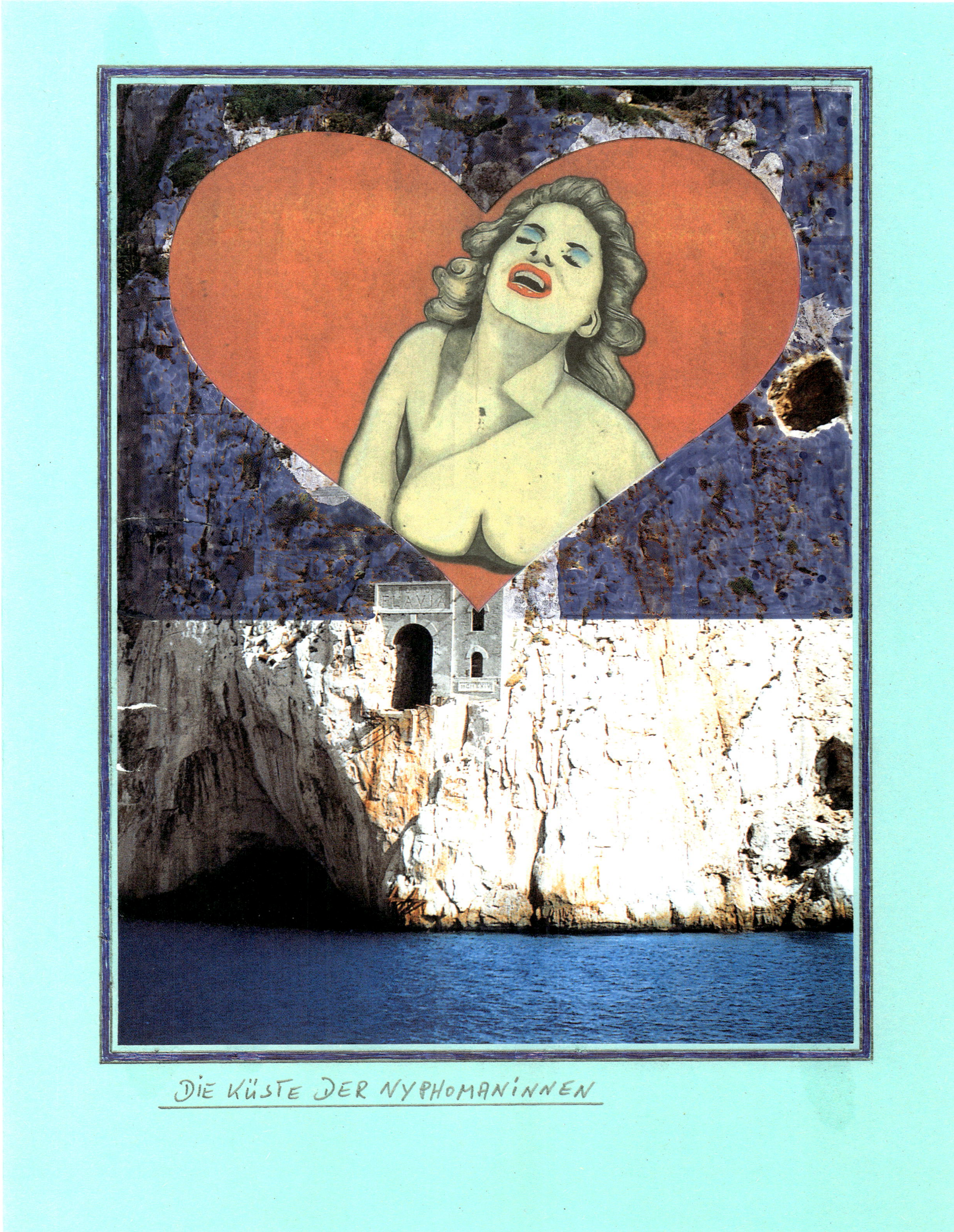

Nymphomaniac coast, 2011

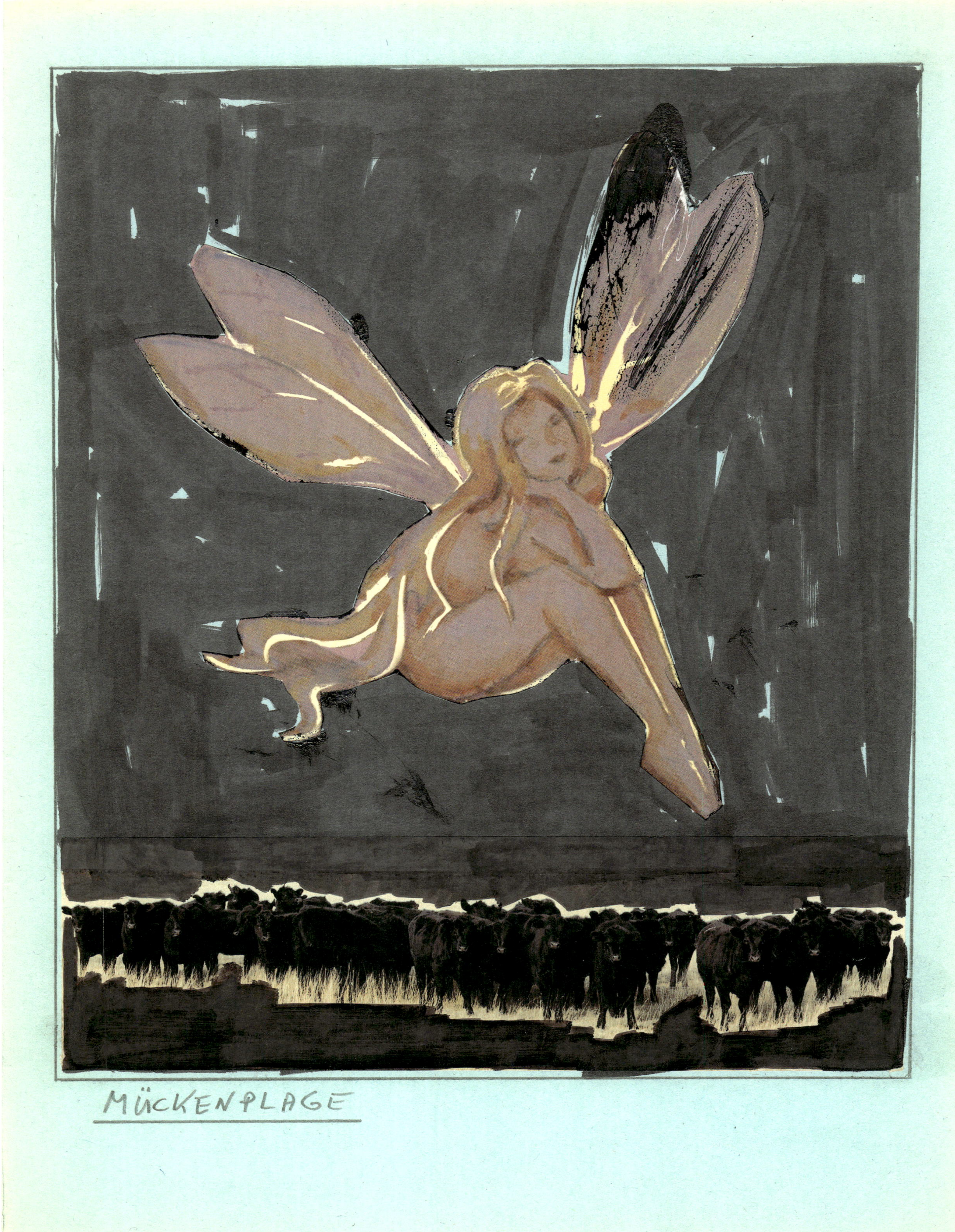

Plague of mosquitoes, 2011

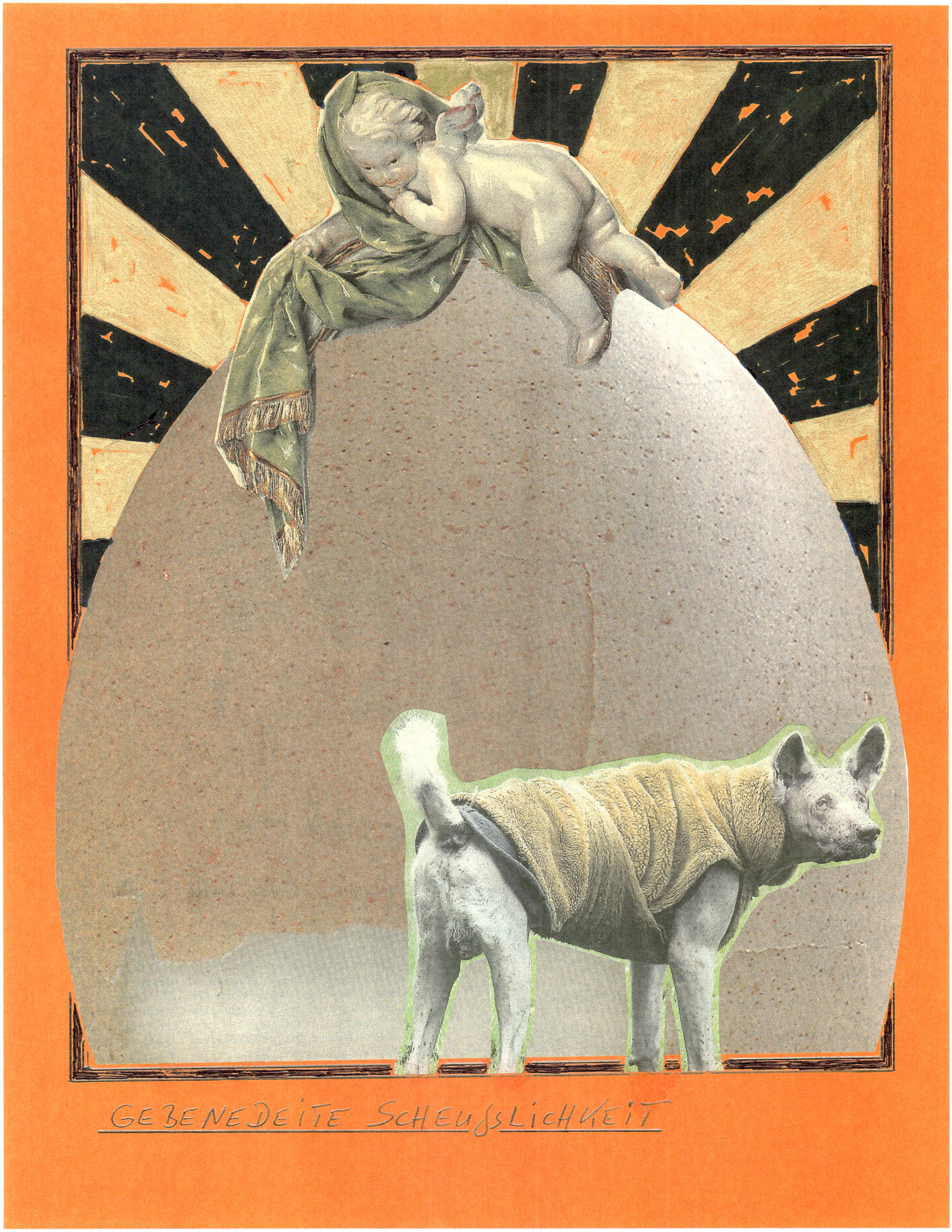

Blessed ghastliness, 2011

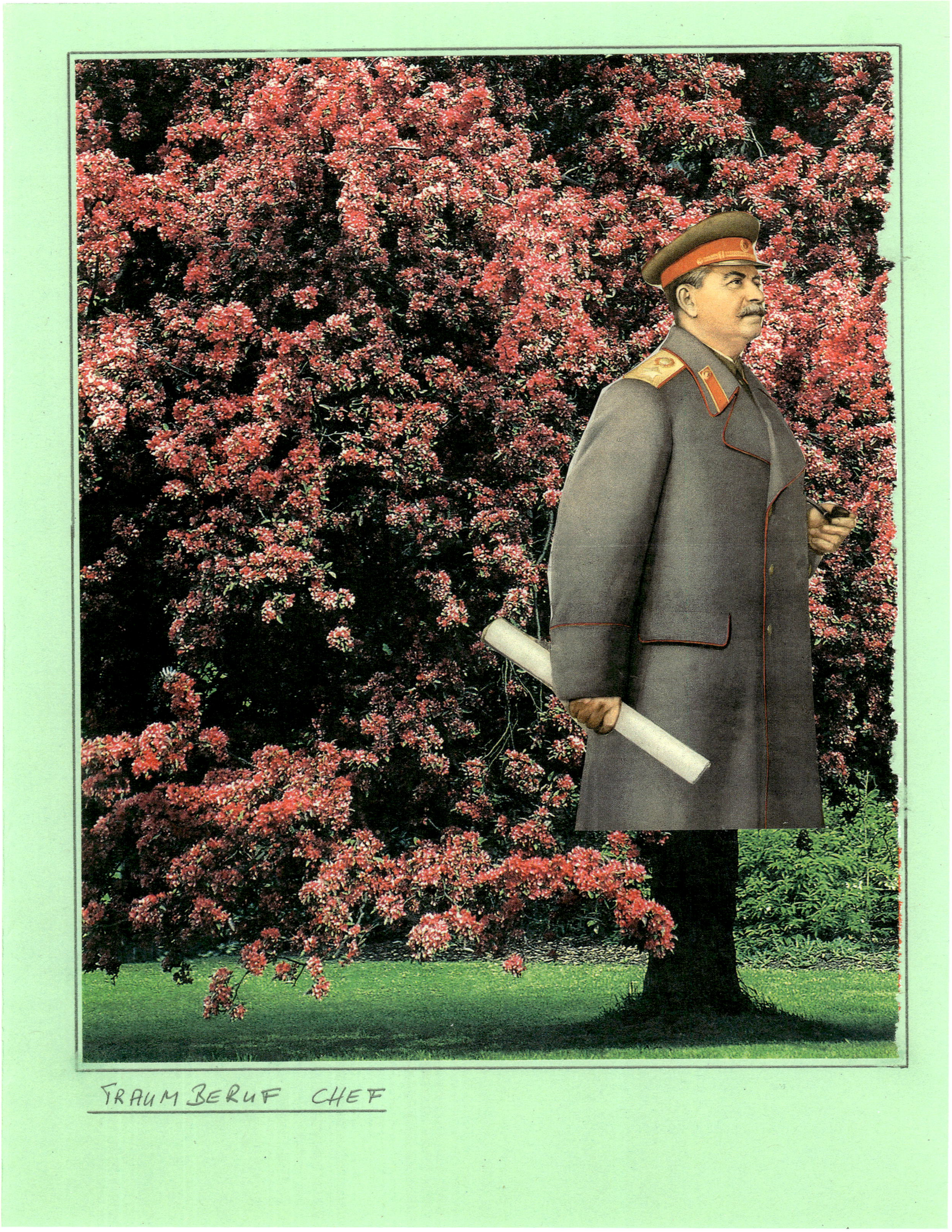

Dream job Boss, 2010

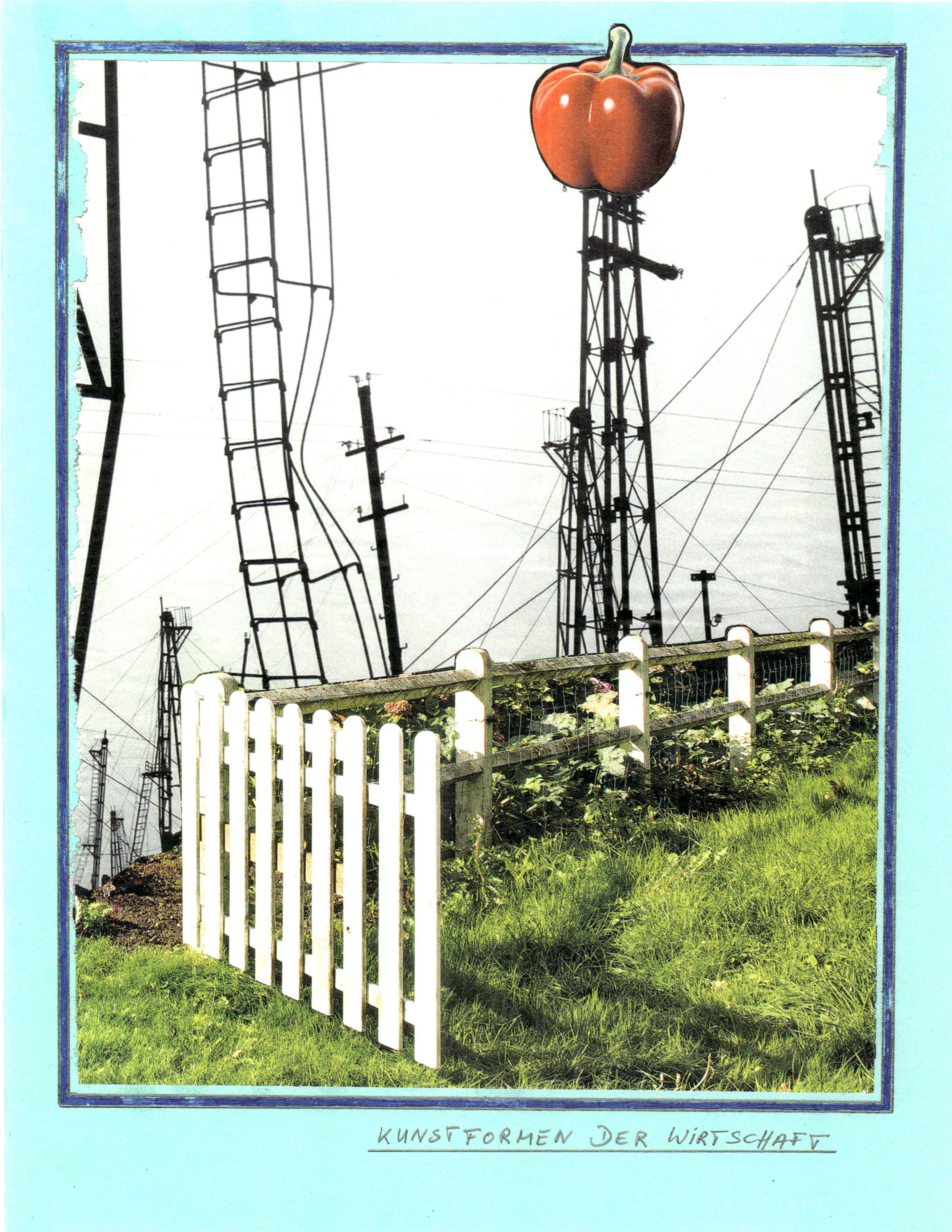

Art forms in business, 2011

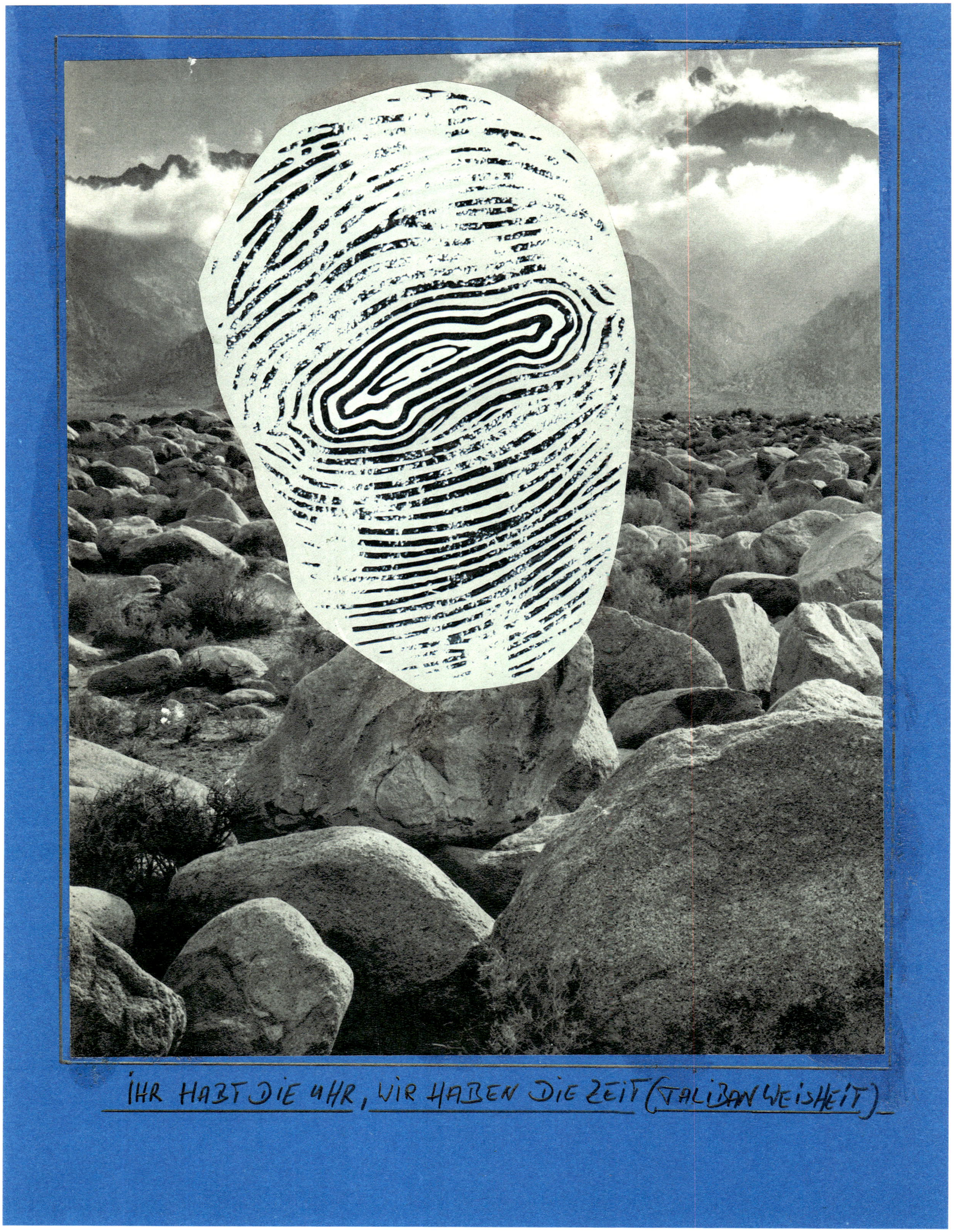

You have the clock, we have the time (Taliban wisdom), 2011

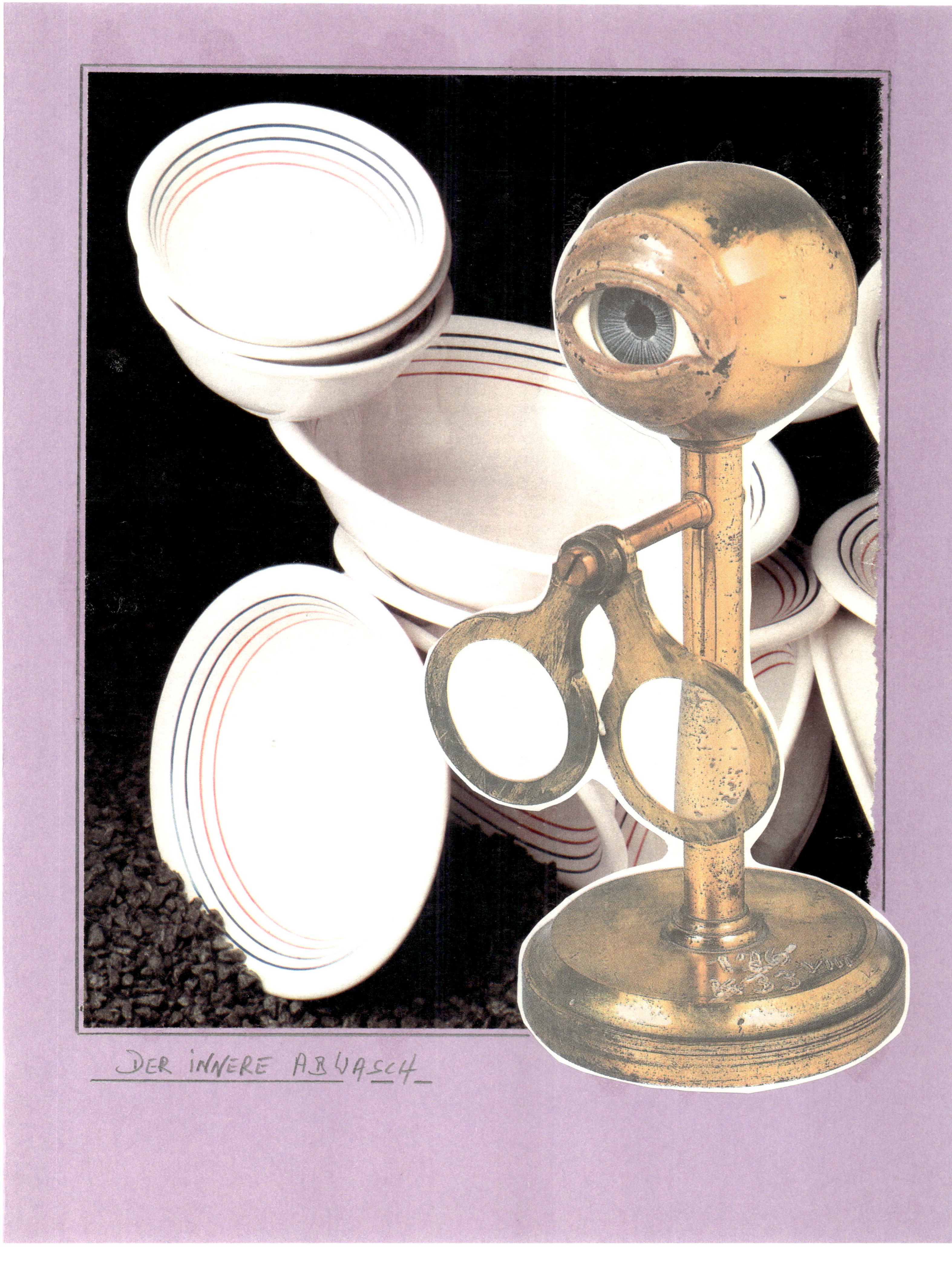

The inner dishes, 2012

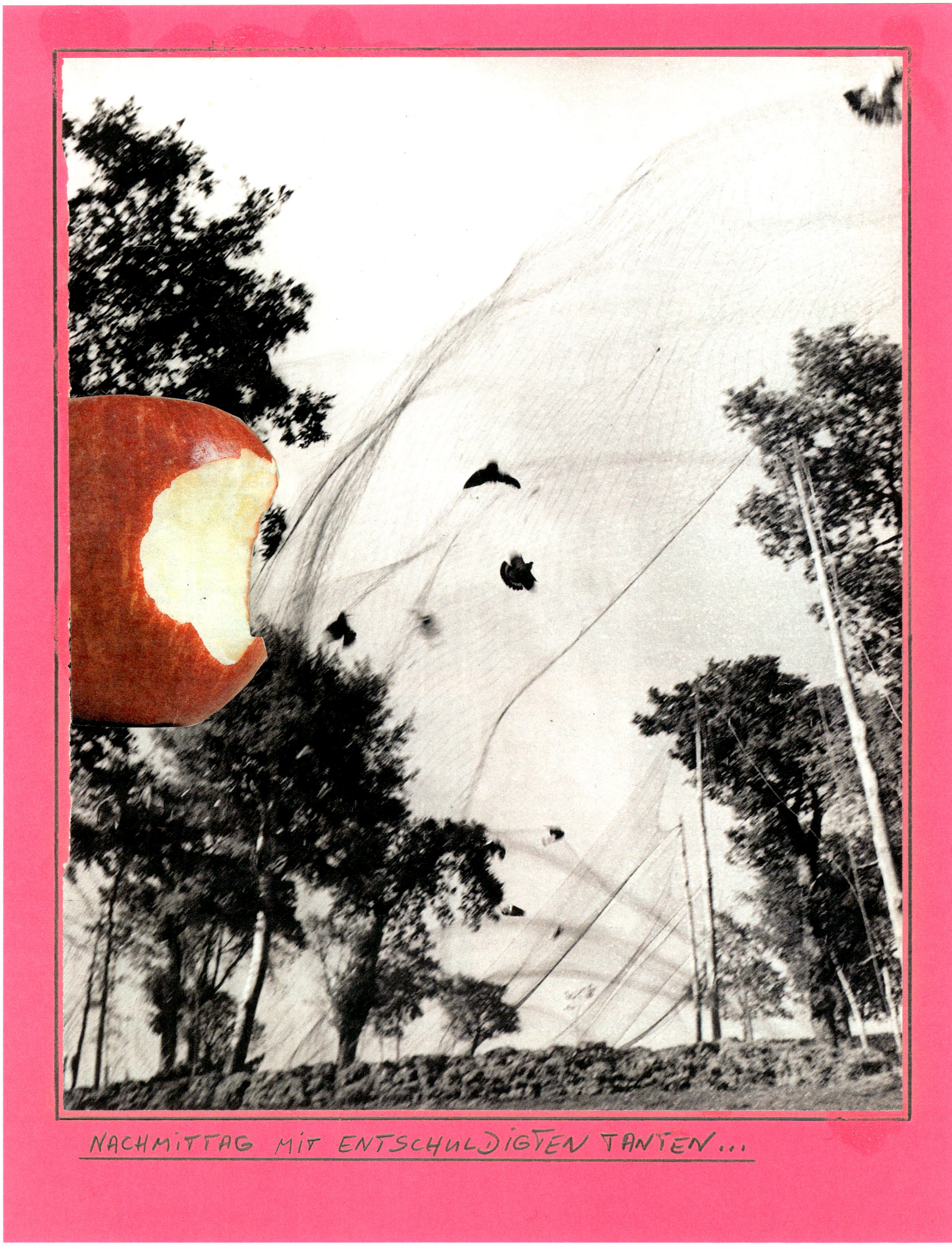

 Afternoon with aunts excused..., 2011

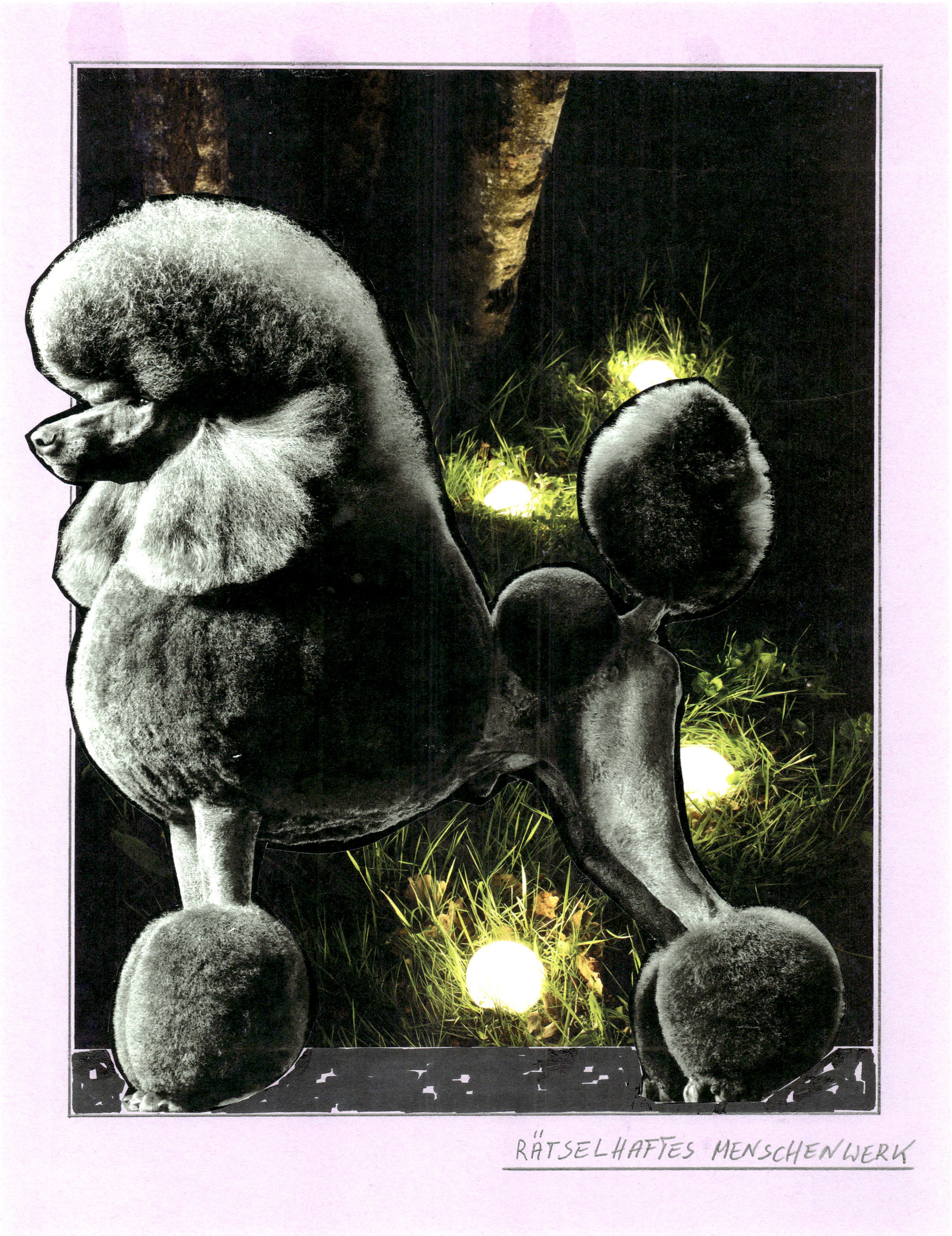

Man-made enigma, 2011

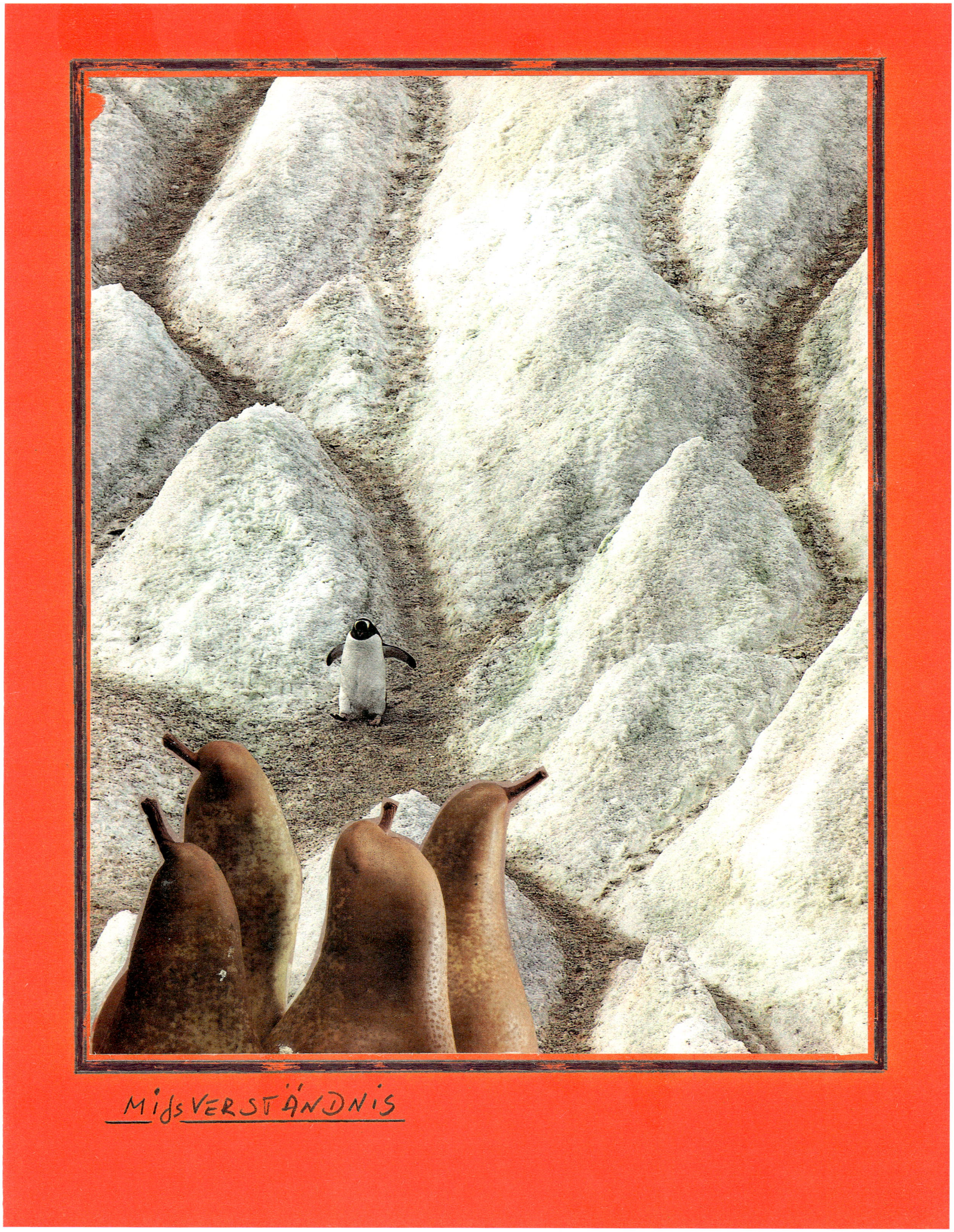

 Misunderstanding, 2011

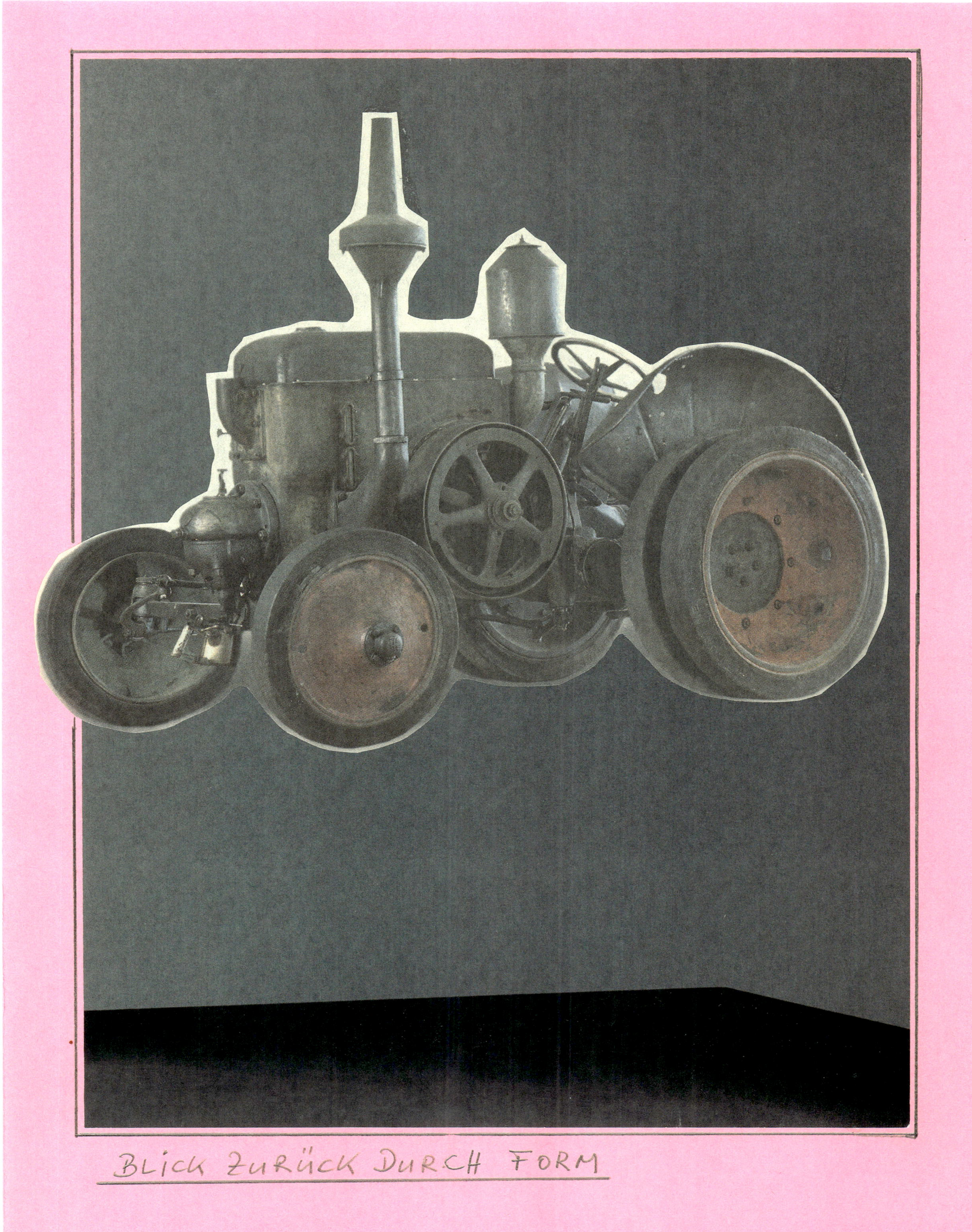

Looking back through form, 2011

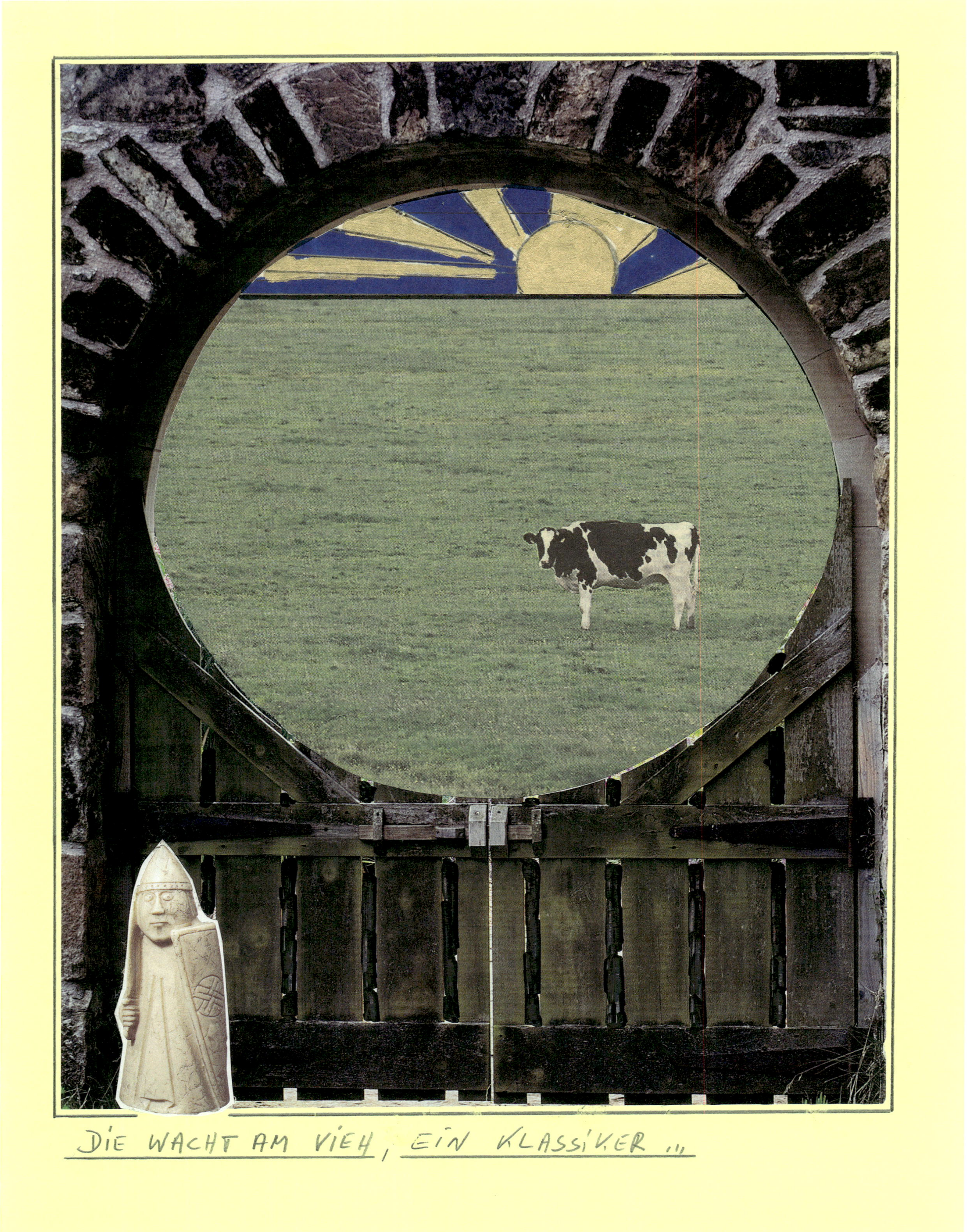

Guarding cattle, a classic, 2011

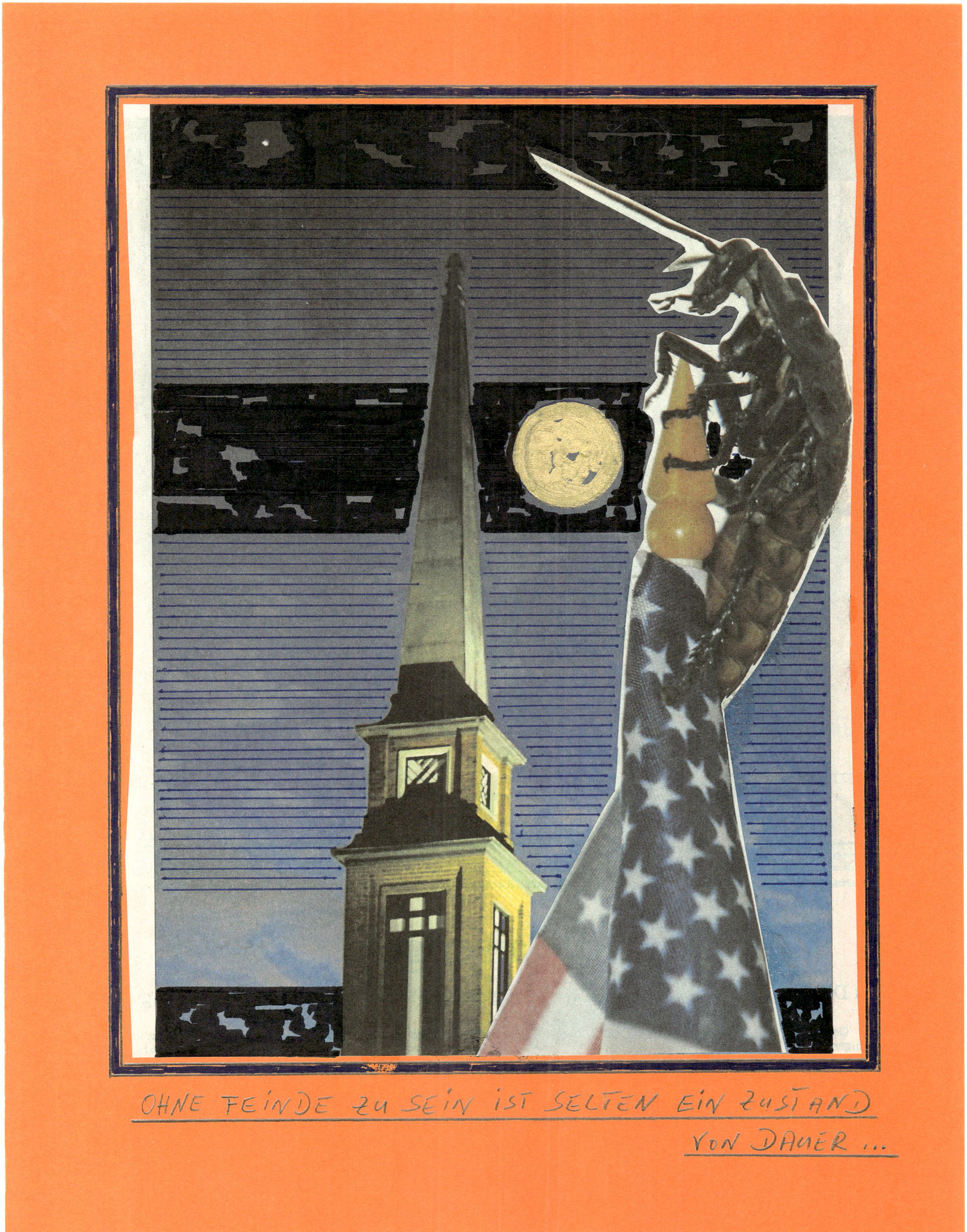

Being without enemies is rarely a lasting condition..., 2011

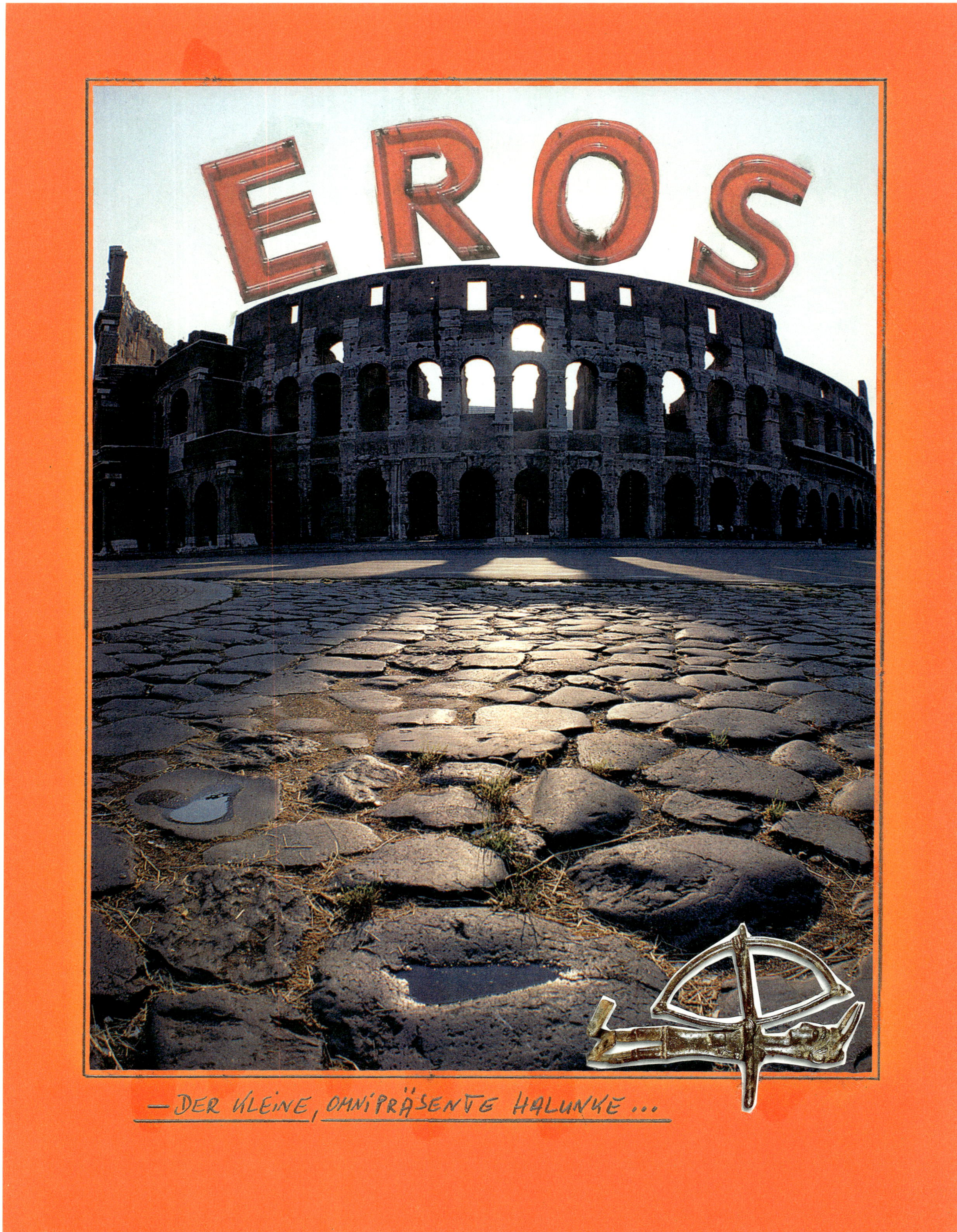

 Eros—the little, omnipresent scoundrel..., 2011

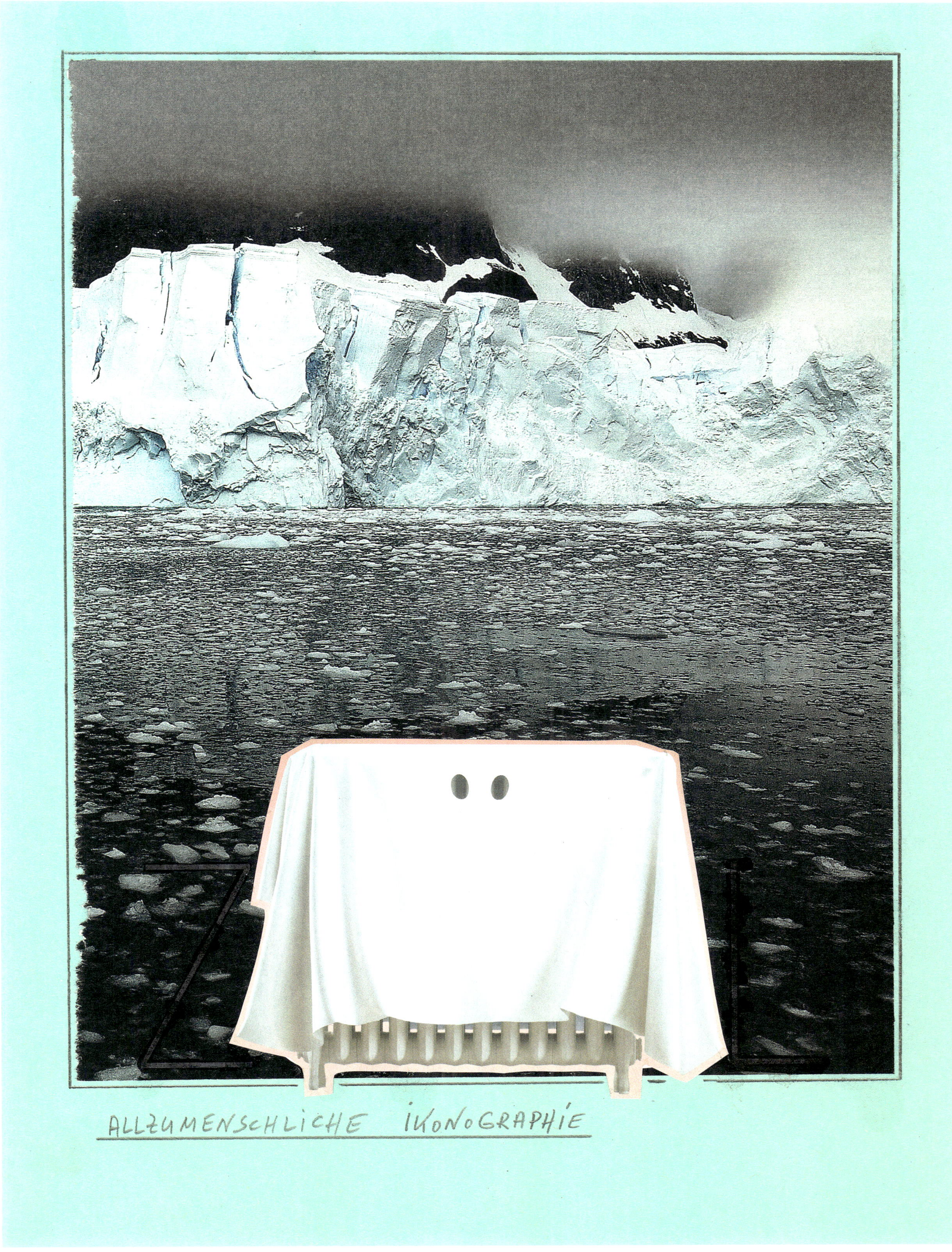

All-too-human iconography, 2011

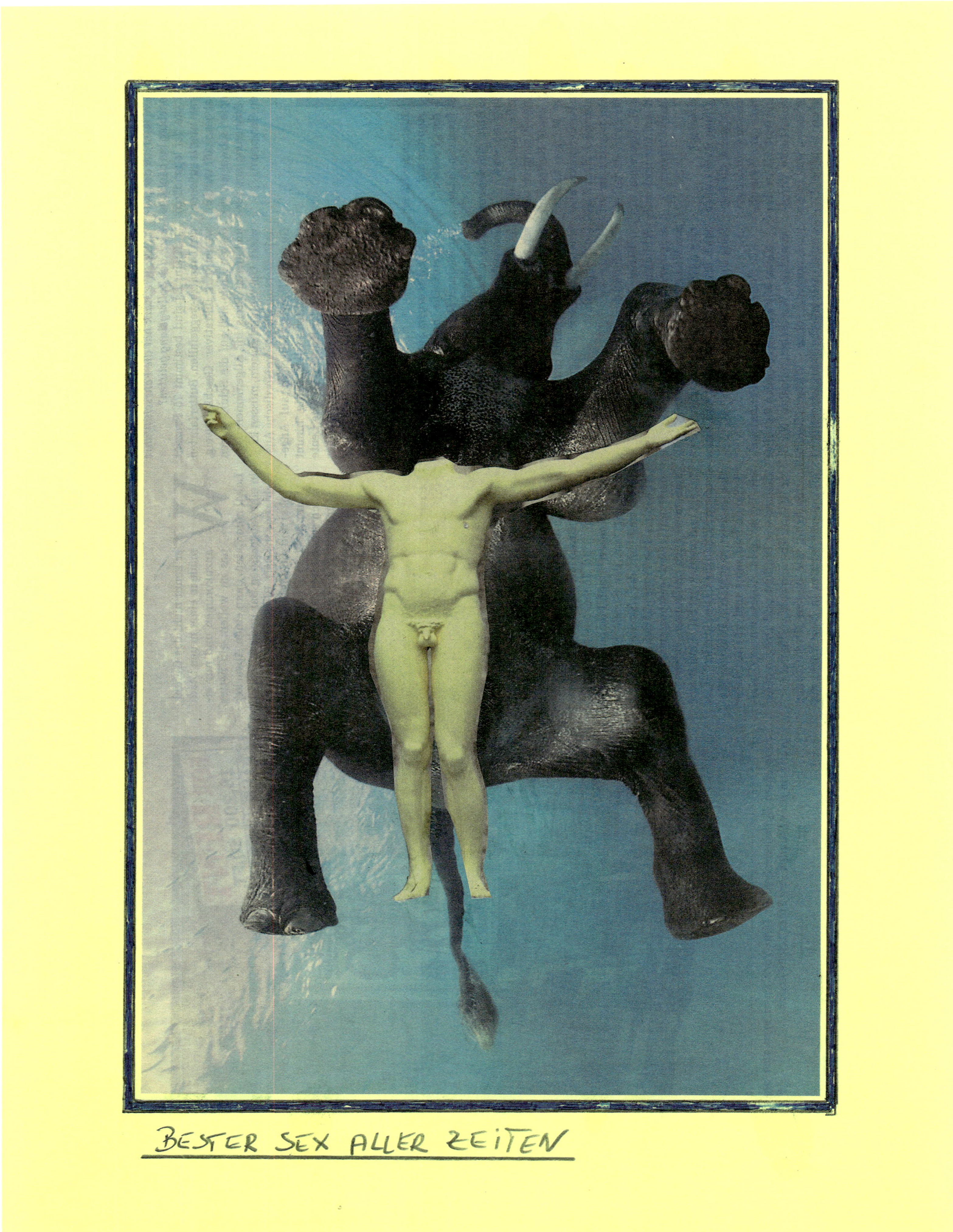

 Best sex of all time, 2011

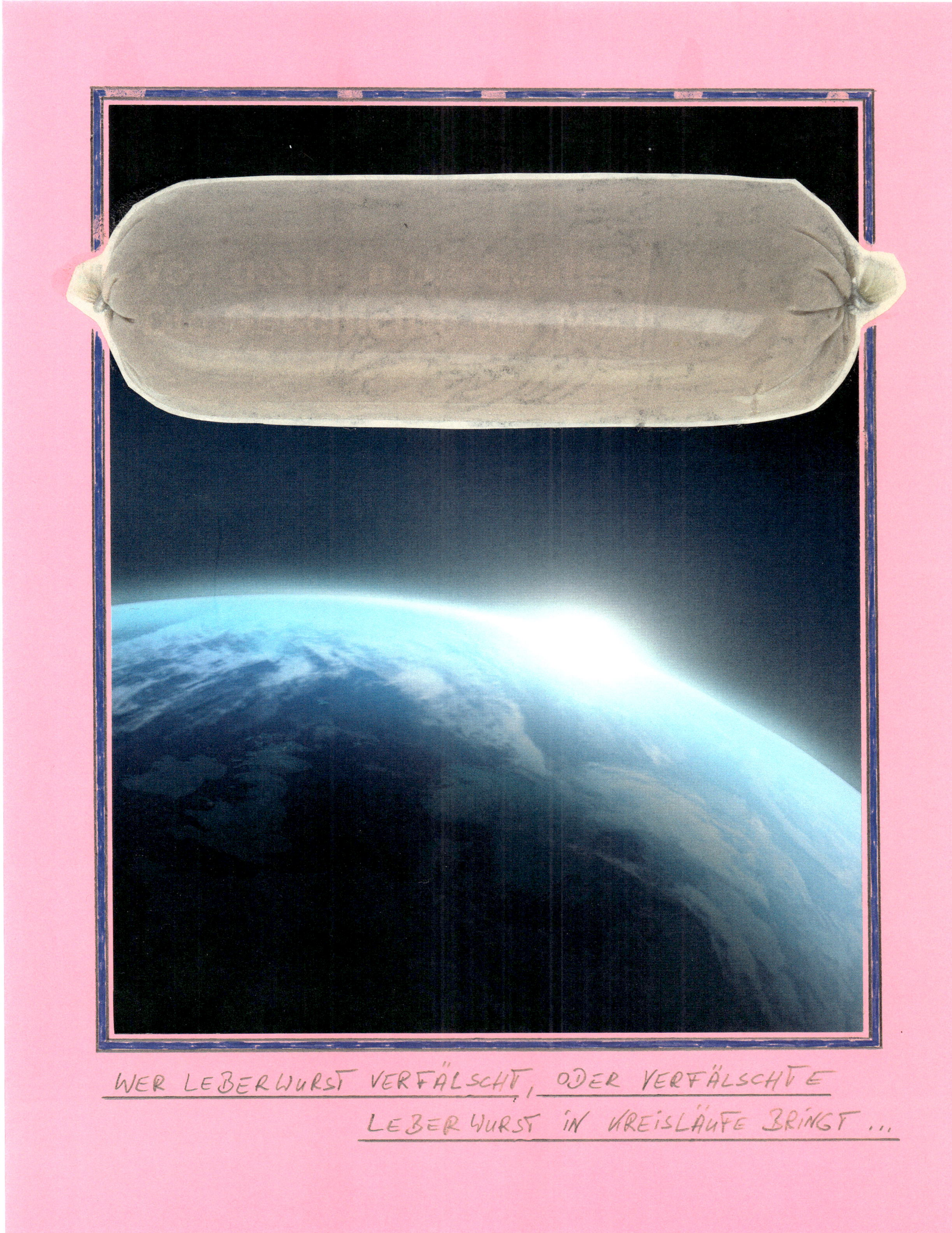

Whosoever counterfeits liverwurst or puts counterfeit liverwurst into circulation..., 2012

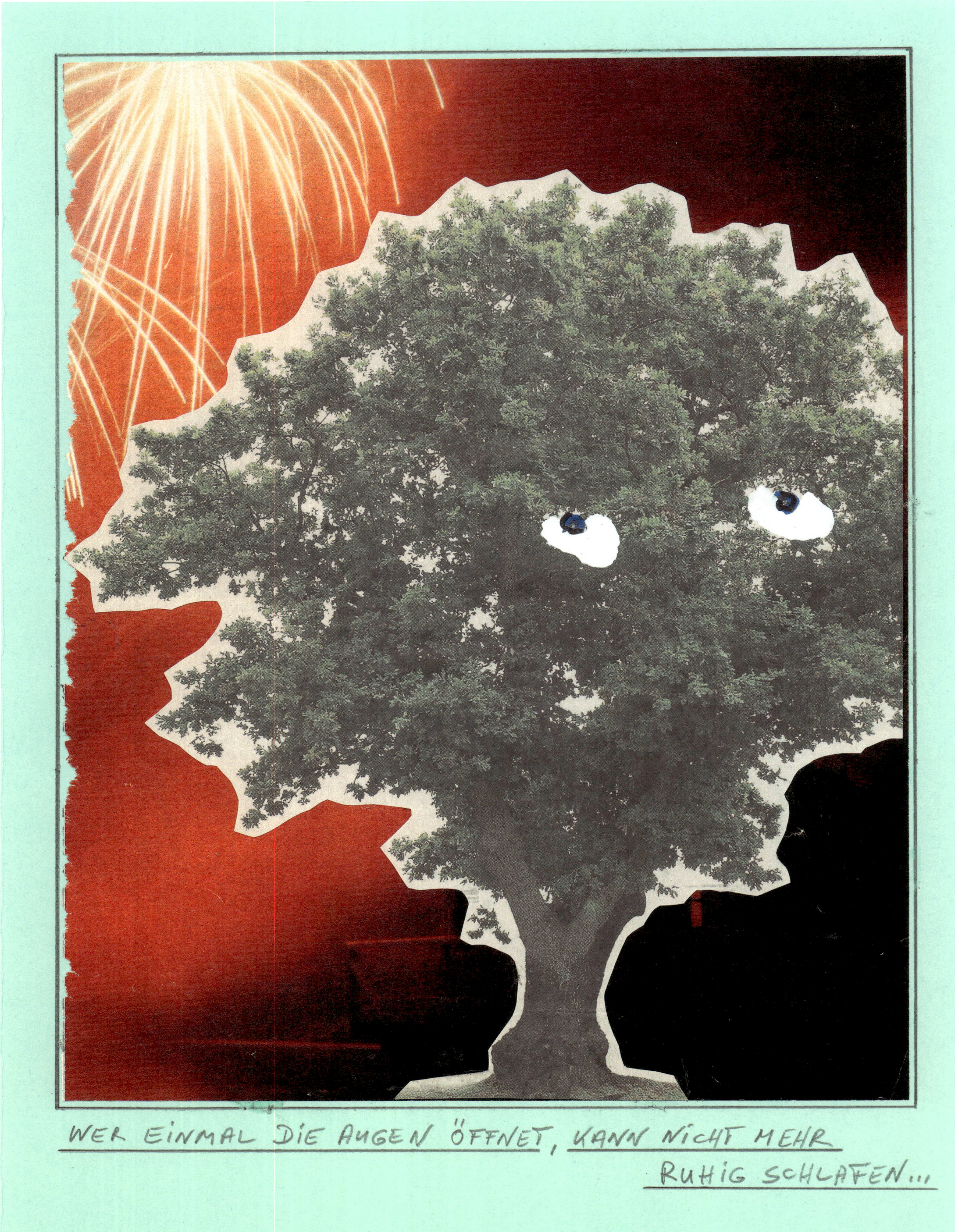

Open your eyes once and you'll never sleep peacefully again..., 2012

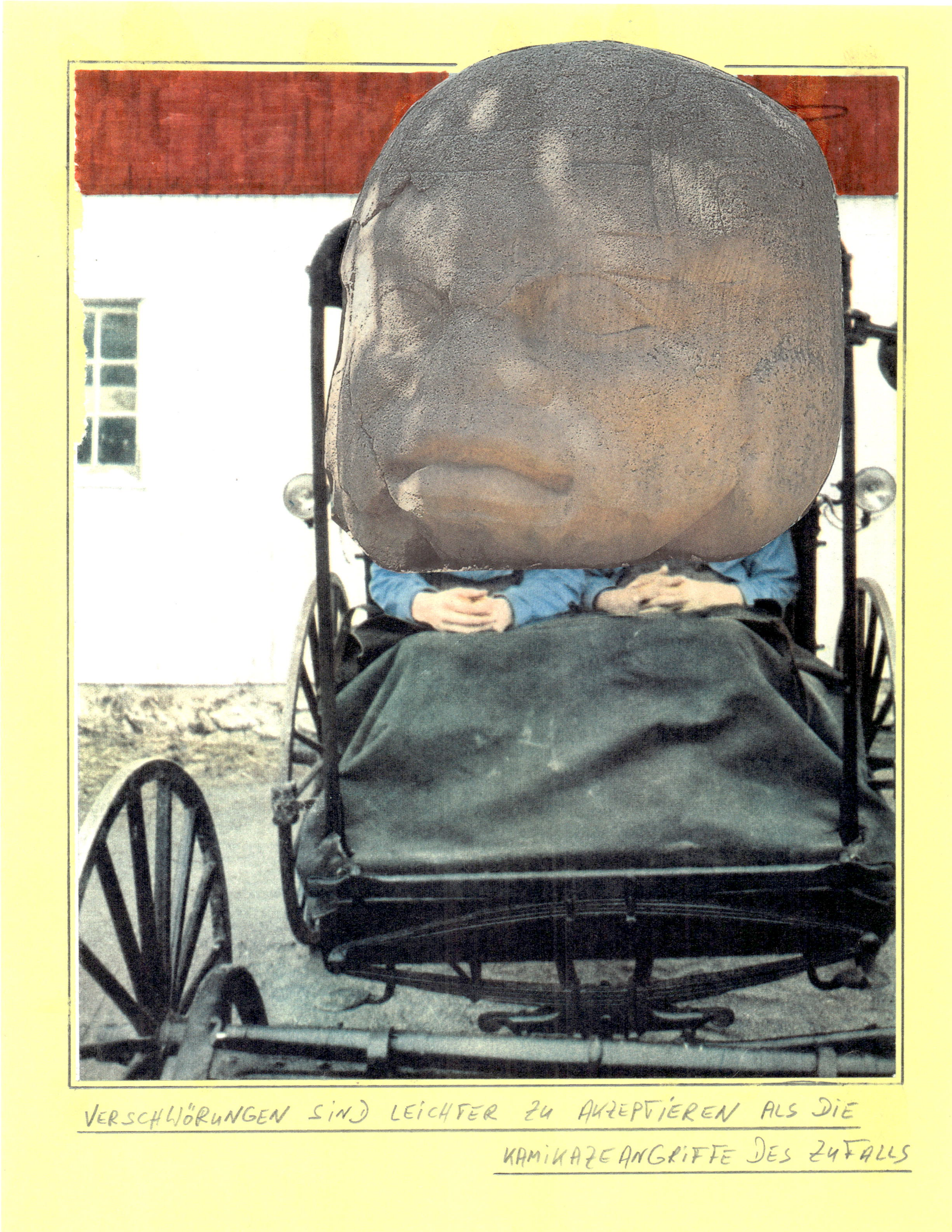

Conspiracies are easier to accept than the kamikaze attacks of chance, 2012

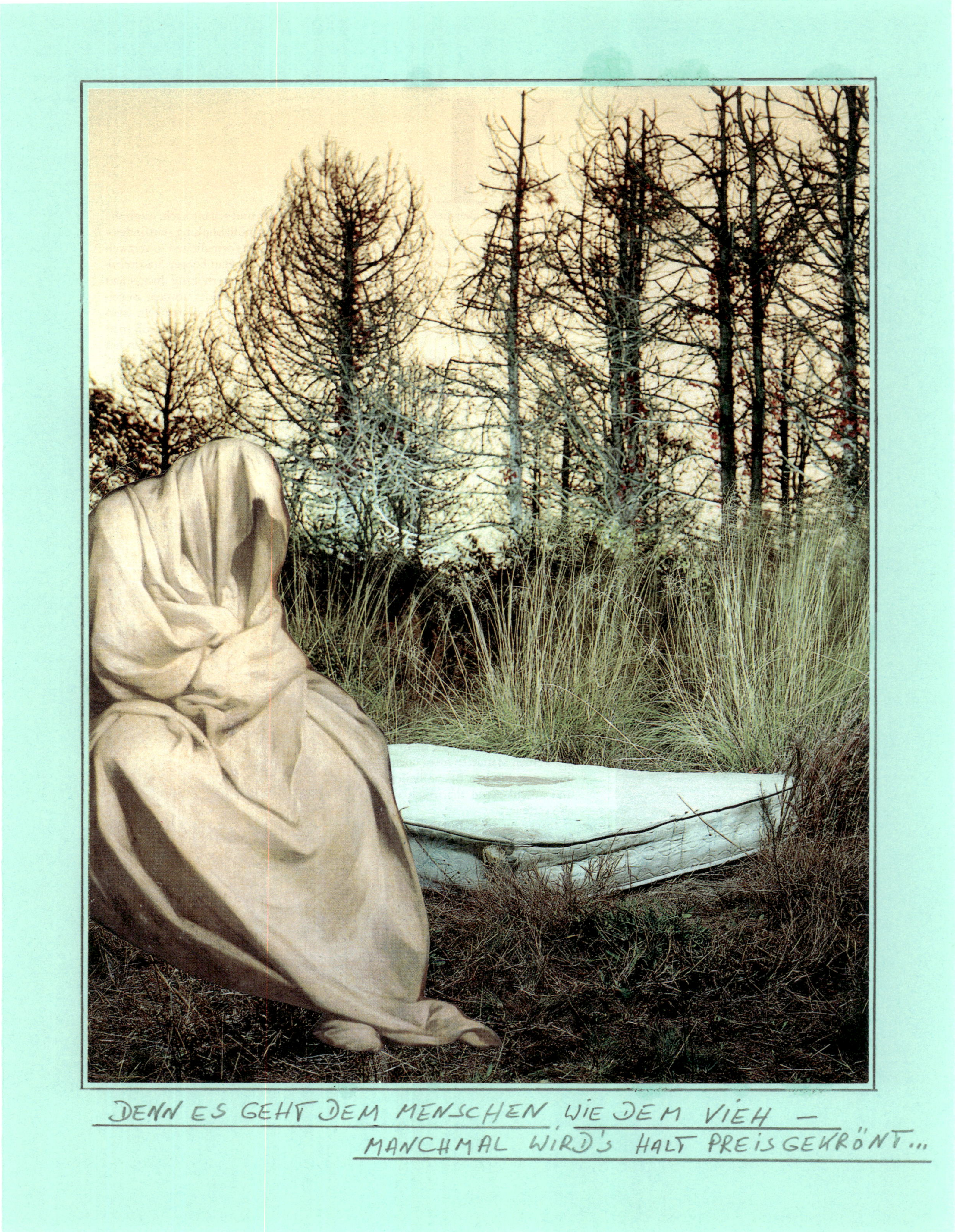

For that which befalleth the sons of men befalleth beasts—sometimes they are prize-winning..., 2012

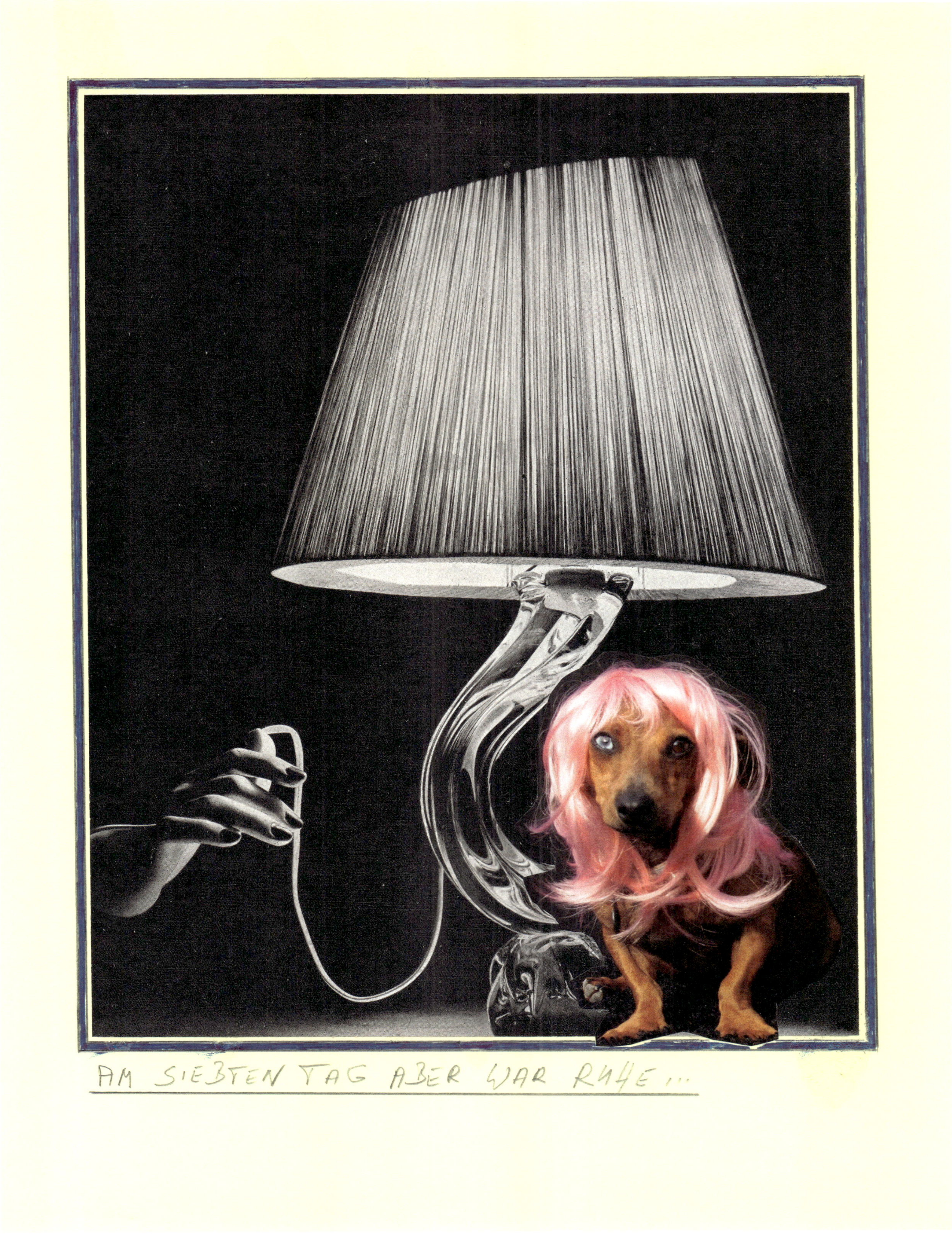

On the seventh day, a bit of peace and quiet..., 2012

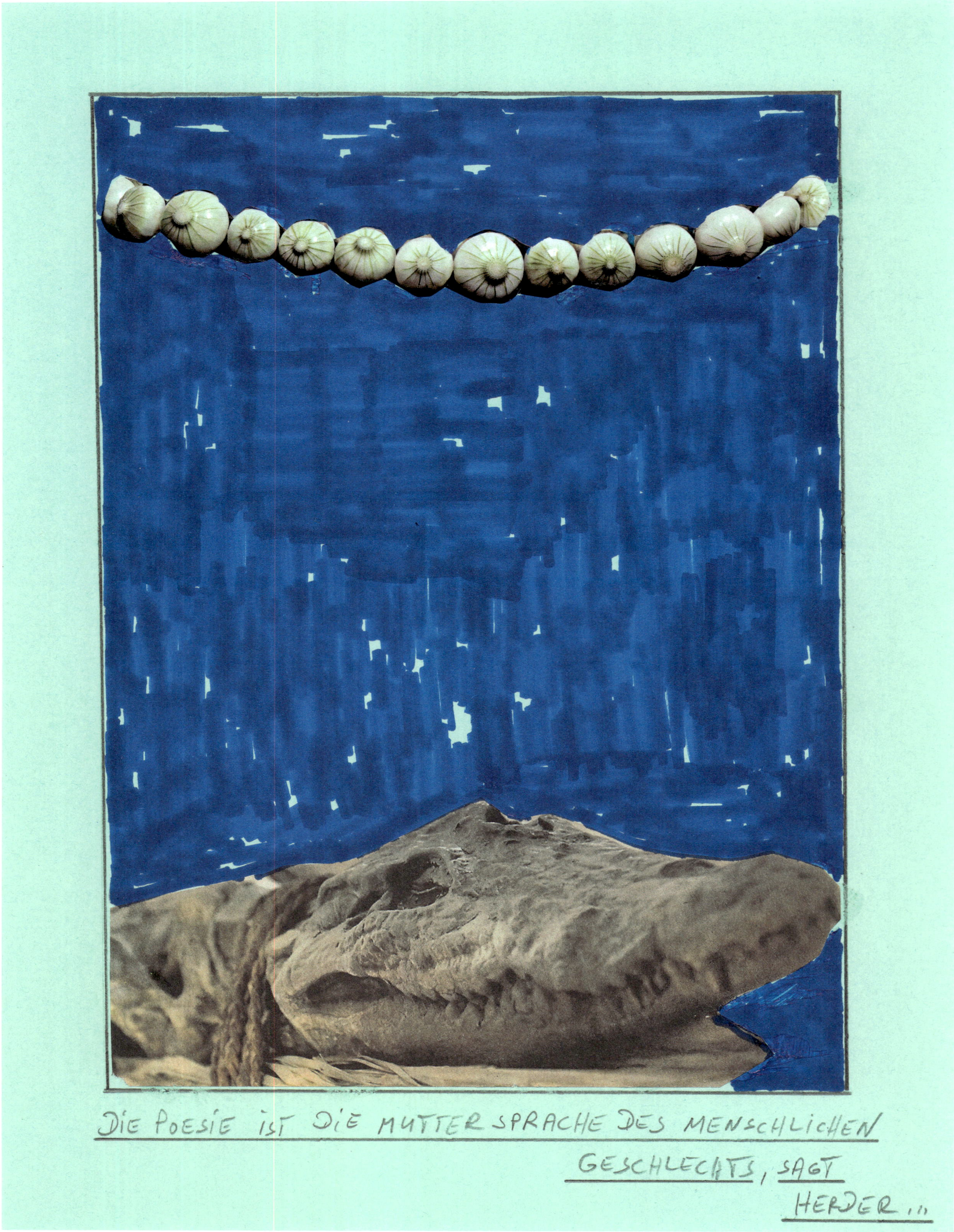

Poetry is the mother tongue of the human race, says Herder..., 2012

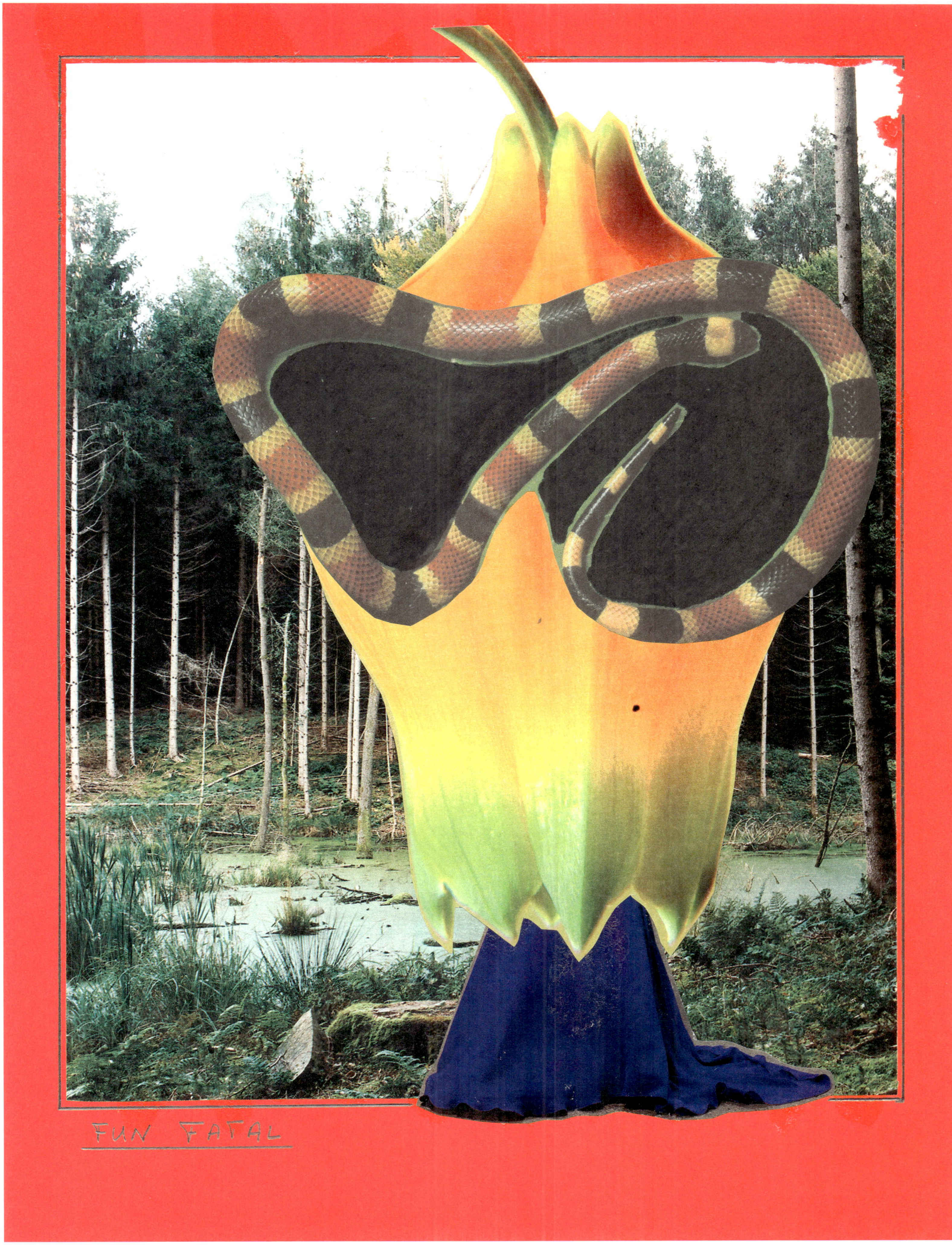

Fun fatal, 2012

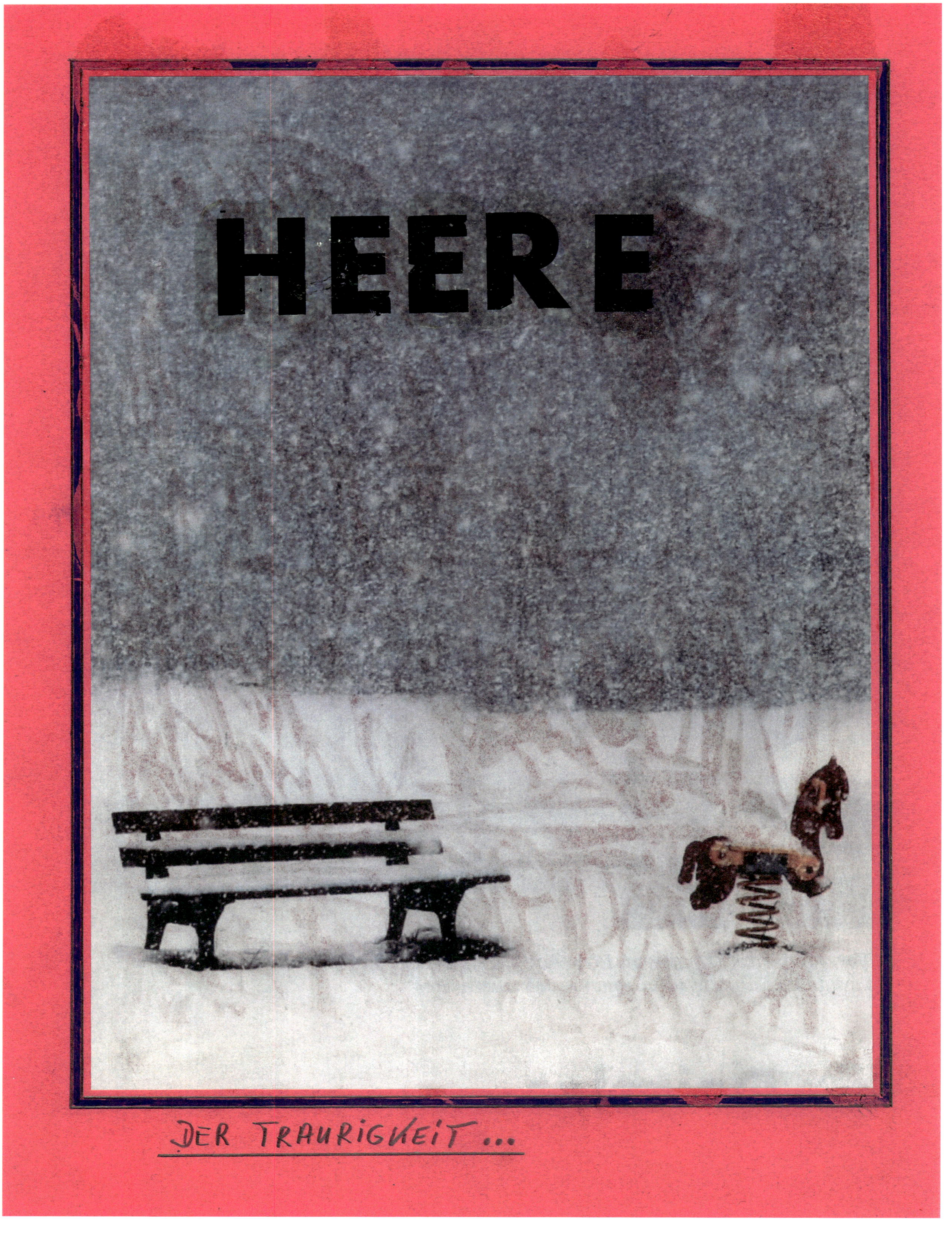

 Armies of sadness..., 2013

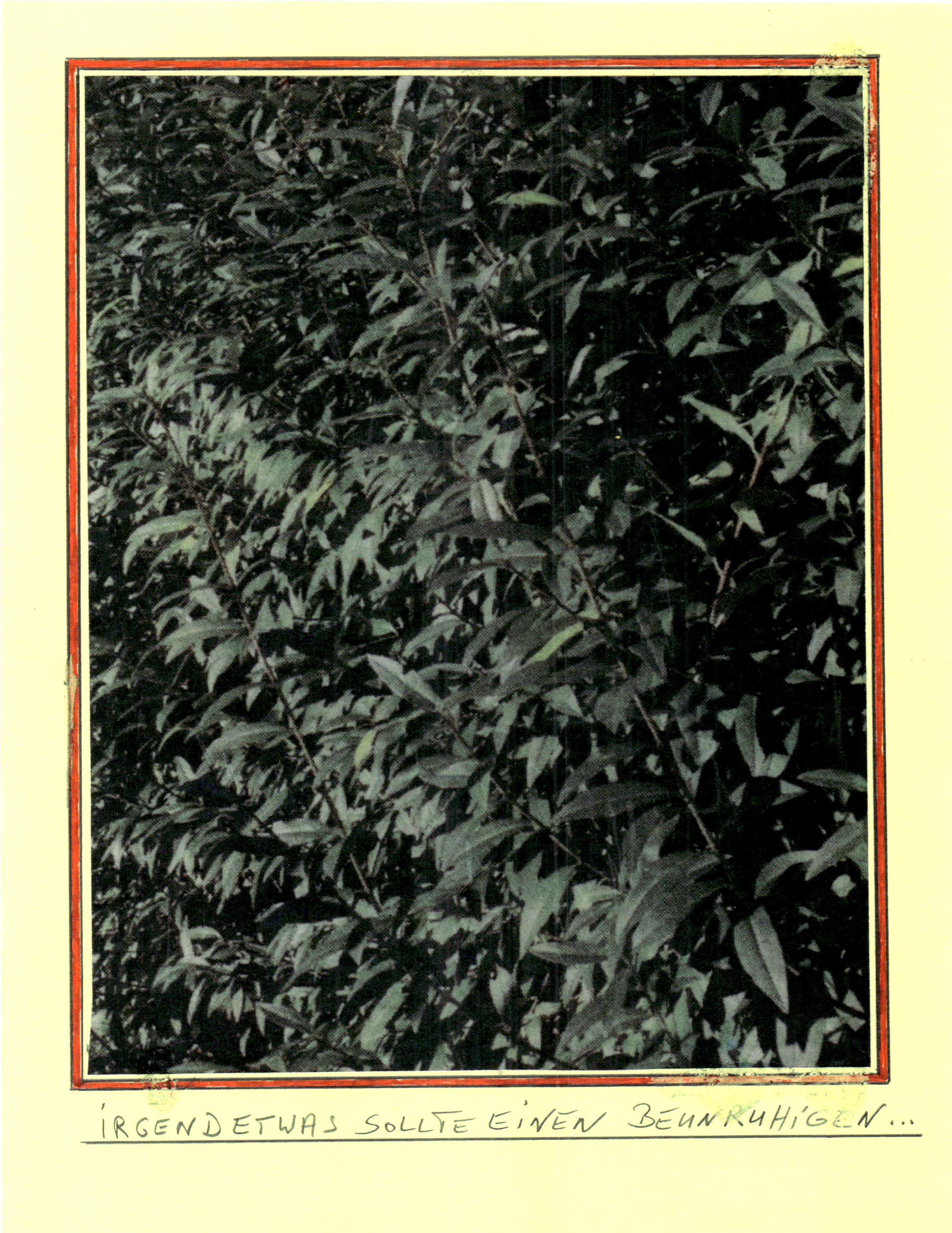

Something should be worrying..., 2013

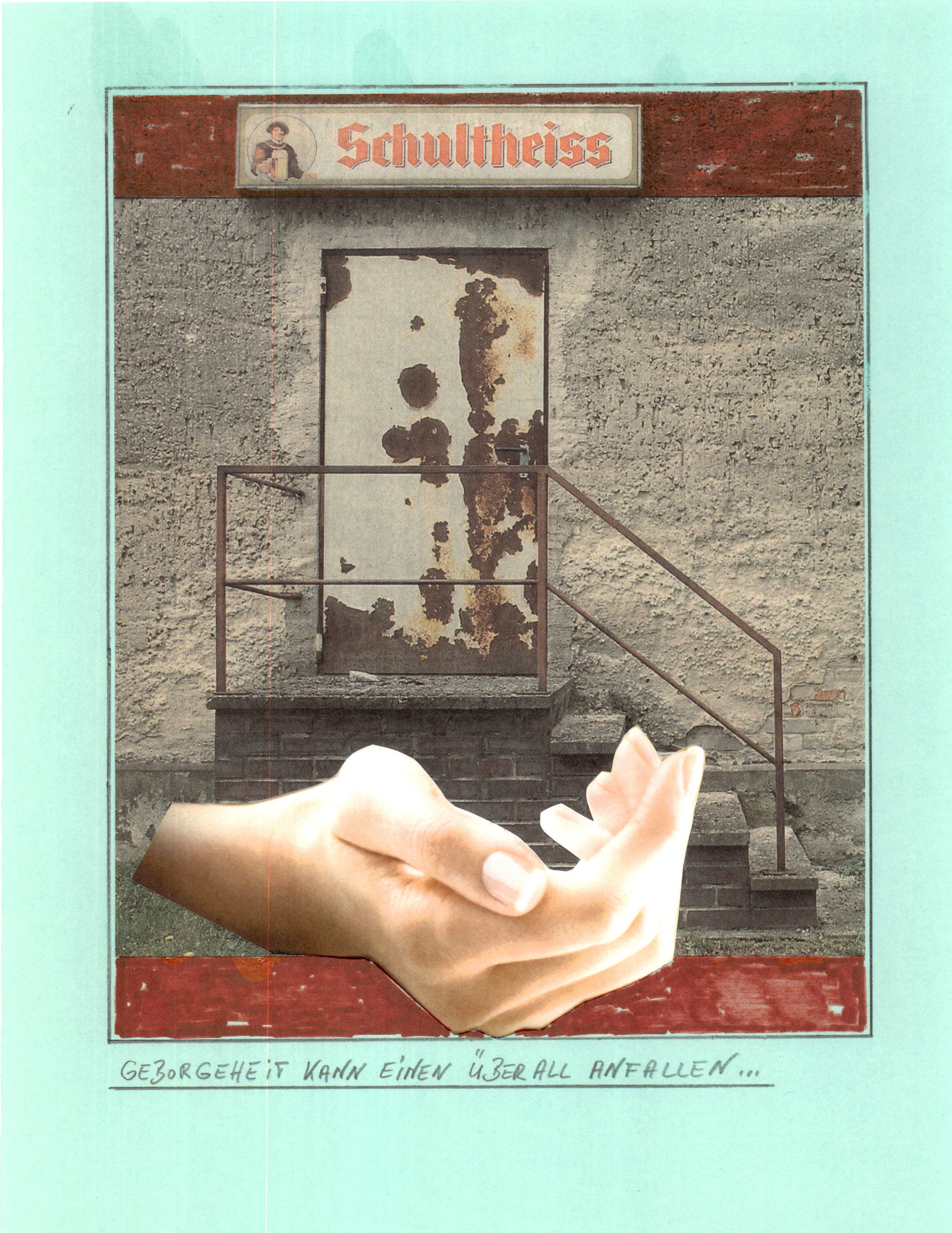

Comfort can assail you anywhere..., 2012

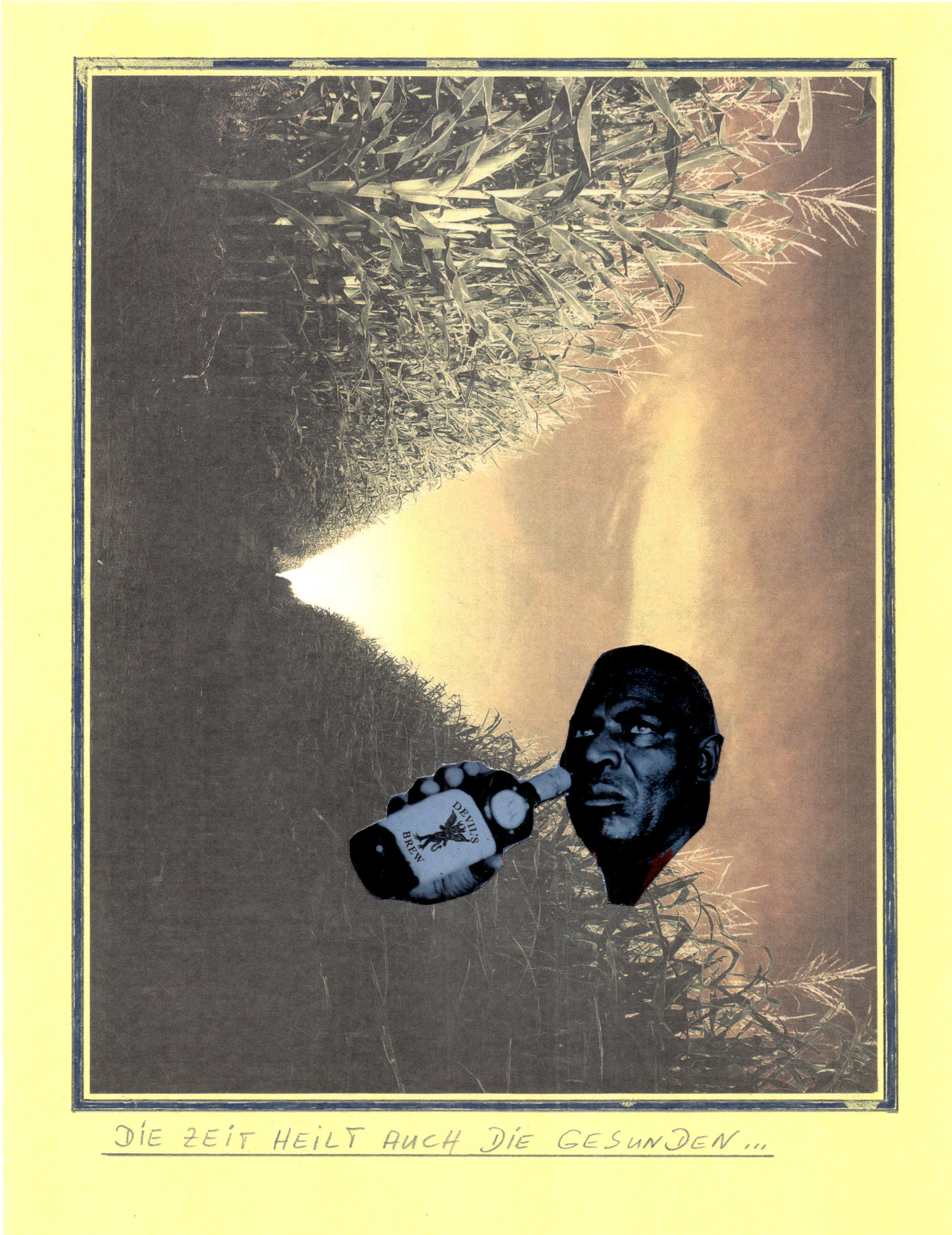

Time heals the healthy, too..., 2012

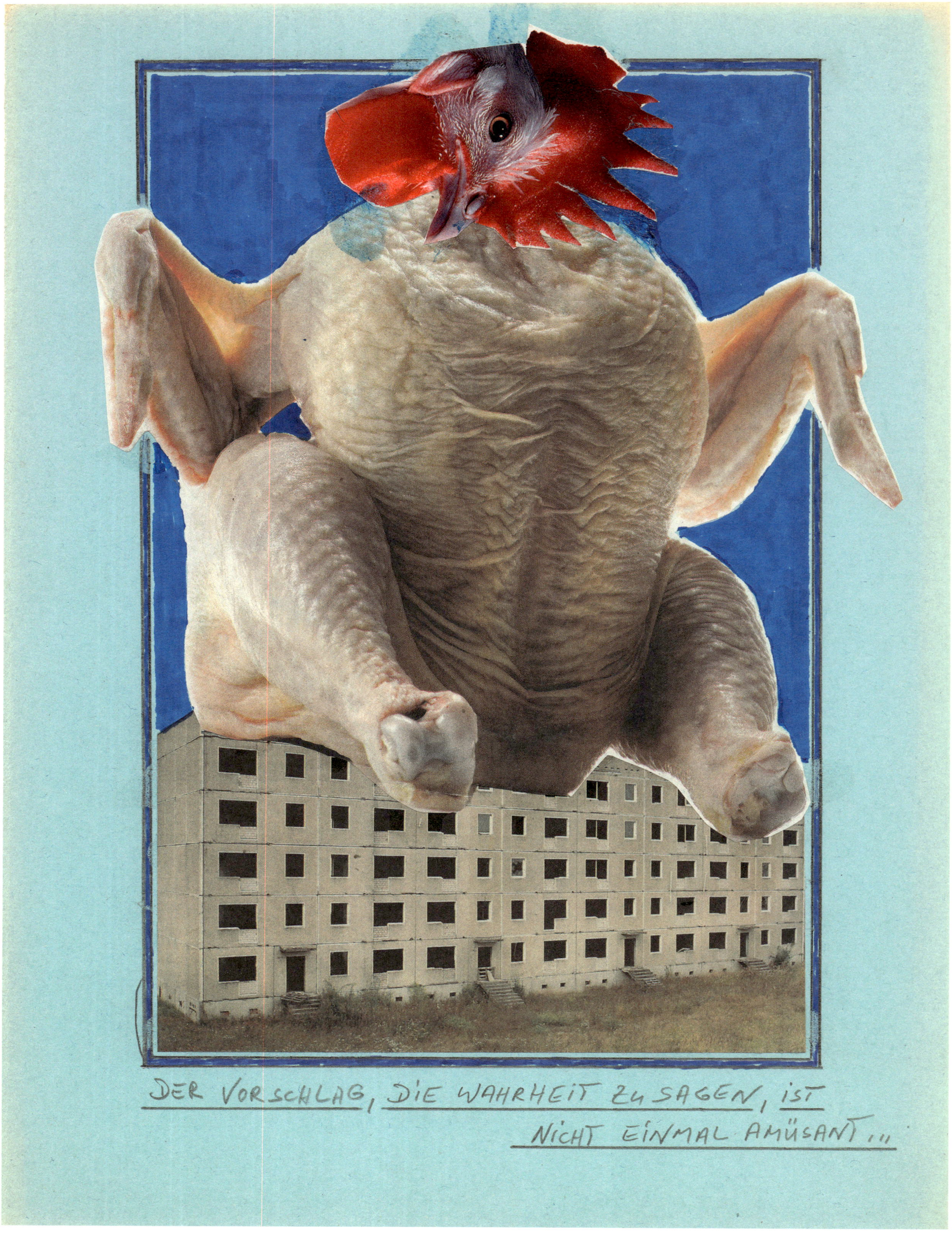

Suggesting to tell the truth is not even amusing..., 2012

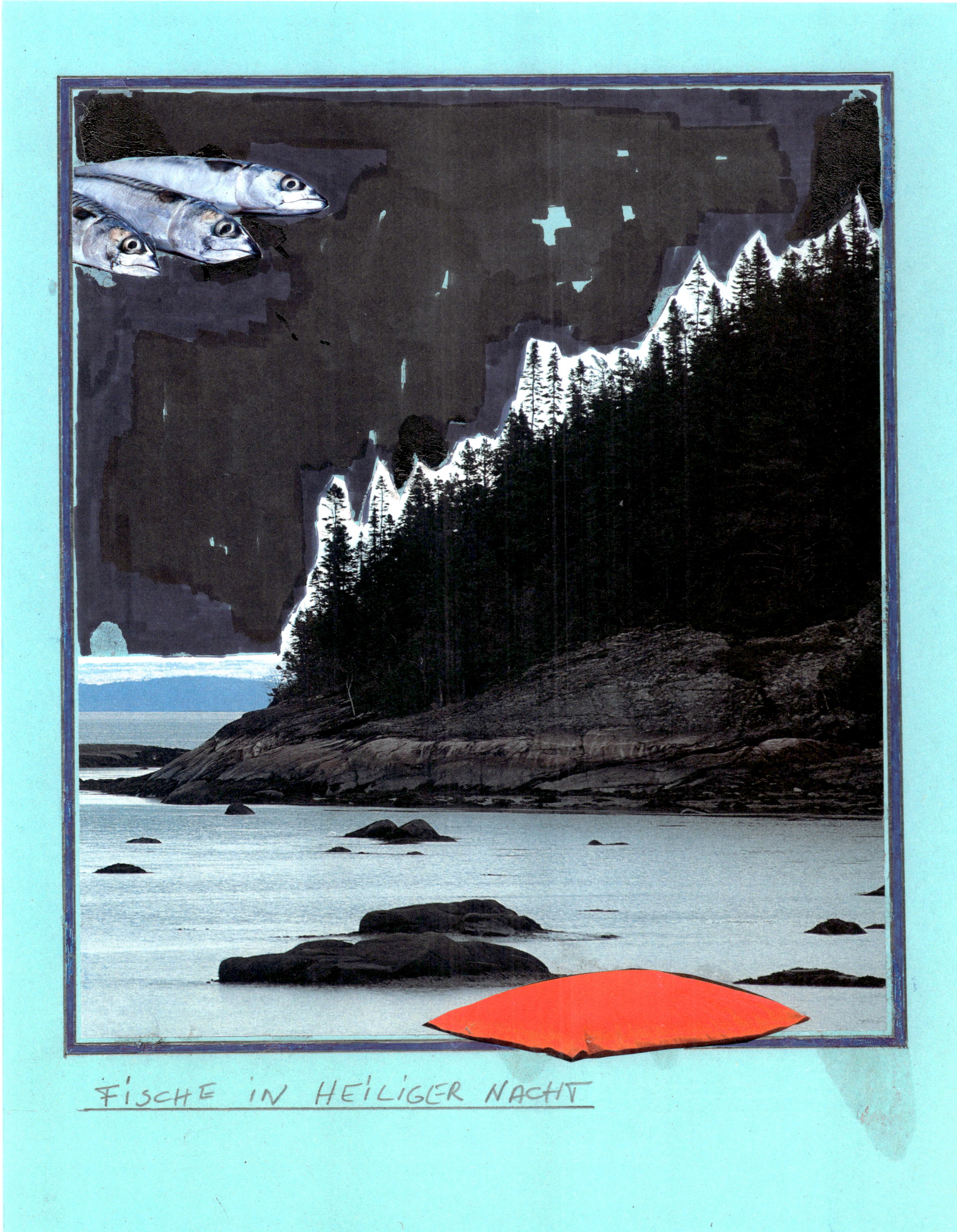

Fish on Holy Night, 2012

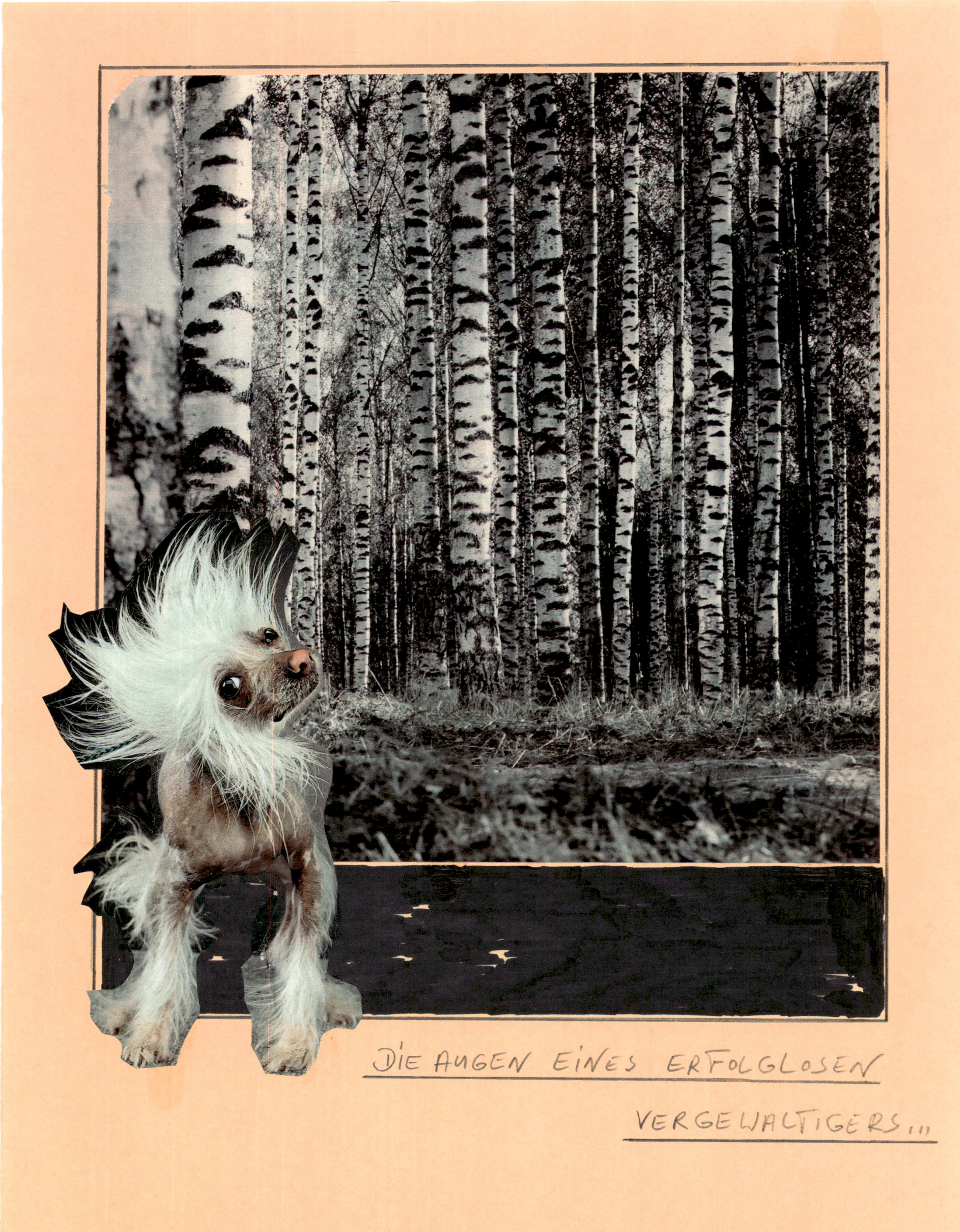

 The eyes of an unsuccessful rapist..., 2012

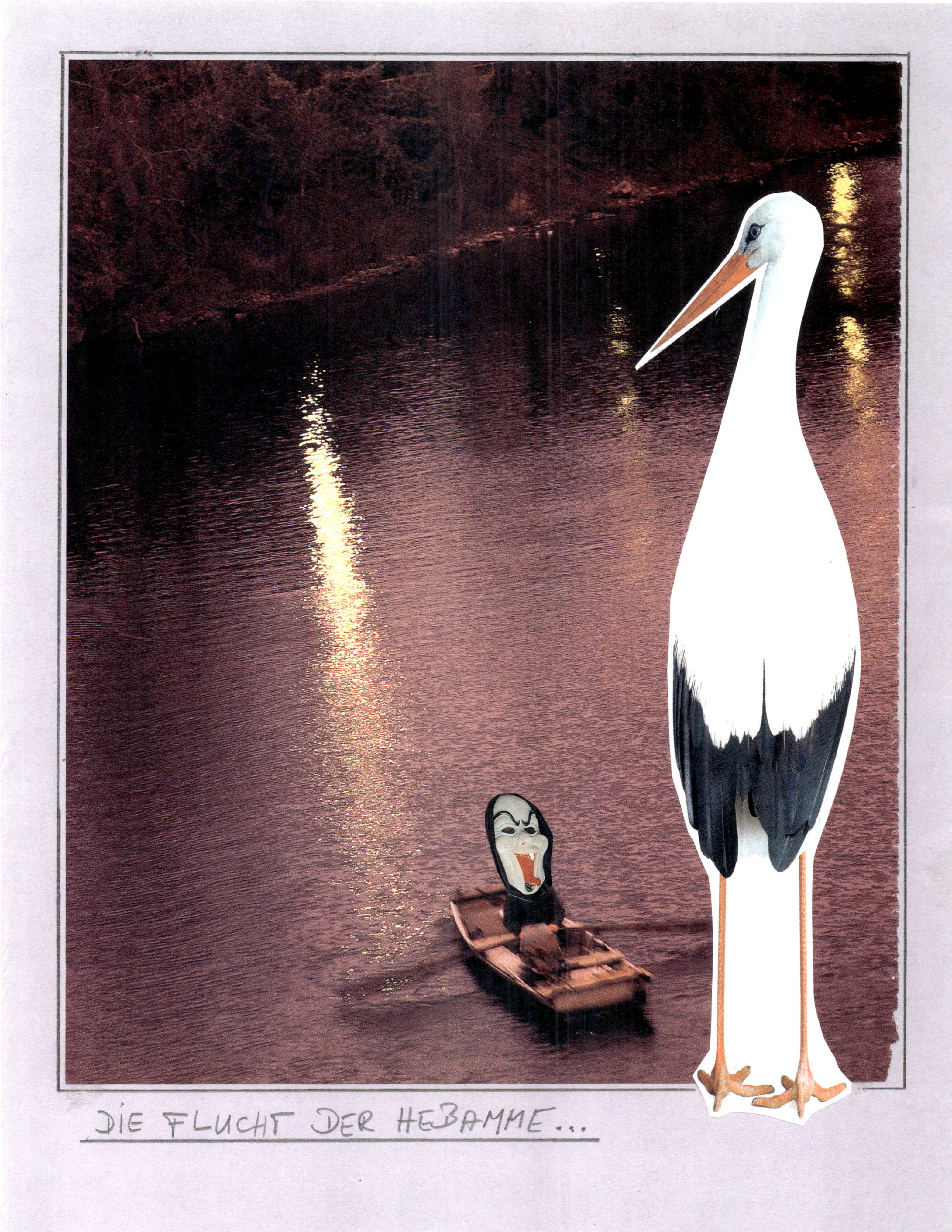

The midwife's escape..., 2012

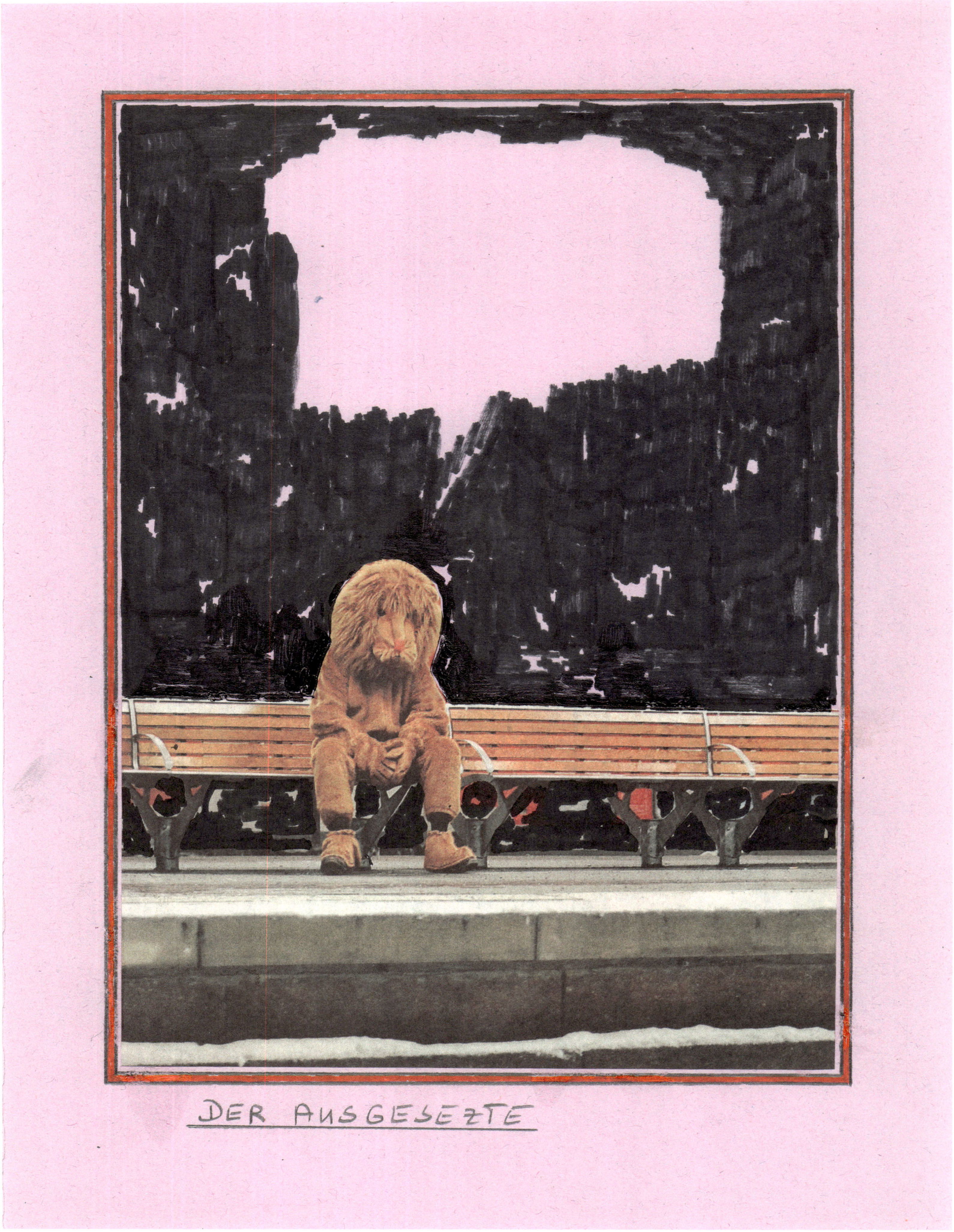

 Abandoned, 2013

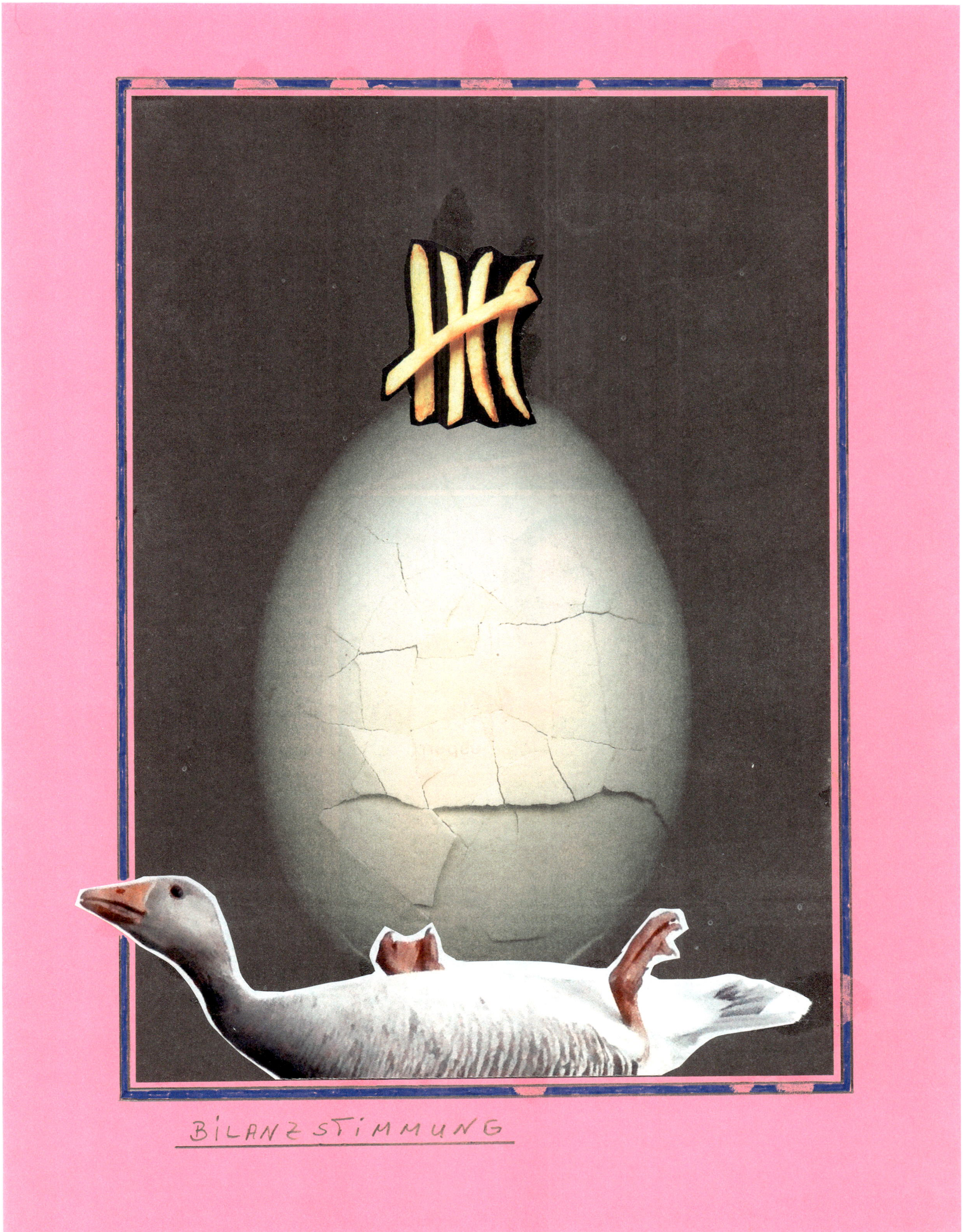

Stocktaking mood, 2012

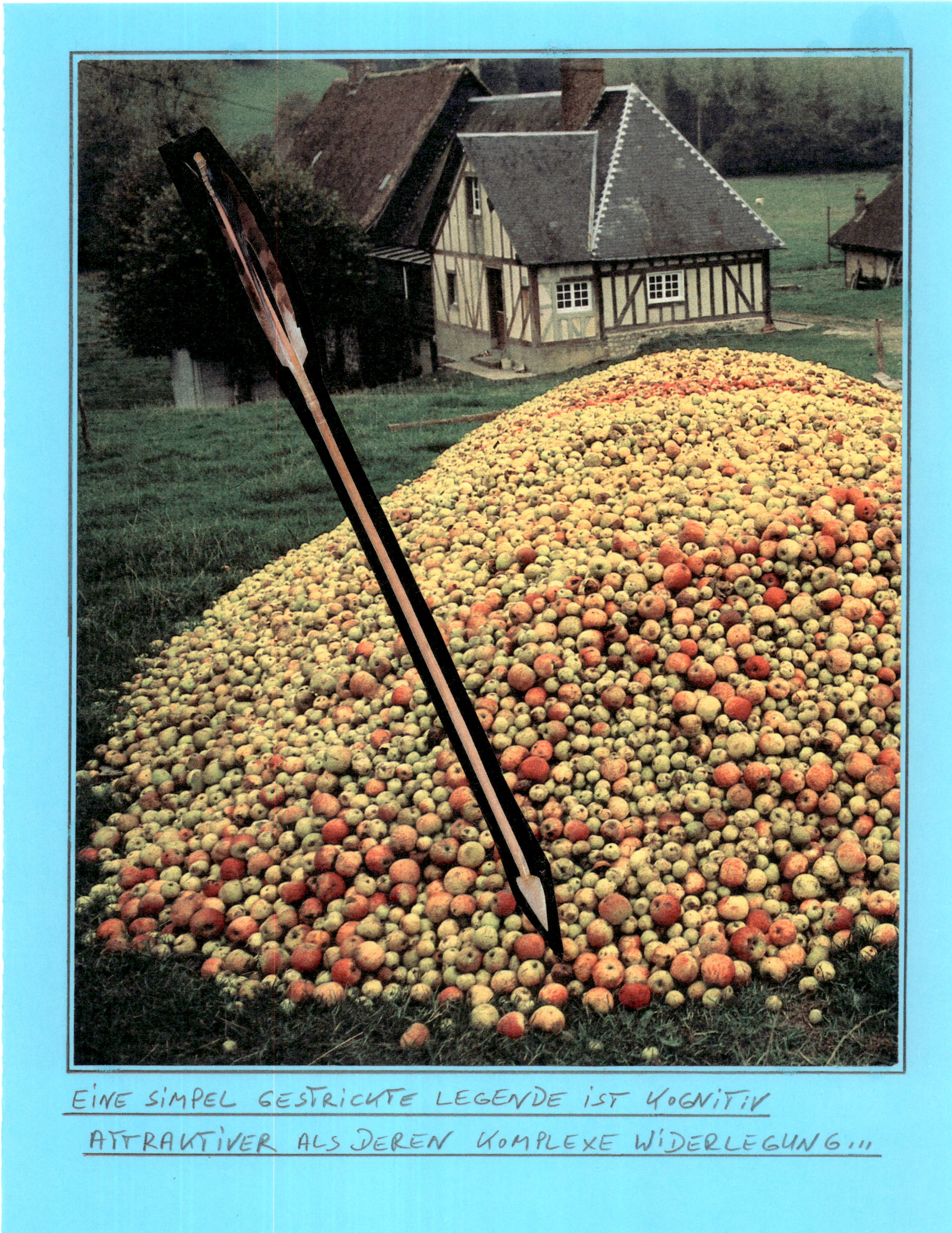

A simple legend is cognitively more attractive than its complex refutation..., 2012

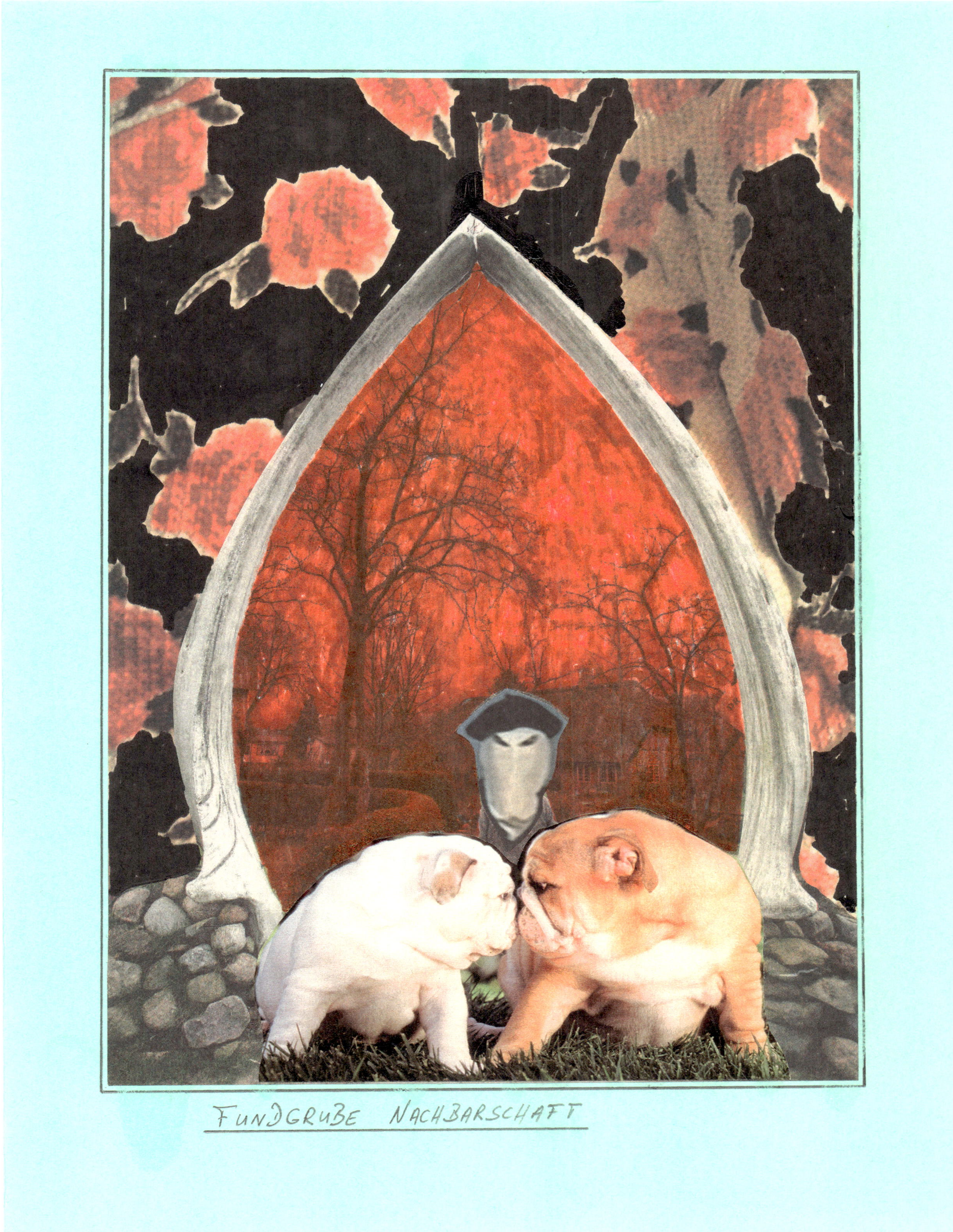

The neighbourhood as treasure trove, 2012

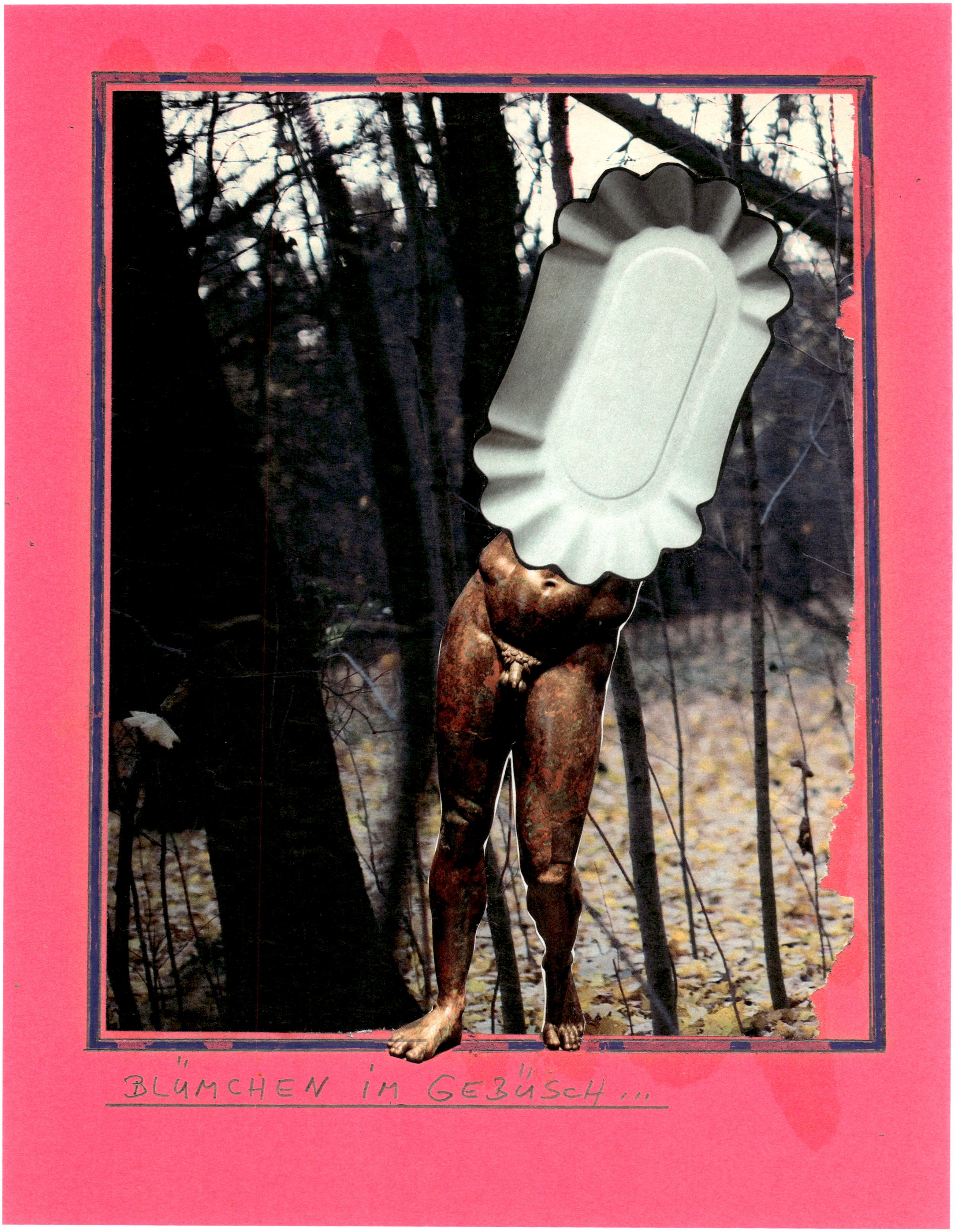

 Little flower in the bushes..., 2012

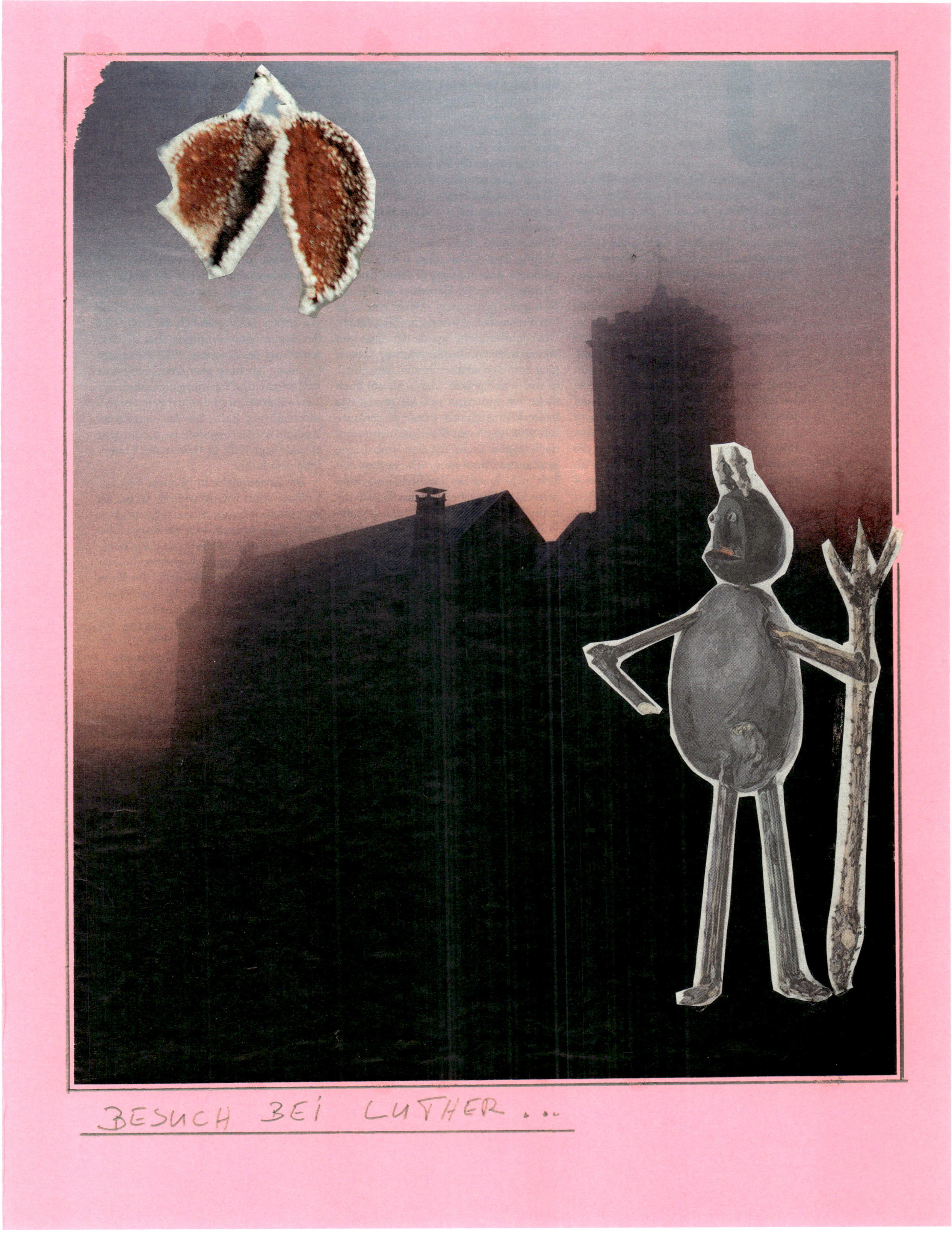

Visiting Luther..., 2012

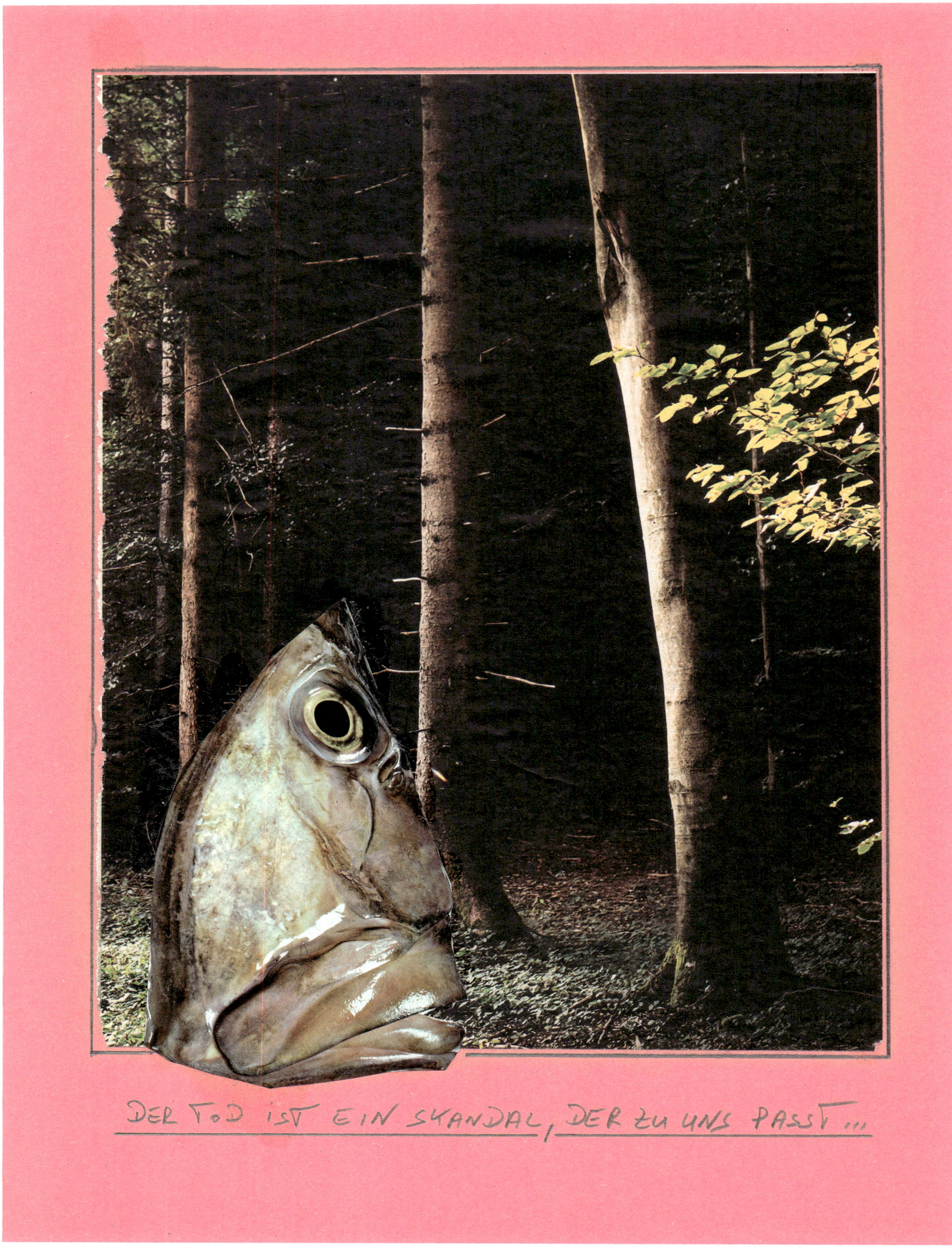

Death is a scandal that befits us..., 2012

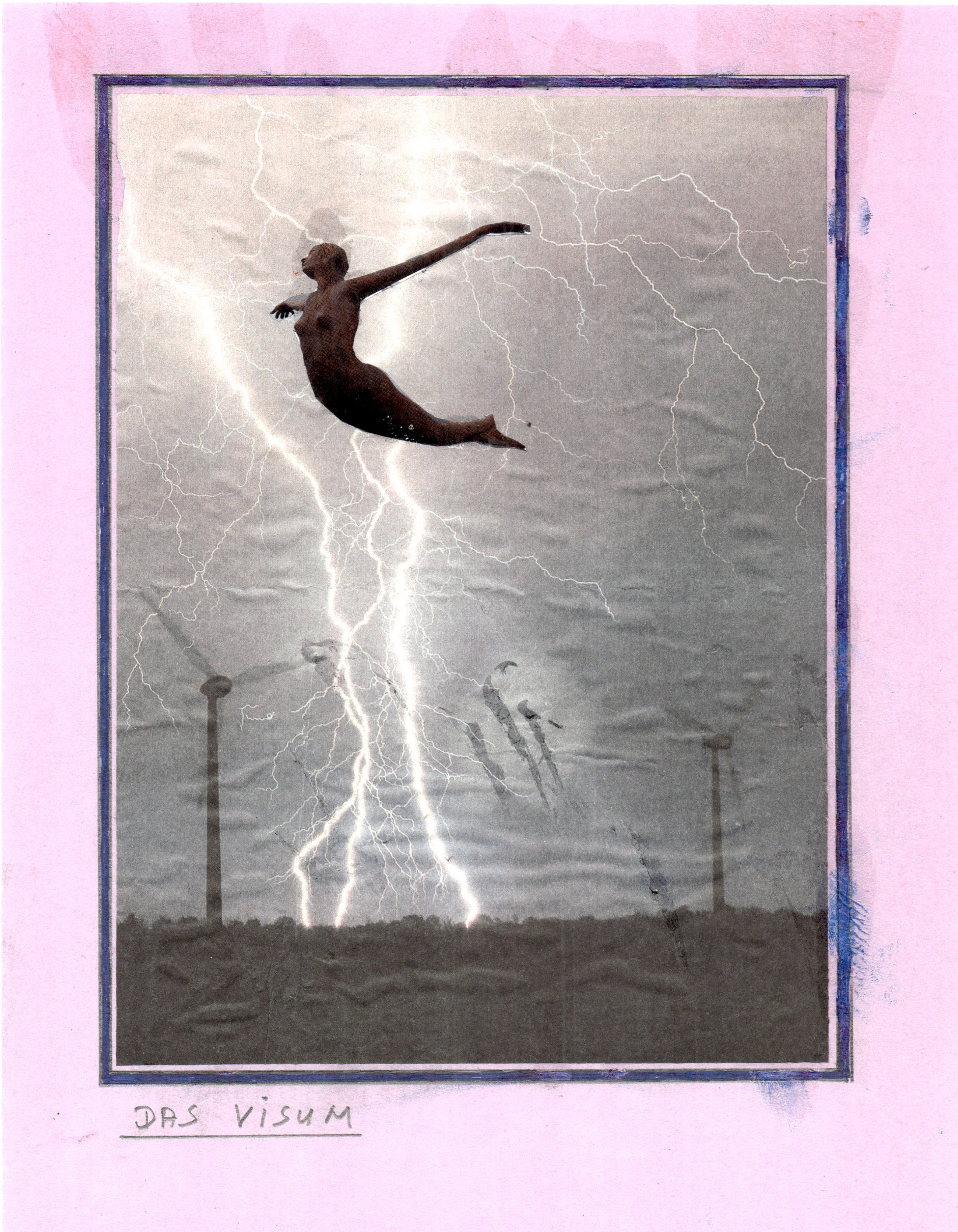

Visa, 2012

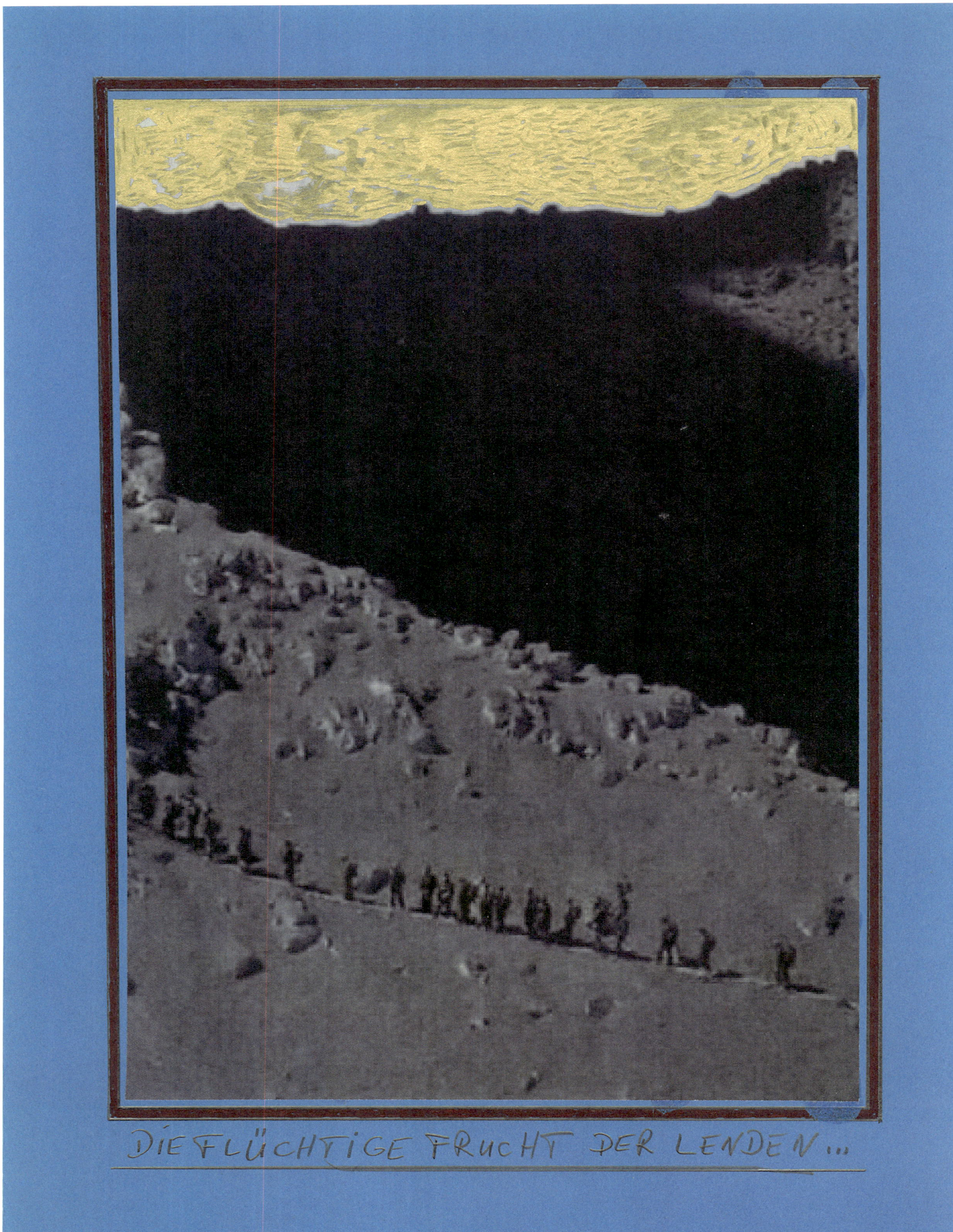

The fleeting fruit of the loins..., 2014

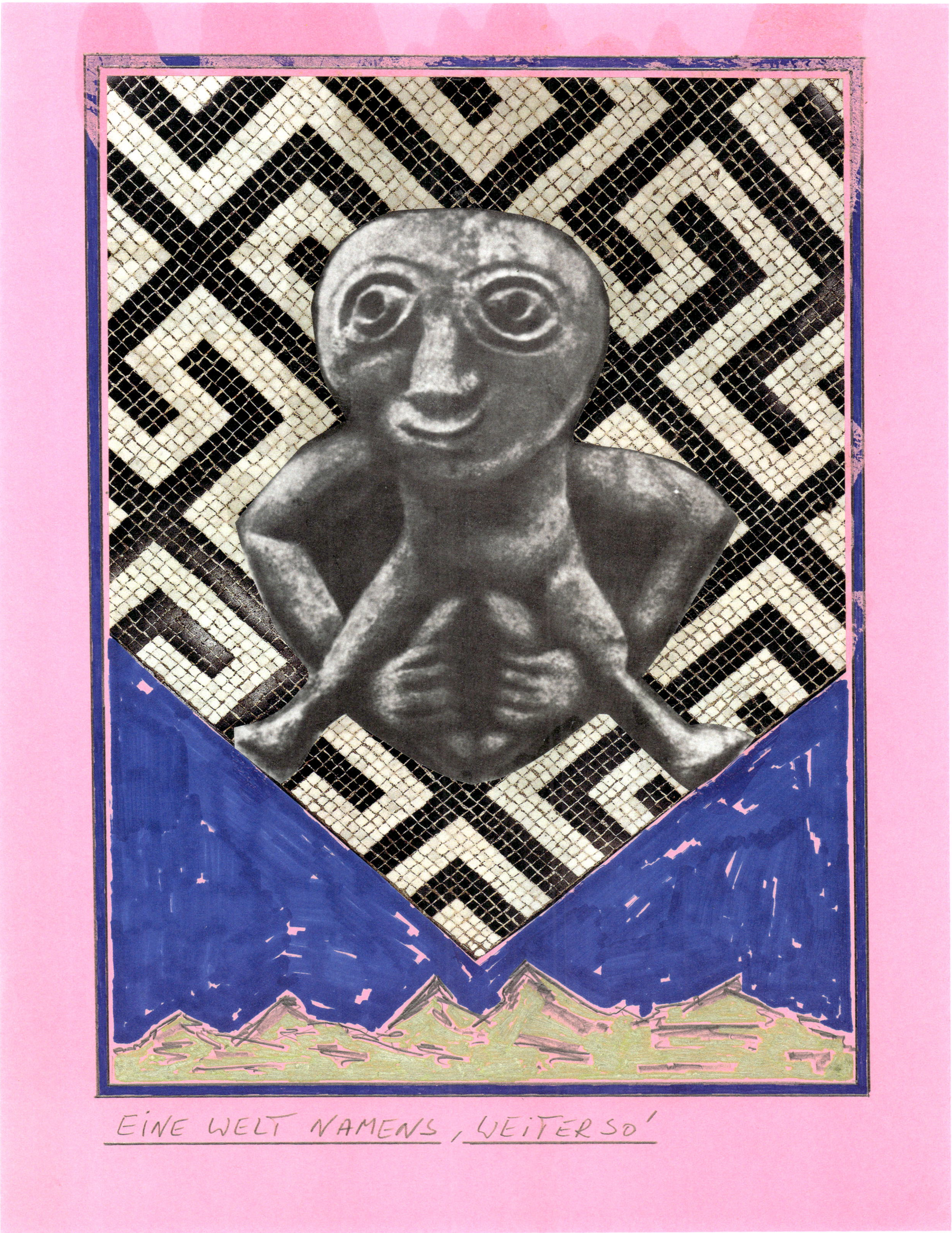

A world called "On and on and on", 2014

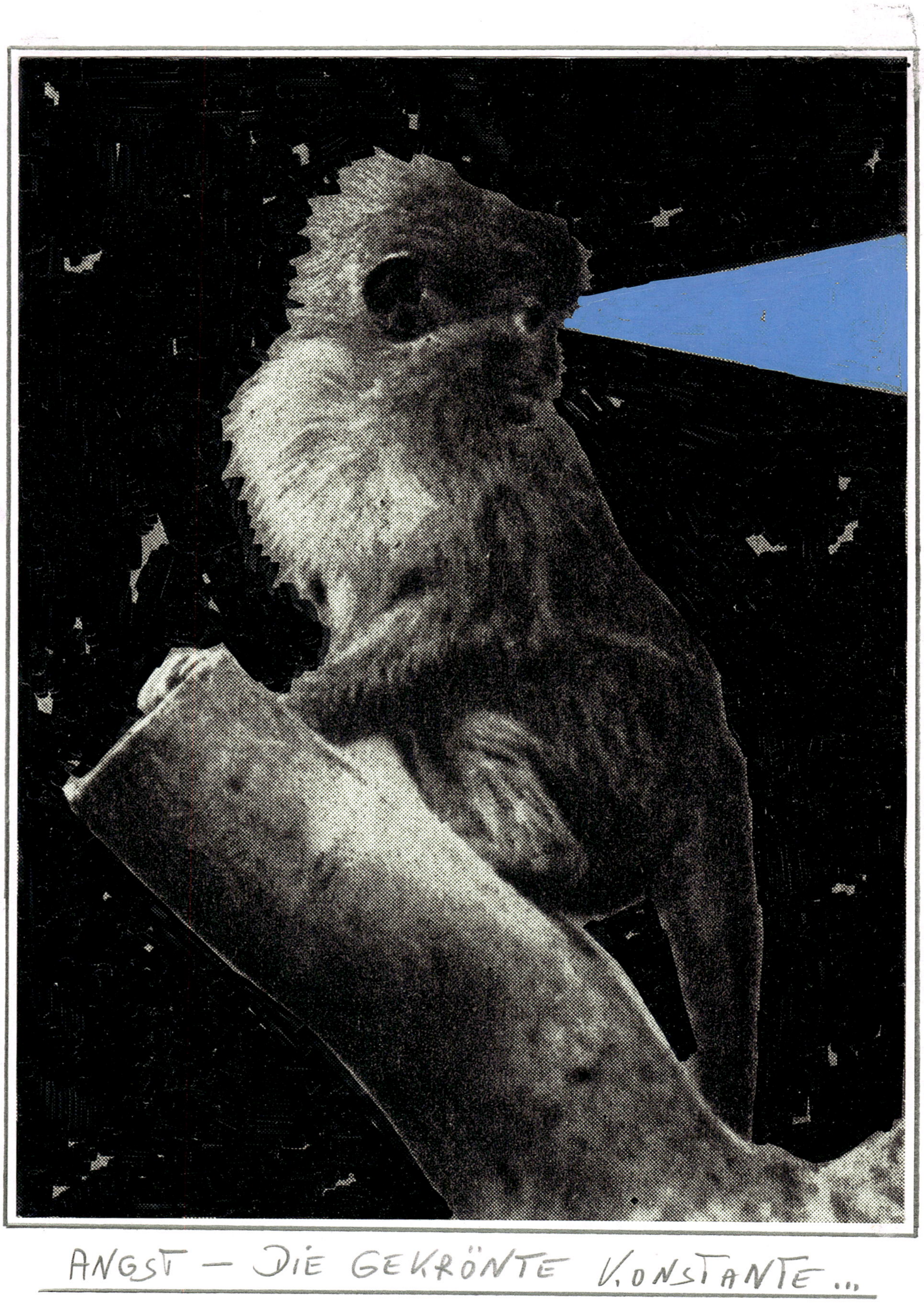

Fear—the crowned constant..., 2015

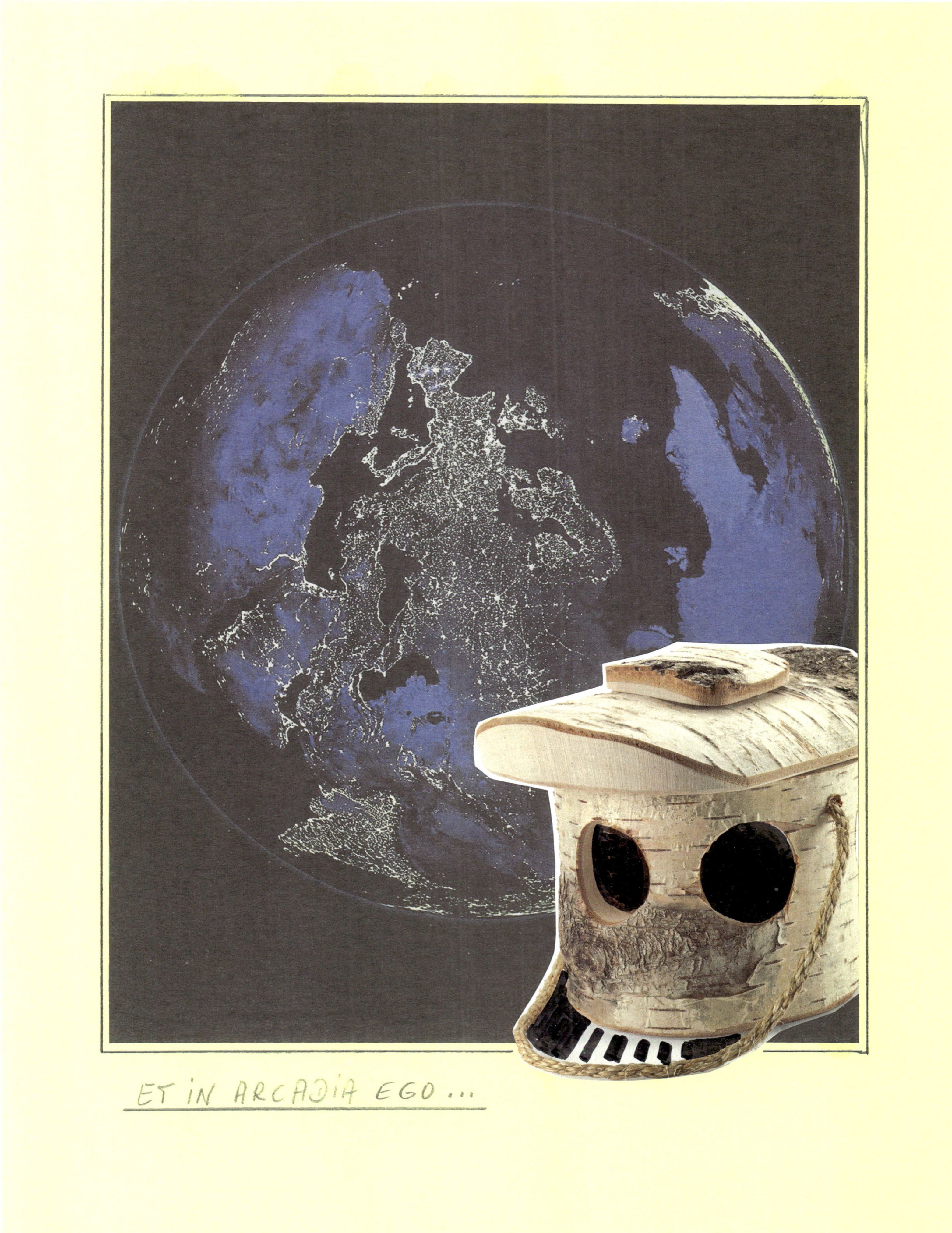

Et in Arcadia ego..., 2014

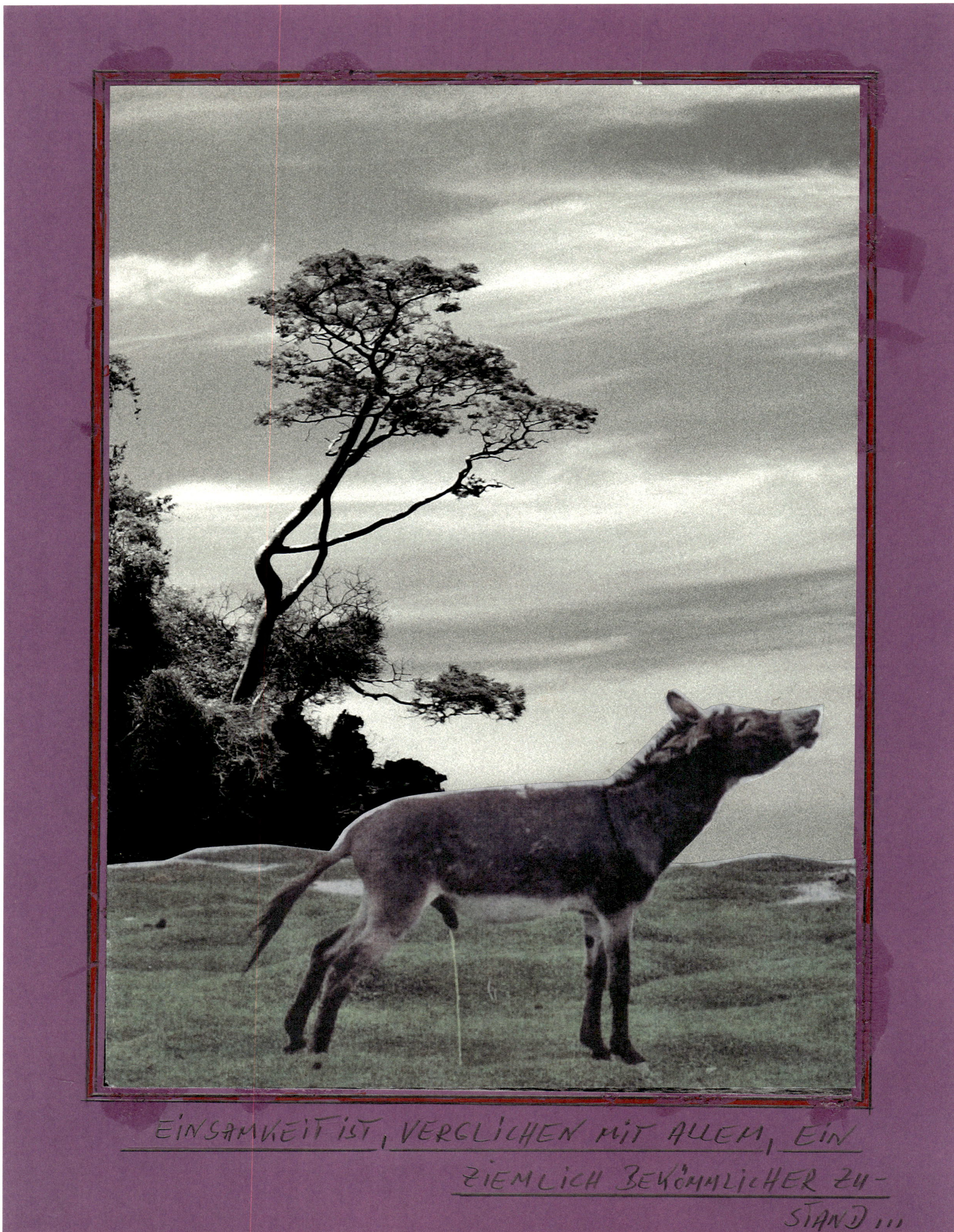

Loneliness is, compared to everything, a fairly digestible condition..., 2013

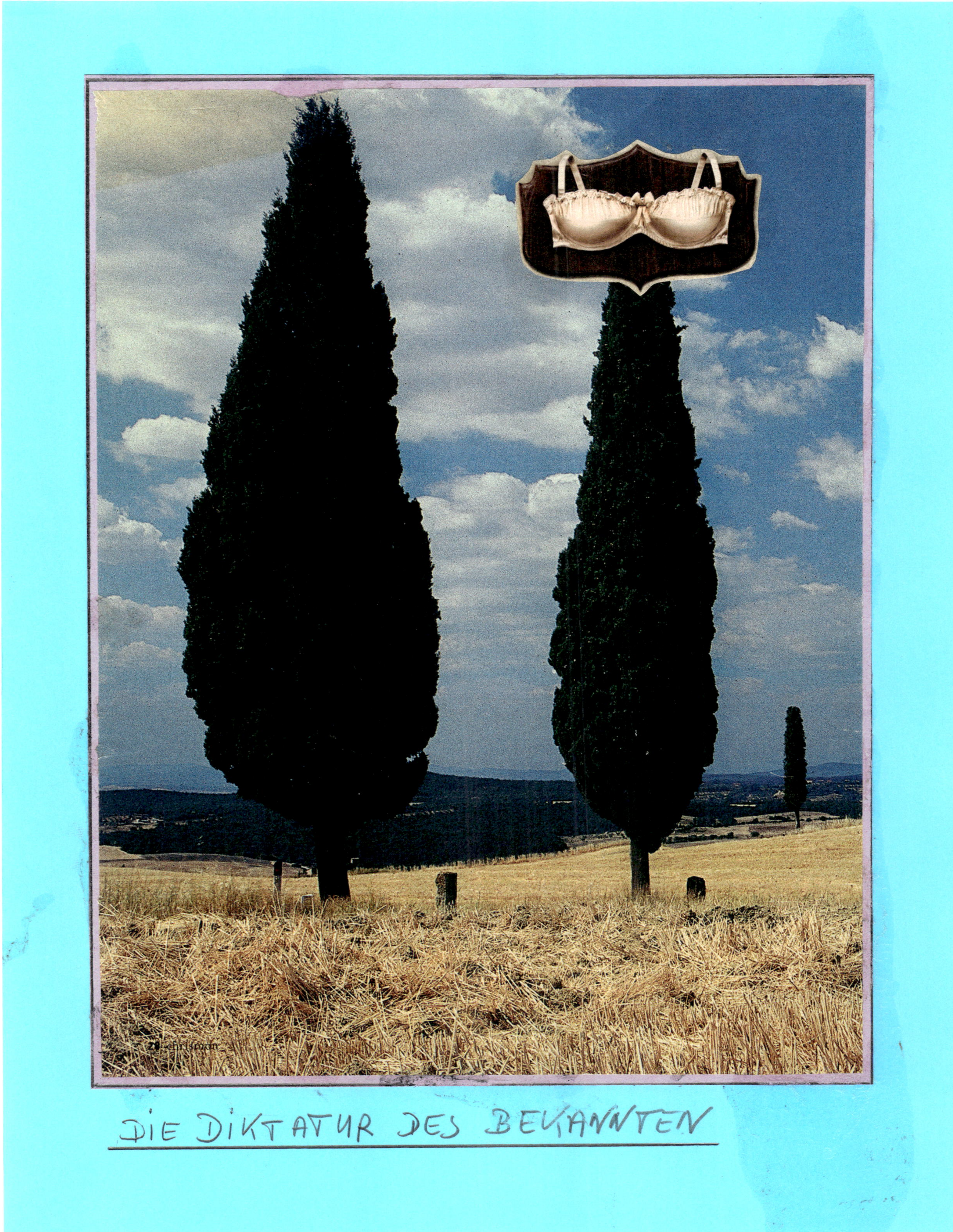

Dictatorship of the known, 2013

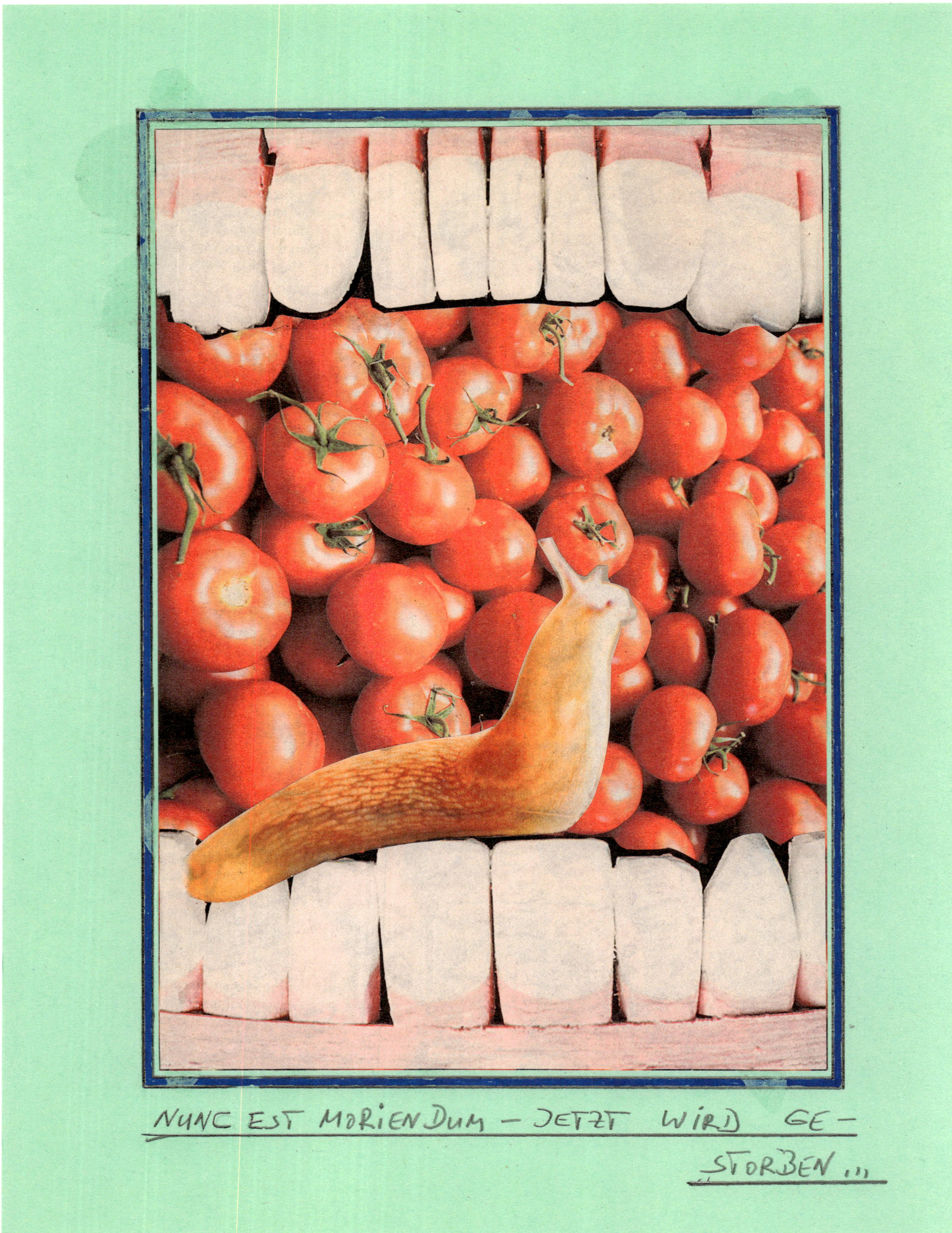

 Nunc est moriendum—now's the time for dying..., 2012

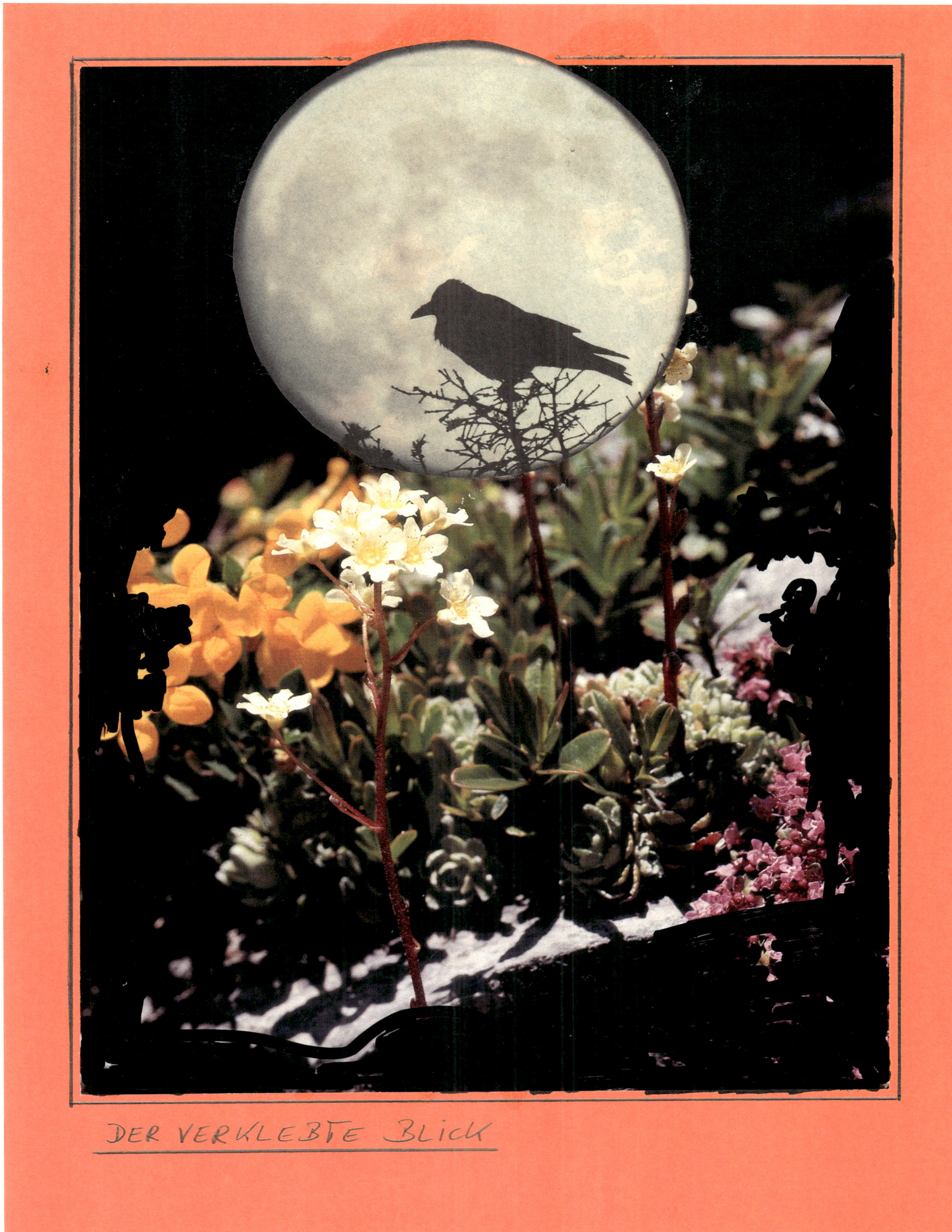

Sticky gaze, 2013

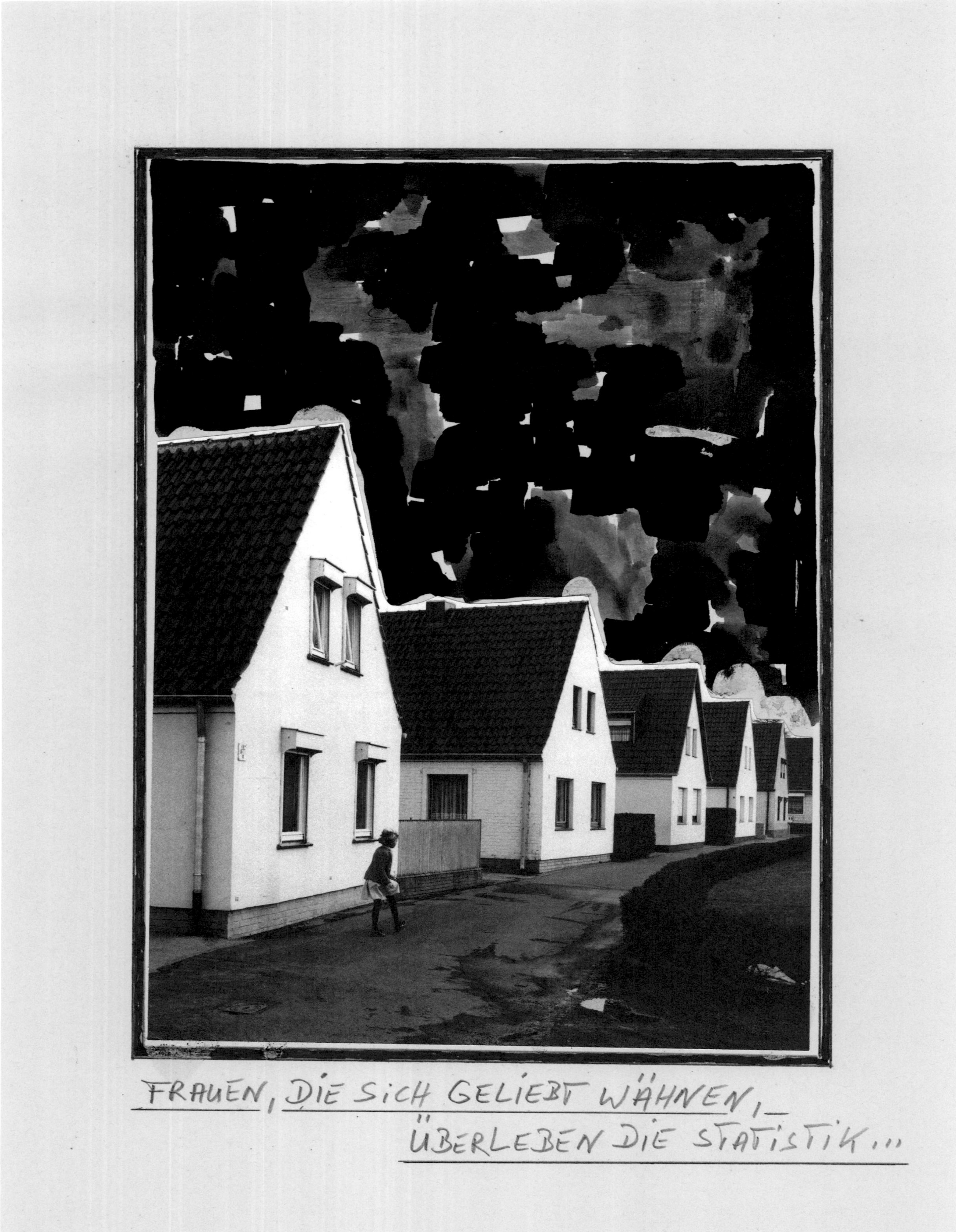

Women who consider themselves loved outlive the statistics..., 2013

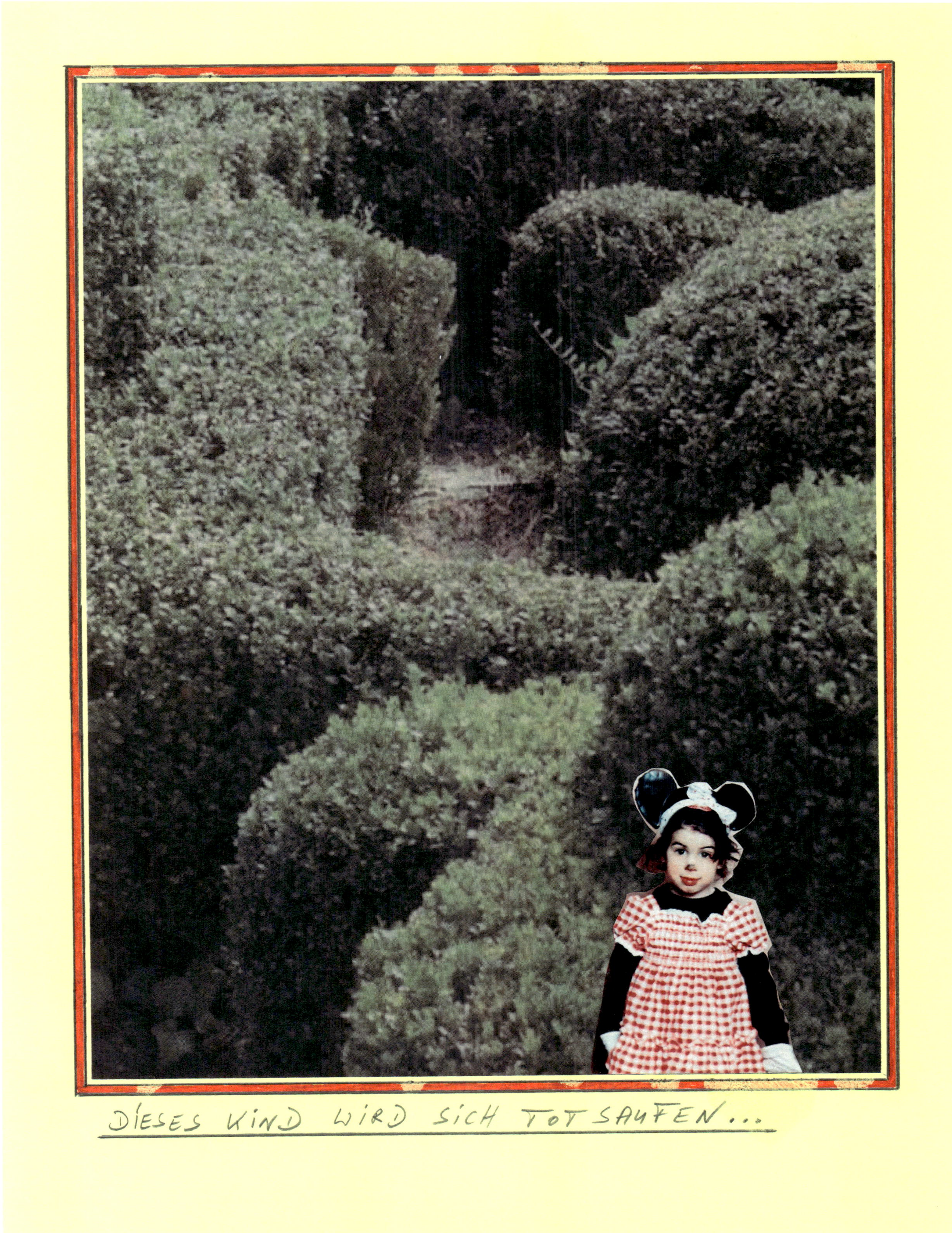

This child will drink itself to death..., 2013

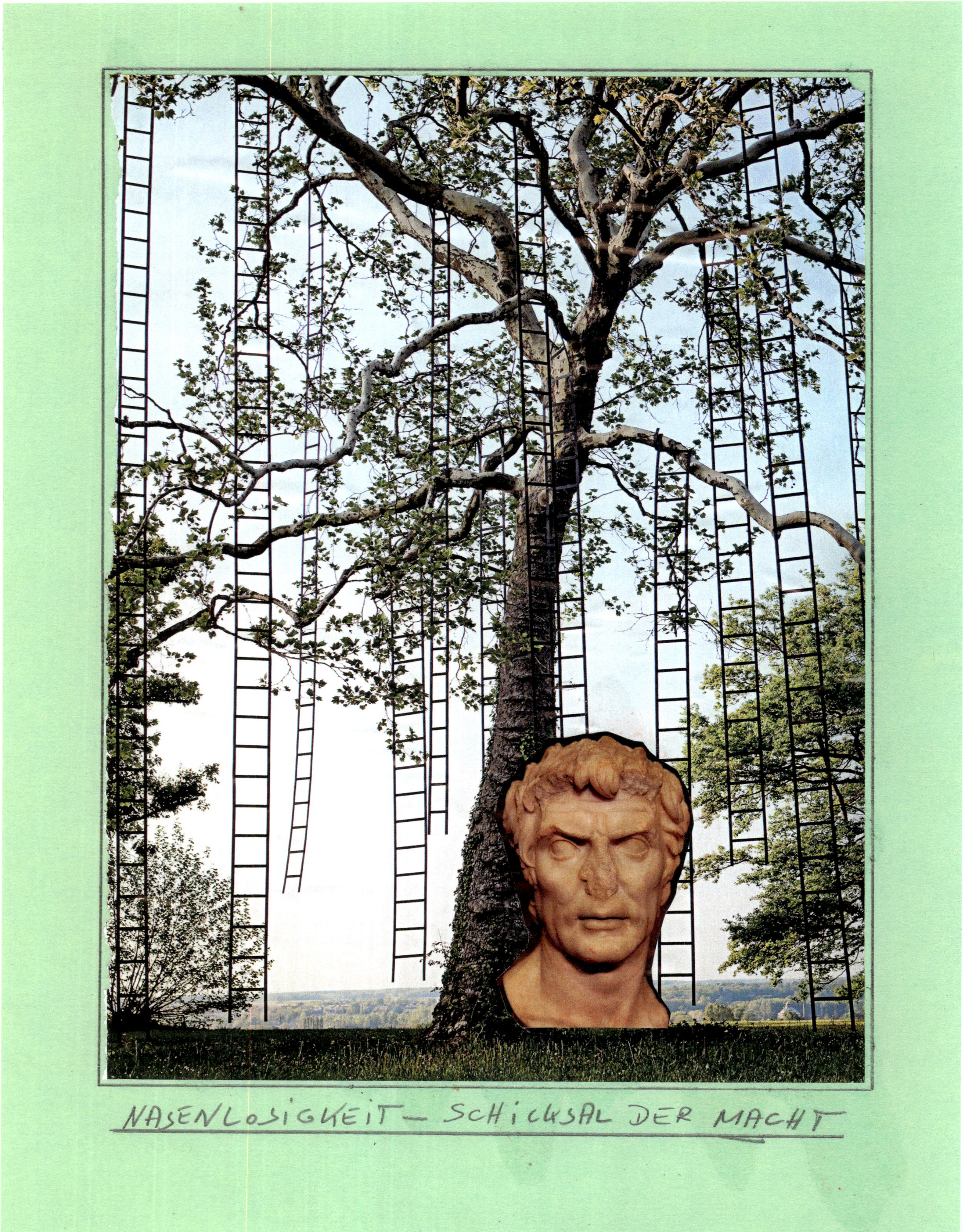

 Noselessness—the fate of power, 2012

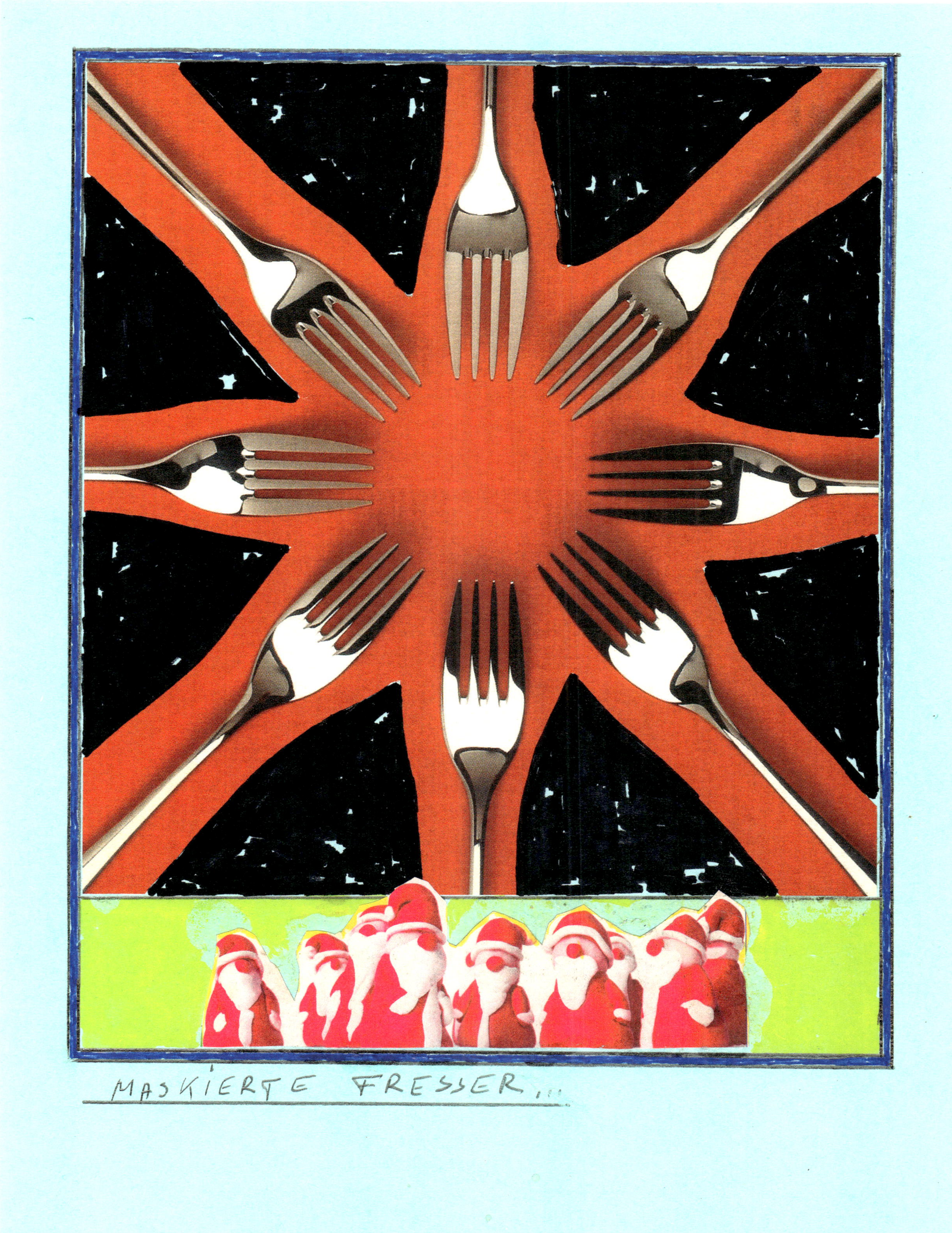

Masked gluttons..., 2012

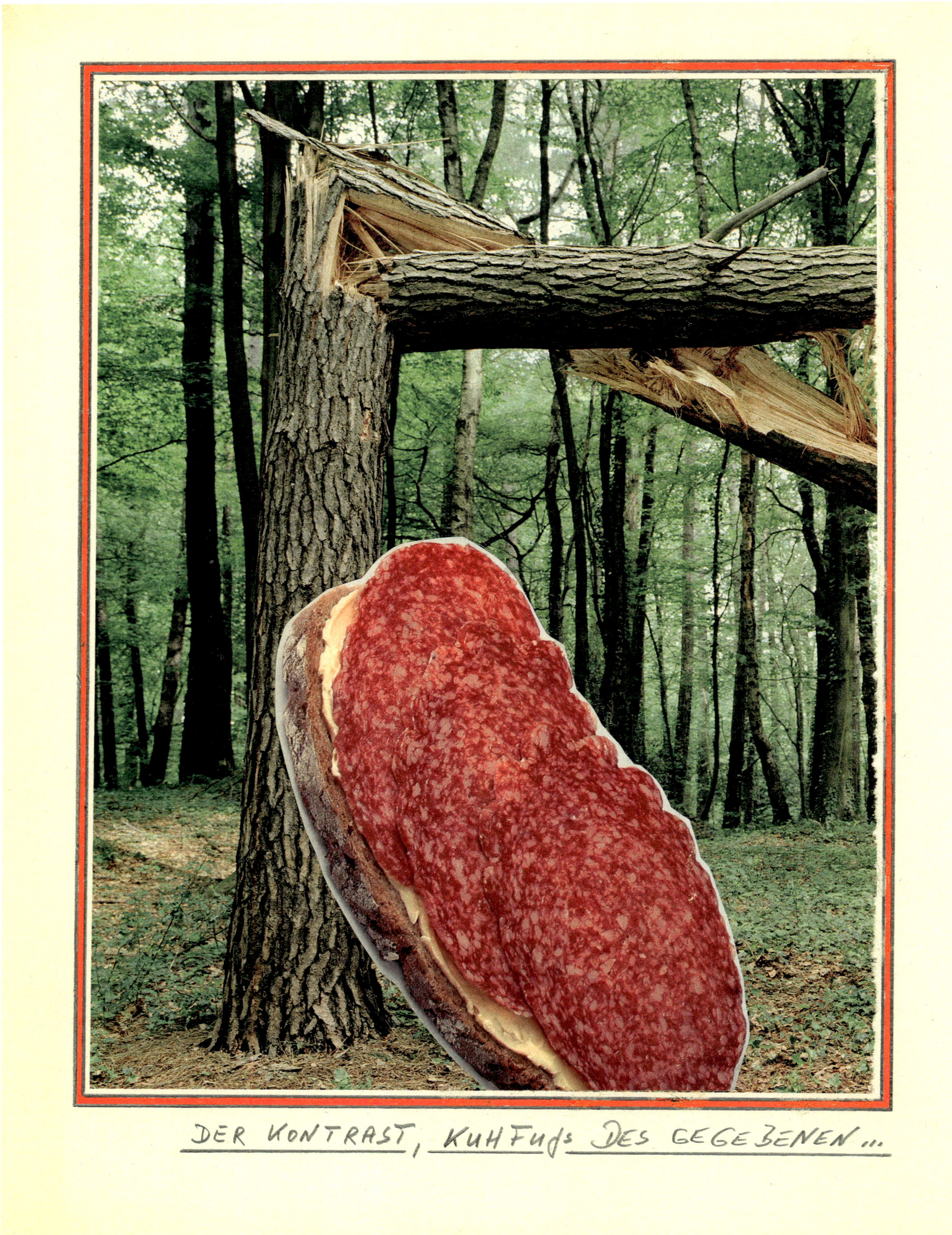

Contrast, the crowbar of the given..., 2012

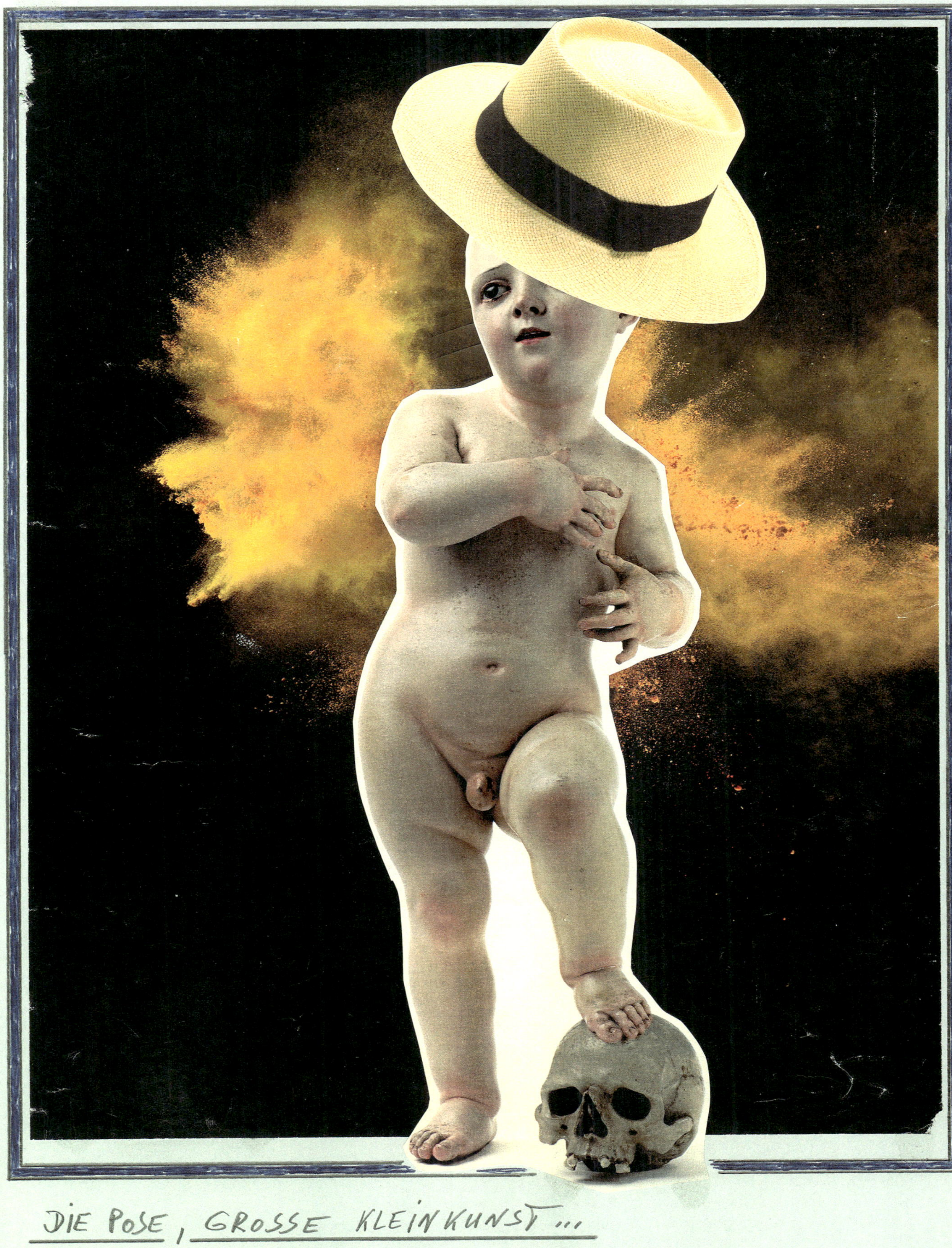

Posing, a great minor art..., 2011

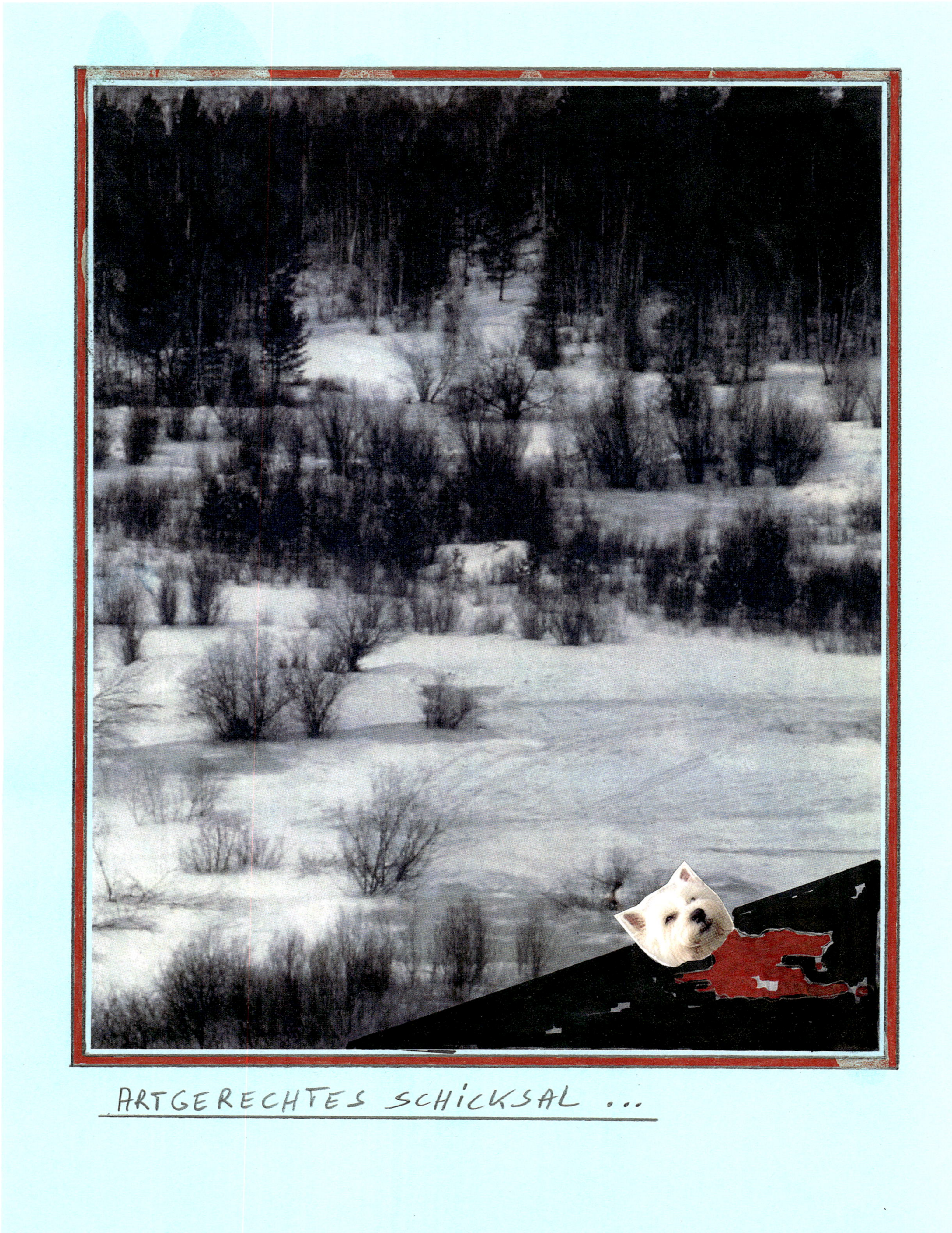

Species-appopriate fate..., 2015

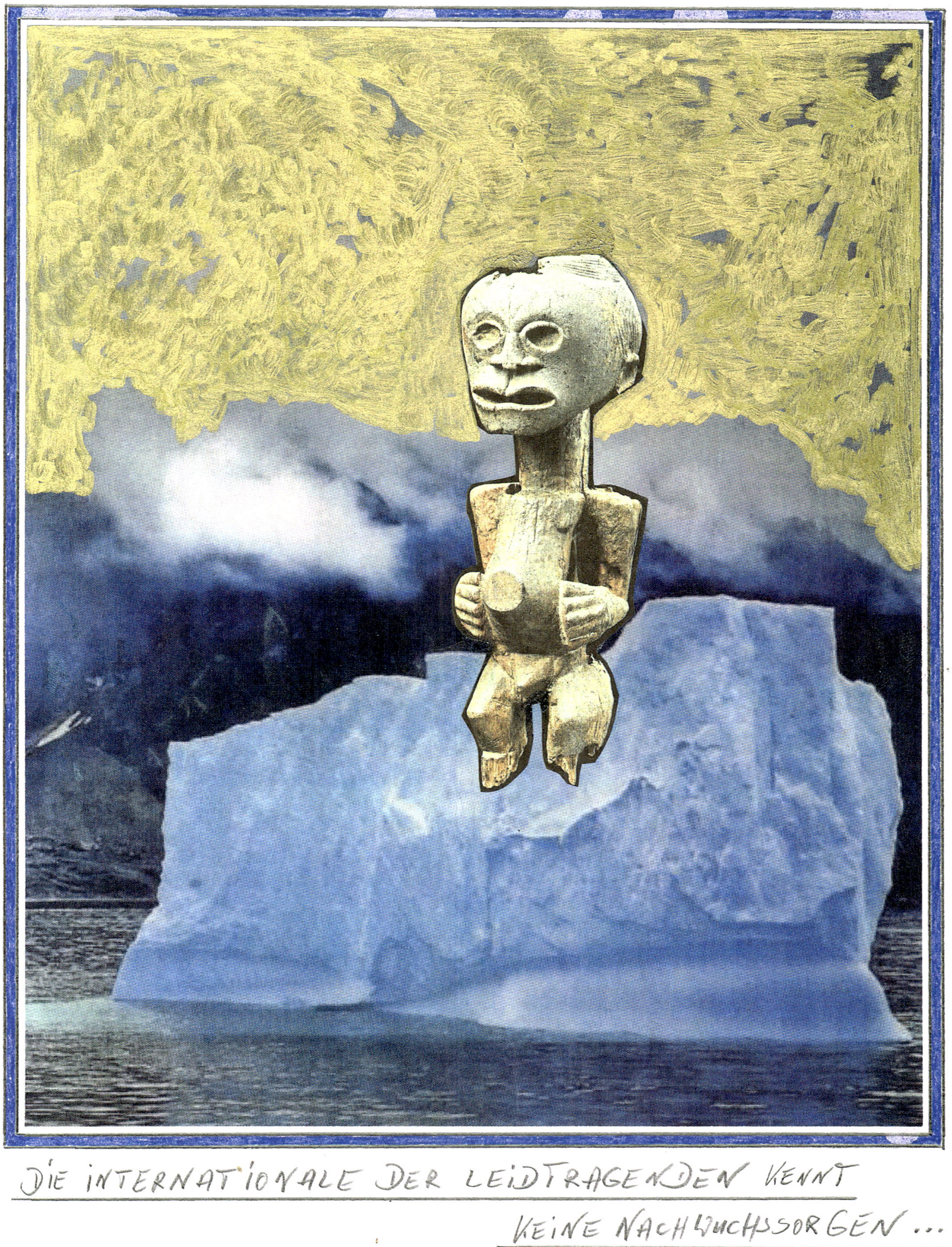

The Internationale of Sufferers has no trouble finding new members..., 2015

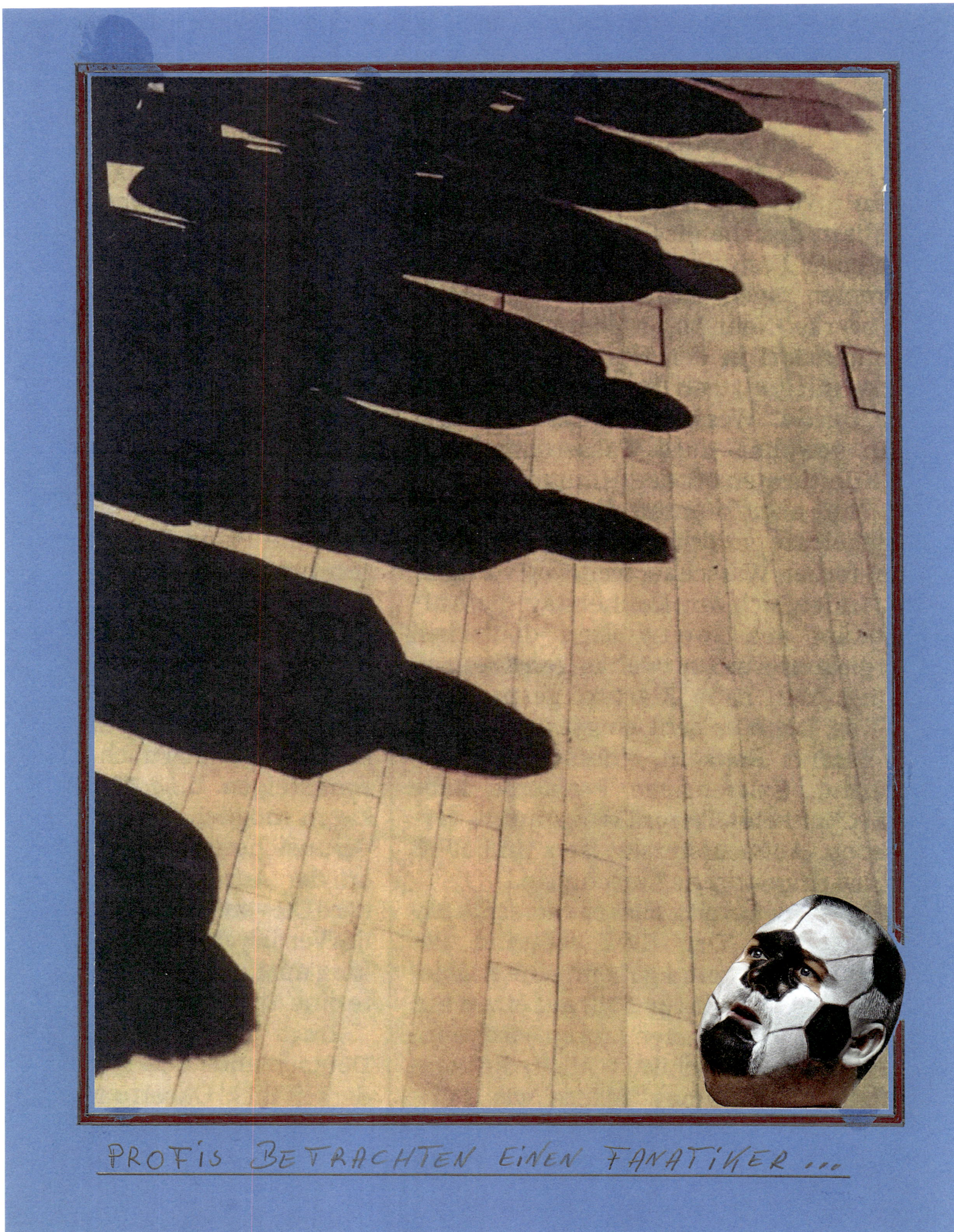

Professionals look at a fanatic..., 2014

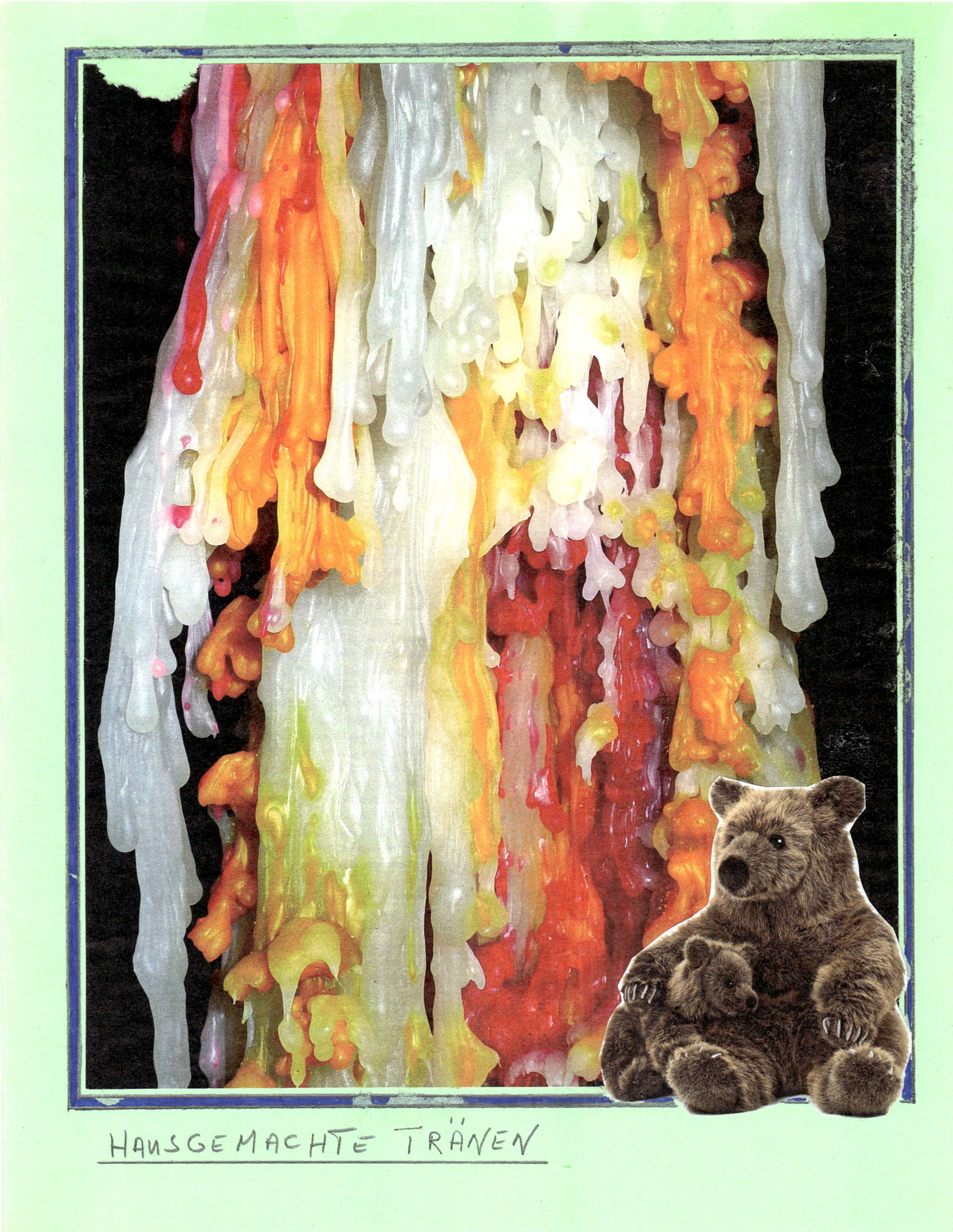

Homemade tears, 2014

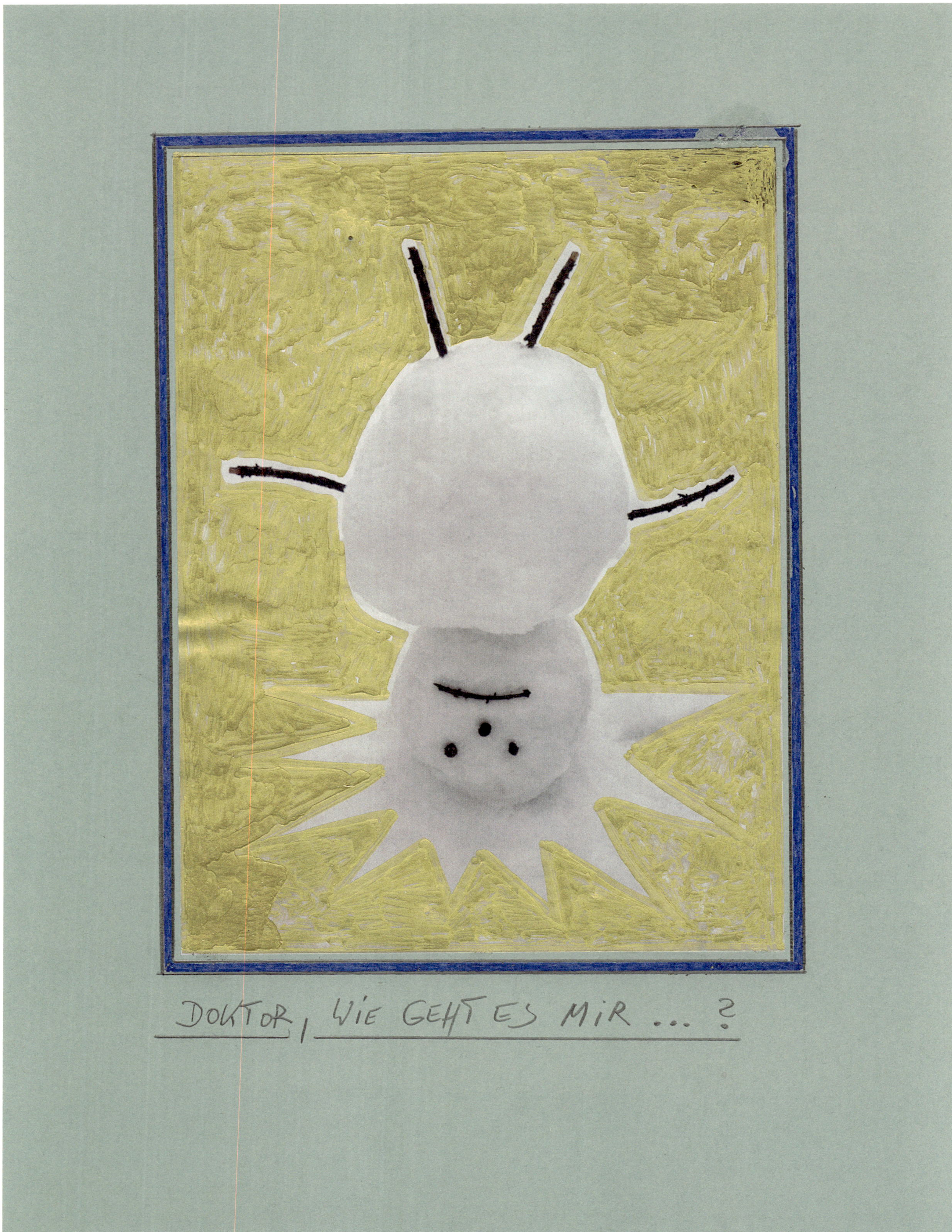

 Doctor, how am I...?, 2014

Countless Revelations The Collages of Werner Büttner

Daria Mille

> In truth you would be distressed if the whole world... were for once seriously to become completely comprehensible. And is even this infinite world not formed by understanding out of incomprehensibility or chaos?[1]

Collage principle

The technique of collage has a long history. Indeed, it can hardly be denied that—as a method involving the principles of fragmentation and citation—collage, and montage, belong to one of the most important forms of artistic and literary production since the beginning of the twentieth century. Introduced by the Cubists as a way of juxtaposing the most disparate levels of reality, collage has travelled successfully through the various 'isms' of the previous century, and continues to play a role in the present one. It has proved to be a suitable means of constructing and deconstructing reality, of representing the self, and also of addressing the nature of perception itself. From an anthropological point of view, collage can be interpreted as a reaction to the contradictory and fragmentary nature of modern life, when subjectivity and the varieties of sociality can no longer be experienced as a coherent whole. In the wake of the division of labour emerging as the basic principle of economic organisation, the essential nature of collage may be seen to have acquired a relevance for the whole of society.

Collage allows some central themes of artistic development in the late twentieth century to be addressed. These include the widely discussed 'death of the author', the uses of appropriation and citation, the question of representation and the problematic relationship of artworks to reality, and especially the overwhelming variety of images with which the media bombard us. The potential and limitations of today's media are shown up well by collage, for this technique is its own message. Its very openness to a multiplicity of interpretations stems from the variety of contexts from which one can extract its constituent elements.

The open-ended image created by the use of collage leaves much room for the exercise of the imagination. The juxtaposition of paradoxical elements, fragments taken out of context and even innate contradictions, can give rise to the grotesque, to caricature and to satire. In his work Comte de Lautréamont, whom the surrealists raised to the status of a founding father of their movement, is often cited as a precocious user of the technique, in view of the unusual metaphors encountered in his *Songs of Maldoror*, and the invention of the paradigmatic 'unexpected' encounter of a sewing machine with an umbrella on a dissecting table. André Breton wrote in his *First Surrealist Manifesto*, "the more the relationship between the two juxtaposed realities is distant and true, the stronger the image will be—the greater its emotional power and poetic reality." The contemporary approach to metaphor and to the role of chance in art would be unthinkable without this surrealist backdrop. Max Ernst said that the Surrealists' exploitation of chance could be understood as "motivated chance", as a subconscious choice made by the artist according to his or her preferences and anxieties. The random encounter, the sudden revelation, could thus be raised to a creative principle in art. Collage stands for staged and moulded contingency, for the realm of the could-be-otherwise, and thus for one of the most important determining factors of modern art, along with openness, unpredictability and plurality. At the same time, collage can make use of any and all aspects of reality, and thus may be said to impinge on all social structures as well as on the life of the individual. In the case of collage, contingency applies at all levels (motivation, production, reception). The failure of metaphysics and the growing recognition of the relativity of all truths have led to a search for new ways of expressing a contemporary awareness of being alive. Such ways can incorporate both reflexivity and the paradoxical, while at the same time allowing room for the shock of sudden insight, a loss of orientation, or even a sense of disintegration to be conveyed.[2]

Hence, on the one hand we can see a strong tendency in collage towards giving expression to the "modern tragedy of metaphysical homelessness", while on the other there is much to substantiate the claim that the joke and thus laughter are what make collage particularly attractive.[3] The essence of the joke lies in "portrayal through paradox". As Freud once proposed, comical effect can be attributed to "the conjunction of opposing concepts", or to "the experience of bafflement which can lead to an epiphany".

The surprise of coming across the known in a new context, the puzzling reality of an unanticipated juxtaposition or of an unexpected meaning, is not only an essential element of the joke itself, but is also a constituent part of the impact of the fragmentary in the case of collage. The sense of astonishment is especially disconcerting when collage takes photographs as its starting-point, since their documentary character signals objectivity. In literary criticism it is common to speak of a "shock" in Walter Benjamin's sense of the term, not only as amazement or bewilderment in the face of contextual transposition but also in the sense of the experience of modern perception, aesthetic impact and "profane revelation".[4] Collage and the joke function on a similar level, based on contextual shifts, ambiguity and innuendo.

Making of

Against this backdrop, it should be no surprise that Werner Büttner, whose art since the 1980s has oscillated between the poles of seemingly humorous provocation and philosophical significance, has devoted himself since 1999 to the technique of collage. It is here that the network of interconnections, in the artist's words, of "mischievous observations on the basis of intuited affinities" can best be understood. In the mid-1990s a collage-like juxtaposition of fragmentary elements was already evident in his painting.[5] The transition from painting to collage became more fluid; some collages were attempted in oil, as he explained, "especially if they then stand around the place surprisingly and solitarily, following the canon of traditional, painterly picture-making".

For Büttner, collage is about the technique of "going beyond oneself, and ultimately of conjuring up revelations". In this respect he can be placed within a long tradition of formulating and revealing hidden messages that give the impression of coming from 'backstage', similar to the technique of automatic writing practiced by the Surrealists. The shock effect inherent in the medium of collage, the 'unpredictability' of unusual pictorial invention, also plays a large role in Büttner's practice. It is a way of challenging one's own limits.

From time to time Büttner adopts the term *bricolage* from Claude Lévi-Strauss to describe his creative process. *Bricolage* and "wild thinking" as "taking and connecting what is there" apply to the non-predefined new order and to the creation of novel structures from readily available signs and events. In the spirit of *bricolage*, Büttner exploits the absurdity of the everyday as articulated in the media, that anonymous flood of printed images, the very same "pictorial rubbish" of promotional brochures, fashion magazines and periodicals of the kind that are delivered to every household. These become the raw material for his collages.

The criteria governing his choice of motifs are anonymity and insignificance: he would never touch "the photo of the year". A "process of destruction and liberation" is then set in motion. "The tools of rebellion are legal weapons and they are cheap: scissors, scalpels, metal rulers and glue. With these one can release the insulted and demeaned motif from its dreary context, from its service as a hired hand to seduce and enslave, to its purpose which is to provoke desire and promote saleability, and liberate it from the status of mere servant for the chaff of bloated bank statements."

The moveable pieces of pictorial scenery are playfully shoved around until a spontaneously discovered surprise appears. Coherence is of the essence, whereas meaning is of lesser importance. The pictorial scraps scavenged from the print media are brought into more 'dignified' interrelationships and glued together to create narrative scenes. "Worlds are called into being only to be rejected, minute by minute.... But some are found to be good for sinful reasons. And allowed out." Digital enlargement transforms the recycled motifs into C-prints with "pomp and fake glamour" but nonetheless as "homely truths". Surprisingly, this co-option of media products and their consequent loss of function and meaning, produces a result that may well have a function. As long ago as 1799, in an introductory text the Kantian philosopher Johann Adam Bergk urged that the latest discoveries in the realm of truth should be expressed in the vernacular, so as to make them more commonly available: "Where could be a better place to do this than in journals?".[6] Now Büttner sets himself the task of casting doubt on illusions and givens, on the semblance of logic of those truths that, basking in the gloss of the magazines, have been reduced to pure titivation of the senses over the course of two hundred years. Instead he advocates "thinking for oneself" as a means of defence against the defamation of the world. "Hopefully one can now get a sense of the conceptual ruses that are sometimes set to work by my hand. There is the rebellious reframing of common truths, a Gnostic stratagem, which basically intends no more than the revitalization of lost attentiveness."

Loose connections

Büttner is especially interested in these: "One seeks loose connections because one does not want to have to think about real human failings. One learns about one's own shortcomings every morning in one's own newspaper." In order to expose 'baser' truths about human nature, Büttner finds support in psychoanalysis as a modern form of shamanistic technique (Lévi-Strauss). Freud had postulated that the process of self-discovery which such loose connections can initiate in the viewer or reader is furthered by—in Freud's phrase—"playful judgement", by jokes and laughter as well as by the relationship between the linguistic title and that which is depicted.

We are often unaware of why and what we are laughing about, and some rationale is frequently sought to explain why we particularly enjoyed a joke. But in many instances a joke aims at finding sense in nonsense, and hints at something serious veiled in amusing clothing. What distinguishes the joke from other forms of humour is that sudden feeling of liberation that the culmination of a good joke sets off. This happens most dramatically in the case of sceptical, aggressive, cynical or obscene jokes, what Freud termed "tendentious jokes". They cleverly mask what they really have to say and conceal that something forbidden is hidden behind their facade. The main thrust of working with jokes is to relieve inhibitions caused by something suppressed and to whet the appetite for enlightenment with the aid of "paradoxical techniques". Working with jokes liberates by unleashing nonsense or through word play, reviving the pleasure that is lost to us for cultural reasons (such as intellectual upbringing or social norms). This brings relief from the pressure of criticism. The targets of Freud's "tendentious jokes" are institutions, people, inhibitions generated by shame or, as in the case of sceptical jokes, our certainty about our knowledge itself, and the unintelligibility and absurdity of commonly used terms.

Büttner's palette of joke-like ideas in pictorial idioms is multifaceted. He does not baulk at corny jokes, base jokes, black and sardonic humour, to release the truths about human nature from their enslavement by the unconscious, and to put them beyond the control of reason. He places special emphasis on sceptical subjects, which expose the unintelligibility of commonplaces, and question our very ability to comprehend or even to grasp the concept of comprehension (*How many drills does a man need in his life?*). The very 'grammar' of collage is based on the technique of the joke plus—as he puts it—"a tower well-filled with gunpowder and a little poetry in the freezer every single day". Double-meanings (*legendary castration above the belt*), word-play (*fun fatal*), depictions of the opposite and the absurd (*frenetic rigidity*) are just some examples of this gleeful grammar.

Excursus into the Romantic

As part of his fascination with denouncing reason, Büttner would love to allow "vegetable reason" to rule the world. In this, he echoes the view of the German Romantic philosopher Friedrich Schlegel who, while exaggerating the concept of 'naturalness', wrote in his *Idyll of Idleness*, "The more divine a human being or a work of man is, the more they come to resemble plants. Among all forms, the latter are the most ethical, and the most beautiful, and without these, the most highly perfected life would be nothing but mere vegetation."[7]

In his collages Büttner reclaims the Romantic view of the world for himself, including the manner of speaking and perceiving: "Romanticism, that is the eternally hypochondriac achievement. That is the enlightenment of the gullible! That is the brain-spiked green minus May! And then there is the forest! It affords bird-happiness for a hundred thousand chicks and keeps a million lovers' oaths warm."

The concept of art as revelation or message can be traced back to the philosophy of the Romantics. The idea that truth results from a concordance between a statement and the world it purports to describe was rejected. In contrast, truthfulness was held to be located in the ability to develop or find forms enabling the world to be revealed. Parallel to this new concept of truth, a new understanding of language developed during the Romantic period. It was understood as a means to recreate and rewrite precepts, to discover for oneself other ways of seeing, and to reveal new aspects of the world. In metaphoric language—not to be understood as a representation of pre-existent reality—the world can always be negotiated and articulated afresh. This understanding of language also stems from the idea of art as experiment, as formulating original meanings and tending towards nonsense.

Büttner's "world-upside-down" arises from "a hotbed of neologisms", from the metaphors, metonyms and oxymora that are cultivated between the poles of what is depicted and the handwritten title. The comical effect of this treatment of language and image is obvious: the philosopher Jean Paul had already designated metaphor, allegory and trope as figurative jokes.[8] Analytical tools fail in their attempt to grasp the nature of collage systematically. The picture-text combination is often random, the parts do not comment on each other, yet appear together and try to evoke both atmosphere and meaning. And again Schlegel's ideas resonate with the collaged world of Büttner: "For the beginning of all poetry is to cancel the course and the laws of rationally thinking reason and transport us again towards the beautiful confusion of imagination, into the original chaos of human nature for which I know as yet no more beautiful symbol than the motley throng of the ancient gods."[9]

Tools: in the triumvirate of estrangement, parody and irony

It is worth casting an eye on the tools or "aesthetic tactics" Büttner employs, in order to trace some of his affiliations. For he himself talks of "speaking with many tongues" and his debt to 'quoting' from past masters as a "favoured device to raise one's own credibility", hinting in this context that the magic of tradition has a hold on him. Büttner's "famous forbears" come mainly from the literary field. With his use of quotation, reflecting "a persistent need to be anachronistic", he does not refer, however, to specific literary motifs but rather to the human condition itself, leading in justifiable cases to a healthy "cultural disobedience". Furthermore, quotation offers a safeguard against the conventional expectations imposed by the world and our times. Above all, Antiquity, the Renaissance and the Romantic period play an important role in articulating his "aesthetic tactics" aimed at questioning, at times even overturning "habitual world views".

Estrangement is both a key to understanding the impact of collages and a literary stylistic device. The literary theorist Victor Shklovsky defines estrangement, also known as the alienation effect or defamiliarisation, as a stylistic method that involves lifting something out of the usual context in which it is normally recognised, thus making something habitual seem strange and unusual.[10] A critical distance from the depicted can be attained by way of 'decoupling' the habitual processes of perception, through "making things seem strange". As a result, new ways of seeing familiar things are opened up, making the contradictory nature of reality apparent.

In a bygone age Marcus Aurelius applied this method in his book *Meditations*. These were intended to help him live his life according to Stoic principles. Things were to be broken down to their basic components, and any object close to oneself was to be viewed from a distance and regarded as an enigma. This would make it possible to observe things correctly "for what they really are". "Confine thyself to the present. See through what you or others encounter. Divide and parse every object into the formal and the material. Think of your last hour".[11] For literary figures in this tradition such as Leo Tolstoy, penetrating the nature of things required freeing oneself from 'supposedly' false beliefs and ideas, and ultimately learning to accept suffering and mortality.[12] If we ask ourselves questions that at first sight sound like riddles we uncover the dogmatism, reification and torpor of our reasoning. This aesthetic tactic is an important feature of what Büttner calls "cultural disobedience".

In his *Essays* Michel de Montaigne formulated a similar proposal, namely that one should adopt a naive, wide-eyed perspective to help one plumb hidden depths and gain an insight into the natural order. He aspired to attain genuine self-knowledge and the truth about the world. His attention was focussed on human perception and comprehension. For him, the 'ego' should be regarded as volatile and as unfolding through time. One should accept the human condition and the trials of existence: the horizon of human life is becoming and not being. This critical and reflective attitude of unremitting scepticism towards any superficial knowledge, together with the readiness to question any statement of fact (whether referring to society or to the everyday), led to a belief in the relativity of any claim to truth. Thus Montaigne developed the foundation for what the distinguished literary scholar Karl Heinz Bohrer would later term a "self-thinker" as opposed to a "systems-thinker".[13] Montaigne especially appeals to Büttner, for he put emotion before intellect, imagination before reason, experience before rules. With this he also anticipated Romantic philosophy: Bohrer thought his "being in the moment" harbours the imaginative and appealing power of poetry, which for him outshone the power of judgement.

Another branch of this network of 'construed affiliations' leads from Büttner to the grotesque, to parody and thus to the popular cultural humour of the carnival. Here he particularly values the emancipatory role of laughter. It is not for nothing that François Rabelais is "the only doctor in whom he would place his trust, full to the brim". From Rabelais, Büttner learnt to laugh in the right place at the right time at authority, at certainty and at stupid, disagreeable things. The Russian philosopher Mikhail Bakhtin scrutinised the carnivalesque subtext of Rabelais' pentalogy of novels, *Gargantua and Pantagruel*, and analysed the significance of Carnival as a manifestation of a counterculture. Laughing at all authorities during the carnival season opens up new ways of seeing things, exposes dogmatism and taken-for-granted postulates. The lighthearted provocation and laughter of a collective popular assembly is directed against official institutions, hierarchies and the sacred, indeed against the whole established order of things. The way governments and truths change, and the loss of utopian potential caused by the authorities, are greeted with raucous hilarity. Although such hierarchies can only be turned on their head for the duration of the carnival, at least an alternative to the ruling order can be envisioned for a while. Bakhtin explained "... laughter was just as universal as seriousness, it was directed at the whole world, at history, at the whole of society and the whole of philosophy. It was the second truth about the world, whose competence was not transgressed; it was the festive aspect of the world in all its moments, a second epiphany through play and laughter."[14]

The verity of such a second epiphany is the truth of ambivalence and thus of relativity, the truth of crisis and of change. The carnival turns out to be a staging of the myth of ambivalence, as death and mortality release their grip on the world; through the sublimation of death, the world is overcome by laughter. The official and restrictive 'cultural order' of laughter's enemies, the *Agelasten* (for the Greeks; "those who don't laugh"), is outlined in Bakhtin's sketch of cultural history as a culture of dualisms, which "seeks disambiguation through restrictive practices of sublimation and repression".[15] This restrictive culture banishes laughter and founds its system on "cosmic angst" and the "fear of one's own death". According to Bakhtin, the confrontation between this official monovalent culture and the culture of laughter—the culture of ambivalence—is a constant parameter in cultural history. The rationality of the carnival in Bakhtin's opinion is the "rationality of duality". In contrast to official culture it is not oriented towards *one* truth.

The Dionysian side of the carnival can also be interpreted as a time of plunging into the wilds. In order to experience culture from outside, one has to become part of the wildness of the carnival and explore the wild in oneself, one's animal nature. "Whoever wanted to live inside the fence consciously must have left that enclosure at least once in his lifetime... must have roamed the woods as a wolf, a 'wild man'... for only there could he gain information on what may have been familiar to him, and yet was unknown: his everyday nature."[16]

At the level of language cultural ambivalence can find expression in irony. Irony, which like parody and estrangement has been known since Antiquity, lends a critical dimension to parody, by revealing difference within apparent similarity. Parody operates at a semantic level and irony at a textual level.[17] Contemporary irony, employed as a defence against the whole Occidental tradition, has its roots firstly in Socratic maieutics, which used irony to elicit "correct knowledge" through persistent questioning, and secondly in the Romantic period which revivified irony after it had fallen into disrepute in the Middle Ages as an empty rhetorical device.

Irony, whether as a mode of communication or as a philosophical asset, cannot be ascribed to a particular discourse nor be declared a concept. Its function of overstepping boundaries depends on its independence and its critical potential, resulting from ambivalence and keeping a distance. It is diametrically opposed to common truths, to that knowledge which does not involve the recipients in its articulation. Irony causes difficulties for speech that wants to be understood. Schlegel describes it as "a permanent Parekbase", as when the chorus stepped out of the dramatic event to address the audience directly, and often in unrestrained language. This can be interpreted as pointing on the one hand to the function of irony as disruption and on the other to a level of critical self-reflection deliberately inserted into a work.

The most important thing about irony, according to the literary theorist Paul de Man, is that it should be recognised as such by the recipient. In this case it leads to uncertainty about what meaning is intended. Irony causes an uncontrolled hiatus in a system. It is opposed to definiteness and rigidity.

Balancing up

Büttner allows things to float. By refusing to pin them down, he hinders any attempt at an unambiguous answer. The language of his collages is the language of "the world-turned-upside-down" idiom of the carnival with its immanent metamorphoses, turning everything on its head, ambivalence pure. His collages revel in physicality, excess and tomfoolery. Their meaning is eccentric, always referring to something else, abjuring identity as if hidden behind a mask. Büttner also builds on the ideas of many bright minds, developing a complex, syncretic approach in his collages. By reinterpreting truths plundered from the world of the media he makes us aware of 'common' truths about the world. In the mirror which Büttner holds up to us, it is possible to identify elements assembled according to certain syntactic rules, but nothing is recognisable—apart from the fact that beyond the structures and hierarchies chaos rules, and that the world is possibly ruled by something other than reason. The apparent connections are broken. And thus Büttner advances into the territory of the contingent and accidental, always aware of the tragedy involved.

Using his own tools he counters the imposition of abstraction and reduction in meaning. Abstraction supports the rule of the already-established power brokers, with their systems of predefined knowledge and authority vested in official institutions, which rely on their ability to impose prohibitions and exclusions. Büttner's recipe to counter the trials of existence, to deal with the haphazardness of individual failure and at the same time halt "the human march into abstraction full of contradictions and mystifications" is as follows: accept the inconsistencies and always be a stranger to your own life. "So perhaps—when you spot the barrel of mystifications and contradictions approaching—you can make a big leap to one side."

1 Schlegel, Friedrich, "Über die Unverständlichkeit", in Eichner, Hans, ed, *Kritische Friedrich-Schlegel-Ausgabe*, Munich, Paderborn and Vienna: Schöningh, and Zurich: Thomas, vol 2, 1967, p 370.
2 Cf Zifras, Jörg, "Kontingenz und Tragik. Eine moderne Figur und ihre ästhetischen Konsequenzen", in Liebau, Eckart and Zirfas, Jörg, *Dramen der Moderne. Kontingenz und Tragik im Zeitalter der Freiheit*, Bielefeld: Transcript, 2010, p 10.
3 Cf Zifras, *Dramen der Moderne. Kontingenz und Tragik im Zeitalter der Freiheit*, p 25.
4 Cf The interpretation of the term "shock" by Bohrer, Karl Heinz in "Schein und Chock", as used by Benjamin, Walter, in Joachimides, Christos and Rosenthal, Norman, eds, *Zeitgeist*, exh cat, Martin-Gropius-Bau, Berlin: Frölich und Kaufmann, 1982, pp 30–35.
5 Büttner, Werner, "Zum Sicheren Geleit", in Pakesch, Peter and Schlebrügge, Johannes eds, *Fama & Fortune Bulletin: Ratiopharmaka, aber auch Herzmittel, und für die Augen eine bekömmliche Tinktur*, Vienna: Fama & Fortune Bulletin, no 28, May 2002, p 3. NB All subsequent unattributed quotations are from the writings or quotations by the artist.
6 Bergk, Johann Adam, *Die Kunst, Bücher zu lesen. Nebst Bemerkungen über Schriften und Schriftsteller*, Jena, 1799, p 385, cited in Schumacher, Eckhard, *Die Ironie der Unverständlichkeit. Johann Georg Hamann, Friedrich Schlegel, Jacques Derrida, Paul de Man*, Frankfurt: Suhrkamp, 2000, p 185.
7 Schlegel, Friedrich, "Lucinde", in Eichner, Hans, ed, *Kritische Friedrich-Schlegel-Ausgabe*, Munich, Paderborn and Vienna: Schöningh, and Zurich: Thomas, vol 5, 1962, p 27.
8 Cf Paul, Jean, *Vorschule der Ästhetik*, Hamburg: Felix Meiner, 1990, pp 182–191.
9 Schlegel, Friedrich, "Gespräch über Poesie: Rede über die Mythologie", in Eichner, Hans, ed, *Kritische Friedrich-Schlegel-Ausgabe*, 1967, p 319.
10 Cf Shklovskij, Viktor, *Theorie der Prosa*, Frankfurt: Fischer, 1966, p 7f.
11 Aurel, Marc, *Selbstbetrachtungen*, Frankfurt: Insel, 1992, p 110.
12 Cf Analysis of estrangement in Carlo Ginzburg, *Holzaugen. Über Nähe und Distanz*, Berlin: Wagenbach, 1999, pp 11–42.
13 Cf Bohrer, Karl Heinz, *Selbstdenker und Systemdenker. Über agonales Denken*, Munich: Carl Hanser, 2011, pp 7–26.
14 Bakhtin, Mikail, *Rabelais und seine Welt. Volkskultur als Gegenkultur*, Frankfurt, Suhrkamp, 1998, p 134.
15 Lachmann, Renate, "Vorwort", in Bakhtin, *Rabelais und seine Welt. Volkskultur als Gegenkultur*, p 19.
16 Duerr, Hans Peter, Traumzeit. *Über die Grenzen zwischen Wildnis und Zivilisation*, Frankfurt: Suhrkamp, 1985, p 107f.
17 Cf Hutcheon, Linda, *Irony's Edge. The Theory and Politics of Irony*, London and New York: Routledge, 1995, p 4f.

Reality is a surprisingly cheap stool-pigeon
Werner Büttner in conversation with Andrew Renton

Andrew Renton: Looking at the new pictures, there are several elements that are consistent in your work. There's often an image that is familiar if not recognisable. Or recognisable if not familiar. And a title that may be helpful or playfully misleading—especially in a form of word play that resists translation from German. So what is the starting point for a new work? Is it a pre-existing idea, a title or an image?

Werner Büttner: Mostly it starts with a remarkable image which convinces me that it is worth getting painted. In the early days I collected, *comme il faut*, ideas for paintings by sketching them with pen and paper. For the past 14 years I've been using my collages. The collage is a marvellous medium to get results that can shock yourself. You have a lot of cutout images and you slide them over and around until you have something where you have to say: "Wow, this is crazy, unseen, unbelievable, but has a certain soundness." Then you glue it together and search for a correspondingly alien title. And if a collage has the quality, the charisma, the fitting destiny to become a painting, I'll try. But sometimes reality perplexes me and I see a painting right through my window like the *Magersüchtige, Entenfütternd* (*Anorexic, feeding ducks*), 2014—which spares me some glue. Reality is a surprisingly cheap stool-pigeon.

AR: Collage is a medium that juxtaposes realities—bits and bobs from the real world forced into unlikely relations. Even at its most complex, I think collage remains readable as a medium because of the raw materials. I remember you once quoted Magritte to me, "I only paint what I have not seen before." I know you weren't talking about yourself at the time, but is producing something 'unseen' the job of painting?

WB: Well, Magritte meant he wanted to paint what he has not seen painted before. The poor bastard had to defend himself his whole life against the silly imputation that he "painted dreams". So the job of the painter is at least to paint unseen paintings. Since painting has existed now for a mere 40,000 years it's not too difficult a task. As James Ensor put it: "As long as the sun shines, you will live, beloved little panel painting." It seems to me to mean that every generation paddles in the same pool of passions, but pictures its adventures differently. This is, of course, just an extremely foggy revelation of the job of the painter.

AR: And yet this doesn't quite explain the continued pull of painting. And 'figurative' painting at that.... All your paintings are about the materiality of paint and not simply the business of image-making. I'm thinking of the splash of paint that is flicked onto the surface at (I presume) the end of your working on the canvas....

WB: Oh dear, this is a delicate question. You are laying hands on my fragile empire of contradictions. In one respect I adore the magical qualities of oil colours, in another I detest its over-eagerness to serve fraud and cheap thrills. I have to mistrust its charms and allurements and make sure it submits to my arbitrary intentions. If it says, "I'm colour, I'm free, I represent just myself", it enters the murk of meaninglessness. I'm not allowed to allow this. The splashes you mentioned have a handful of purposes.

They are, of course, a distinguishing mark, a melody which helps the visitor to identify the author. Visitors love to identify immediately and precisely. The splashes also hide badly painted parts. I loved this immediately. They irritate eye and brain and construct an additional 'phantom-plane'. And you're right, they are the last act after the mumbling of the signature. A gesture of contempt, justified by the power of contradictions.

AR: And, dare I say it, a little bit of abstraction in a field of representation...? Resisting figuration, even in your early days, was never an option?

WB: I satisfied my abstract desires when I made the series *Die Probleme des Minigolfs in der europäishen Malerei* (*The problems of mini golf in European painting*), 1982. The possibilities of abstract painting are hair-raisingly limited. You cannot mock or insult Creation, you cannot mock or insult contemporary art with it. You cannot praise your favourite phenomena with it. Nor is it of any help when you want to idolise or worship. You cannot picture adequately with it your pool of passions. Not to speak of your *Lebensgefuhl*, which might be in English your "sentiment of life". I know many colleagues who went into the desert of abstraction and have been suffering and mourning all of their lives. And secretly they all dream of painting a daffodil, a daisy or a steamy tit.

AR: You mentioned that early series. I sense that you and your contemporaries were mocking and insulting the legacy of painting you inherited. Can you talk about that time?

WB: Unfortunately one of my problems is the fact that I only remember important things that touched me. This might make the fishing in my memory a bit unrewarding. I hardly remember, let alone understand, the young dog I obviously must have been at times. The tragedy of reaching a ripe old age alienates you from what were once welcomed states of being. So the official art historian's version goes like this: The 'tristesse', lack of sensuality and over-long reign of terror of Minimal art, had wearied every collector in Germany. This hunger for pictures plagued and pestered them. Some 80 new painters showed up and tried to assuage the hunger. I was one of them, I suppose. I was not attending art school. Martin Kippenberger and Albert Oehlen did. From time to time, I visited them at the Hamburg Art School (HfBK) and sometimes we drank a few decent beers with Ulrich Ruckriem, Franz Erhard Walther and Sigmar Polke. Maybe we even talked while drinking the beers. The art schools at this time were humane, senselessly experimental and generously giving time to students. No stress, no recipes.... And art students knew about responsibility for their own fate. Because 96 per cent of those who studied art would not make a living out of it.... It was rough, but lively. But, you know, as I mentioned in the beginning, man is no trustworthy witness to his own life.

AR: You speak about an absence and hunger in that late era of Minimalism. So what were you looking at then? Or were there no heroes to turn to?

WB: There are always a lot of heroes when you are trying to become what you finally have to be. At that time, for me, there were two interesting painting positions from whom one could have expected satisfaction—Jörg Immendorff and Sigmar Polke. Immendorff brought the crude KPD/ML [Kommunistische Partei Deutschlands/Marxisten-Leninisten] aesthetics, the primitive style of a German communist sect, to bourgeois households. Out of this limited propaganda he then developed a crazy oeuvre which ended in a perverted, clown-like fiasco. Polke, for me, started as a hippie-like trickster, juggling with bamboo, flamingos and German sausages in an as yet unseen playful attitude. He ended up as an arrogant orthodox alchemist who thought that pop-eyed chimeras were all the bourgeoisie deserves. I did not learn from their highlights. That's not possible. But I learned a lot from their personal and painterly disasters, for which I'm really still grateful. So much for those living at that time. But there were also fruitful discussions with the dead—Ensor, Goya, El Greco, Rabelais, Montaigne, to name an exact full hand. The dead have charms, they have no abilities to disappoint....

AR: Last year's survey of your work brought together paintings from as early as 1980 until the present day, and of course there are shared affinities that transcend shifts in style. You mentioned earlier that you have been reliant on the collages for the past 14 years. What prompted the shift in technique? Was there some expressionist hurdle or debt to overcome? Those earliest paintings feel quite fast or raw....

WB: The new collage-based paintings have ingredients (figures and things) that need a bit more accuracy to reproduce them in oil, and call up a closed little world of convincing meaning and feeling. Apart from time-consuming painterly accuracy in the newer paintings I see no stylistic change. I still try to be fast, raw and furious. Because I still think that there are a lot of better places to be than in front of an easel. And far and wide I see no-one who could save me and do the job in my stead. My style is still a child of my dear eye and brain—impatient and vengeful.

AR: So talk me through a couple... *Die Markieiung des Abgurnds* (*The marking of the abyss*), 2012, for example, which lends the show its title. It's an imponderable romantic German landscape that might make Caspar David Friedrich proud. The dog cocking its leg into the valley is either monumental or pure bathos. And that leaf on the tree that is so disrespectful of perspective... (I guess Friedrich would have liked that too!)

WB: But instead of a tiny human being lost in wonder, while faced with the sublimity of a fading world, we have a miserable dog marking a miserable territory. Which clearly indicates that Caspar David Friedrich is not smelling funny, but is dead indeed. And the disrespectful leaf seems to be the proud pennant in a "desert of freedom", as Nietzsche uttered....

AR: I like the fact that you say "seems". That is, as much as your work is formally composed, the meaning of your juxtapositions are not set from the beginning. Do you prepare yourself to be surprised?

WB: I always hope I'll have interesting and surprising accidents while I'm working. To me, an abortive attempt has to be warmly welcomed. To avoid routine, to avoid craftsmanship, to avoid virtuosity, to avoid seriality, to do as much wrong as necessary to create a good picture. And if you try to do everything wrong you can do no wrong. Clever take-off, isn't it?

Werner Büttner's prosaic biography in tabular prose

1954
Born in Jena, East Germany.
Happy childhood in the Workers' and Farmers' Paradise.

1961
Abducted to West Germany by his mother.
First experiences with meritocracy in Munich's run-down Hasenlbergl neighbourhood.

1968
Abducted to West Berlin by his father.

1973
Studied law at Berlin's Freie Universität.

1977
Officially struck from the university register.
Relocation to Hamburg with the heroic resolution: "stable job, fixed abode, steady girlfriend".
Founded several letterbox companies with a debt to the avant-garde.

1977
"Liga zur Bekämpfung des widersprüchlichen Verhaltens" (League for the Fight against Contradictory Behaviour) with its official newspaper *Dum-Dum* with Albert Oehlen.

1980
Samenbank für DDR-Flüchtlinge (Sperm Bank for East German Refugees) with Georg Herold and Albert Oehlen.

1981
Kirche der Ununterschiedlichkeit (Church of Undissimilarity) with Albert and Markus Oehlen et al.

1985
Meterverlag (Metre Publishing) with Albert Oehlen.
Lovely and not-so-lovely experiences with women.
Lovely and not-so-lovely experiences with the art system.

1989
Professor at Hamburg University of Fine Arts (HfBK).
Refines the pedagogical method of "vernalization", borrowed from botany: "accelerating the development of seedlings by cold shock treatment".

1991
The art market collapses with no real constructive contribution on his part.

2006
Now lives, surprisingly enough, in Geesthacht, the place caressed by the foul waters of the River Elbe, the place with the densest population of nightingales in northern Germany, the place where Alfred Nobel invented dynamite....

Werner Büttner
A short biographical note

Given his fortunately aborted legal training at university, a lawyer's taste for amusing but trenchant wordplay and word-manipulation has nevertheless infused Büttner's innate sense of fun, his gift for satire and for unmasking the absurd and his rebellion against the norms and fashions of the art world. His childhood of contradictory experiences—his first fictitious letterbox company then having the title "The League for the Fight against Contradictory Behaviour"—led him to defy the unfavourable judgement of his close friend Albert Oehlen, who had indeed attended a conventional art school, and pursue a painting career without any formal art school training whatsoever.

With Oehlen and the late Martin Kippenberger, Büttner staged performances and cultivated a practice of rebelling against good taste and polished execution in painting. For a time 'Bad Painting' and plebeian subjects ruled their practice, but by the time Harald Falckenberg, the Hamburg-based collector and patron, had made their acquaintance in 1998, their respective roles had been well established. Falckenberg would later record their earlier roles in his brief memoir: "Martin was the practical one, and game for everything. Werner the theoretician who formulated texts on art and saw to their propagation, and Albert the painter-god responsible for questions of style and execution in art."[1] Their work has continued to be exhibited together for the last 30 years, although the work of each has gradually found its own distinctive character.

Galleries have been admirably consistent and loyal to their style. Max Hetzler was the first to give them exposure at his several galleries in Berlin, Stuttgart and Cologne, Ascan Crone in Hamburg, Sabine Knust in Munich, Peter Pakesch in Vienna, and the Grässlin family of dealers and collectors in Frankfurt. An essential part of their work, and especially so in the case of Büttner, has been the production of texts and publications to accompany some of their exhibitions. Some would correspond closely to the work exhibited, such as Büttner's *The Problems of Mini-golf in European Painting*, 1983, Galerie Max Hetzler, but others, such the three artists' *Painting is Truth*, 1984, Museum Folkwang, Essen, or Büttner's *Miserere*, 1993, Kunsthalle, Klagenfurt, were properly artist-determined publications with essays and reflections of lasting relevance beyond the occasion of the exhibition.

While Büttner, like Oehlen, has continued to paint and exhibit, the former's growing corpus of collages has accompanied his paintings in exhibitions and publications since the early 2000s. The collages were the subject of a new, scholarly essay, reprinted in this volume, by the young Russian art historian Daria Mille in the extensive monograph *Werner Büttner, Gemeine Wahrheiten*, published by Hatje Cantz to accompany his retrospective at the ZKM's Museum for New Art, Karlsruhe, in 2014.

1 "Medium-range theories. Some details" reproduced in Büttner, Werner, *Coincidence in Splendour*, London: Black Dog Publishing, 2015, pp 247–255, where full details of Büttner's solo and group exhibitions, and his publications, can also be found.

List of Works

All works are collage on paper
All measure 32 x 24 cm / 12 ½ x 9 ½ in

Contributor Biographies

Daria Mille (b 1982) studied art history and arts management in St Petersburg, Weimar and Paris. In 2008 she was appointed Assistant to the Curator and Project Manager for the Moscow Biennale until she took up the post of Research Associate at ZKM | Museum of Contemporary Art Karlsruhe in 2011. She is specialising in contemporary art; her research focus lies in the museology of avant-garde art of the 1920s. At ZKM she is part of the GLOBALE-team, in charge of the programme of exhibitions, concerts, events, lectures and conferences to celebrate the city of Karlsruhe's 300th anniversary in 2015–2016.

Andrew Renton (b 1963) is the Director of Marlborough London. He holds the chair of Professor of Curating at Goldsmiths, University of London. He has himself curated many shows internationally, including the first Manifesta biennial, Rotterdam, 1996; Stay Forever and Ever and Ever, South London Gallery, 2007; Come, Come, Come into my World, Lisbon, 2007; and ArtTLV, Tel Aviv's first biennial, 2008. He wrote a weekly column for the *Evening Standard* on art matters, and is author and editor of hundreds of articles, books and monographs on art, including *Technique Anglaise*, the first book to document the Young British Artist movement, in 1991. He was a member of the jury for the 2006 Turner Prize, and advises many collections, museums and institutions, including the British Government Art Collection.

Gilda Williams is a writer, editor and teacher on art, who moved to London in 1994 to become Editor and later Commissioning Editor of some 50 monographs in the Contemporary Artists series as well as anthologies in the Themes and Movements series for Phaidon Press between 1994 and 2005, including the magisterial *Salon to Biennale: Exhibitions that made Art History, Vol 1 1863–1959* (2011). She now lectures on the MFA in Curating programme at Goldsmiths, University of London, and the MA in Contemporary Art at Sotheby's Institute of Art. She is the London correspondent of *Artforum* magazine, co-author of the *Art Book for Children* (2005), which has been translated into ten languages, and author of *The Gothic* (2007). Recently her *How to Write About Contemporary Art* (2014) was praised in *Art Monthly* magazine as "the little red book everyone in the artworld should have". In Spring 2016 MIT/Whitechapel will publish her reader *On&By Andy Warhol*, a critical history that gathers some 50 essential texts written by and about Andy Warhol over the past five decades.

Acknowledgements

The publisher would like to thank the artist, Werner Büttner, for his collaboration on the content of this book. Special thanks also to Ingo Offermans for his longstanding collaboration with the artist and his generous input on the development of this book.

We would also especially like to thank Gilda Williams for her new writing on the artist, Andrew Renton for his interview with the artist, and Daria Mille whose essay on the artist's collages appears in English for the first time. The artist would like to thank Nicholas Grindell for the congenial translations of his rather strange titles.

Black Dog Publishing's partner on this publication, Marlborough London, has been instrumental in the realisation of this book. As such, the publisher wishes to gratefully acknowledge this partnership and the commitment offered by Marlborough London in our bringing about this important and timely publication.

Colophon

Black Dog Publishing Limited
10A Acton Street
London WC1X 9NG
info@blackdogonline.com

British Library Cataloguing-in-Publication Data.
A CIP record for this book is available from the British Library.

ISBN 978-1-910433-83-6

Translation from the German by Pauline Cumbers and Nicholas Grindell

Edited by Andrew Renton and Philip Wright
Assisted by Francesco Dama

Scans by Dye Transfer International

Portrait of Werner Büttner by Egbert Haneke (page 4)

Black Dog Publishing Limited, London, UK, is an environmentally responsible company. *Werner Büttner: My Looting Eye* is printed on sustainably sourced paper.

reuse recycle reduce

art design fashion
history photography
theory and things

black dog publishing
london uk

www.blackdogonline.com